Structure and Process in a Melanesian Society

Studies in Anthropology and History

Studies in Anthropology and History is a series that will develop new theoretical perspectives, and combine comparative and ethnographic studies with historical research.

Edited by Nicholas Thomas, The Australian National University, Canberra.

VOLUME 1   Structure and Process in a Melanesian Society: Ponam's progress in the Twentieth Century

A.H. CARRIER AND J.G. CARRIER

VOLUME 2   Androgynous Objects: String bags and gender in Central New Guinea

MAUREEN MACKENZIE

OTHER VOLUMES IN PREPARATION

Time and the Work of Anthropology: Critical essays 1971–1991

JOHANNES FABIAN

Colonial Space

JOHN NOYES

The Gifts of the Kamula

MICHAEL WOOD

This book is part of a series. The publishers will accept continuation orders which may be cancelled at any time and which provide for automatic billing and shipping of each title in the series upon publication. Please write for details.

Achsah H. Carrier
James G. Carrier

Structure and Process in a Melanesian Society

Ponam's progress in the Twentieth Century

Routledge
Taylor & Francis Group

LONDON AND NEW YORK

Published 1991 by Routledge
2 Park Square, Milton Park, Abingdon, Oxon OX14 4RN
711 Third Avenue, New York, NY 10017, USA

First issued in paperback 2016

Routledge is an imprint of the Taylor & Francis Group, an informa business

Copyright © 1991, Taylor & Francis.

LIBRARY OF CONGRESS CATALOG CARD NUMBER

DESIGNED BY	Maureen MacKenzie Em Squared Main Street Michelago NSW 2620 Australia
TYPESET IN	Palatino 10/14pt, by James Carrier using Microsoft "Word" 5.0A, DOS version
FRONT COVER	Joseph Karin announcing a distribution of gifts in the mortuary presentation for Pimeses (see pages 172–75). Photo by J. G. Carrier.

ISBN 13: 978-1-138-99657-1 (pbk)
ISBN 13: 978-3-7186-5149-8 (hbk)

Publisher's Note
The publisher has gone to great lengths to ensure the quality of this
reprint but points out that some imperfections in the original may be apparent.

Contents

This is dedicated with gratitude and affection to the people of Ponam Island: Tama Gabriel Kalan, Tine Pimokon Sosi, Njana Pilau Turuwai and Selef Njohang, Asi Sani Pipat, Piso'on Njoli and Pindramolat Mohok, Pelu Sepat Peleheu, and Tony Kakaw, Tine Nja Kaseu and naron, Laisen Sosol (MPLGC), Gerrard Sale and Michael Tapo (komiti), and all of the others whom we cannot list but will remember.

List of illustrations

ix

Preface

We began fieldwork on Ponam Island, in Manus Province, Papua New Guinea, in 1978, our expectations shaped by recent research on the Highlands, where the clear defeat of old-fashioned structural-functionalism had been explained in all that we had read. Societies were shaped by politics and contingency, not by logic and structure. They were led by big men who created kinship and the appearance of social order through the management of exchange and the manipulation of their followers and dependents. And what we had read about Manus led us to expect the same things there.

Margaret Mead's monograph on kinship in the south coast village of Pere, published in 1934, was an attack on structural lineage theory, written even before that theory was fully formed. She argued that Pere had a system of kinship and ranking of the sort that could provide the structure for political and other forms of organisation, but that Pere society did not actually operate in terms of this system. Instead, it was a big man system (though she called them entrepreneurs or financiers) in which the wealthy and powerful constructed kinship and social relations through exchange in order to serve economic ends.

It was obvious from our own experiences and from Theodore Schwartz's 1963 survey, 'Systems of areal integration', that all the different groups in Manus were part of a single social and cultural system, as one would expect of this isolated region with its population of only 25,000 (and that twice the size it had been at the time of Mead's research). So Ponam should have fit Mead's argument and the picture that was emerging from the Highlands.

But Ponam seemed quite unlike the Pere that Mead had described.

We would sit in our thatched house under the palm trees, lulled by the constant roar of the breakers on the reef and the romance of fieldwork on a true tropical island, and read and reread Mead's work looking for clues to understanding as well as enjoying this alien paradise. And such is the romance of fieldwork that we, like many others before us we are sure, became convinced that our predecessor had got it wrong.

Ponam had no financiers, no entrepreneurs manipulating and managing dependents. They did not even seem to have any big men. People asserted that all positions of clan leadership were hereditary, and in fact just about all the recognised leaders seemed to be eldest sons of eldest sons; not that they ever seemed to lead anything. The elective offices of modern government were widely dispersed, not concentrated in the hands of the few. In 1979 the 31 possible hereditary and elective offices on the island were held by 28 of the island's 64 adult men, and the elected officers changed with every election. People claimed that all relations of exchange were conducted in terms of kinship, not patronage and dependence, and as we began to investigate exchange this seemed indeed to be true. People described their lives and relationships in terms of the structured relations of clans and lineages, the links between descendants of brothers and the descendants of sisters, the logic of the rules of inheritance and the ritual obligations between various categories of kin.

The word that came up again and again as people described how things were done was "right", as in 'She has the right to do this', or 'He doesn't have the right to be here now'. "Power", another popular Pidgin word that appears in so many anthropological accounts of the region, especially those from the north coast of the New Guinea mainland, was almost never used. And when it was, it was used only to refer to the ritual power that some categories of kin had over others, not to the political or supernatural power that some men and women might have over others. We toyed with the idea of writing something called 'African models in the New Guinea islands'. (Sadly, we missed our chance. Roger Keesing wrote 'African models in the Malaita highlands'.)

This contrast between the apparently highly logical, tightly structured, descent- and lineage-based system that we saw, and the more fluid political system of evanescent process that we had expected, eventually came to be an important focus of our study of Ponam Island. But having lived with Ponam for many years now, and no longer feeling the romantic impulse to do combat with Margaret Mead, we do not try to choose between these two perspectives, or to argue that one provides a better description of Ponam than the other. Instead, we look at Ponam from both of these perspectives, look at it as a structure and a process, a reflection of logic and contingency.

This book is an extended discussion and application of these two different perspectives. The realms that give content to this discussion of structure and process are kinship and ceremonial exchange, inseparable on Ponam as elsewhere in Melanesia, and central to everything else that Ponams did. It focuses on the rules and processes of managing ceremonial gift exchange, who gave to whom, and how they decided how much to give. Consequently, it largely ignores symbolism and meaning. This choice was directed by the interest of Ponams, which match our own inclinations. Ponams never once attempted to volunteer symbolic explanations for any of the actions of their ceremonial exchanges, nor did they ever try to relate these exchanges to any of the events of what little mythology they had. Moreover, they were only grudgingly tolerant of our attempts to impose such interpretations, and often forthrightly denied them. For example, people rejected even the attempt to impose the very common Melanesian classification of exchange gifts into male and female, or to suggest that certain classes of gifts, for example the baskets that were always given by a woman's family to a man's, had obvious sexual connotations.

This is not to say, of course, that one could not make an analysis that would reveal a symbolic framework underlying Ponam exchange. It is to say, however, that this was not the way that Ponams themselves seemed to think about exchange or the way that they explained its importance to us. In their discussions Ponam focused on exchange as a system of rules, or perhaps more accurately, etiquette. Their exchanges were based upon an elaborate system of obligations and calculations of obligations that wove together different classes of relatives, and it was this elaborate etiquette itself that was meaningful. People reacted to our attempts to impose another level of meaning almost as though they felt that the search for this other level of meaning debased the value of the actions themselves, as though they did not want the actions to stand for something else but wanted them only to stand for themselves. Thus, this is the kind of interpretation we have tried to present.

◆ ◆ ◆ ◆

Because this book is about kinship and exchange on Ponam, it is worth recounting briefly how Ponam Islanders fit us into their system and how we acted within it. These sorts of experiences inevitably affect the fieldworker's perspective and analysis.

During our first year on the island we lived in a house owned by an island club, the Mataungan Association, named after the famous Rabaul group. By staying there we walked unwittingly into the midst of a quarrel between this group and another faction headed by the village councillor (*WT&E*: 44–47).[1] We worked hard to overcome this and to show that we hoped to be friendly with and to work with both groups; and Ponams too seemed to have worked hard to resolve their differences enough to allow us to stay there. Eventually we were divided among these groups, with the village councillor, Damien Self Njohang, taking the role of James Carrier's father, and the leader of the Mataungan Association, Gabriel Kalan, taking the role of Achsah Carrier's father. We both remained close to Achsah Carrier's father, however, and stayed with him and his family in his house on our return trips to the village.

---

[1] This is described in pages 44–47 of the book that is a companion to this one, *Wage, Trade, and Exchange in Melanesia* (J. Carrier & A. Carrier 1989). Throughout the present volume we will have occasion to refer to it, and will do so as *WT&E*.

Although Ponams gave us each fathers and mothers they did not give us wider families, along with all of the problems they knew that would entail. For the first year they did not give us families at all, but when we returned to the island after our first year in Port Moresby they decided to create them. These were not normal genealogical families, however. Instead, the men of the village were designated as James Carrier's family, and the women of the village were designated as Achsah Carrier's, a solution inspired by our own way of participating in ceremonial exchange: Achsah Carrier always gave to the wife's side in exchange and James Carrier always gave to the husband's side. They created these families when we went back to Ponam because Achsah Carrier was then pregnant with our first child and they decided that we should sponsor exchanges as Ponam migrants did. This proved to be the most successful way for us to contribute money to the island, and on subsequent visits we put on first-birth and brideprice prestations.

We mention these prestations here because they were extremely interesting and because being obliged to manage exchanges (even highly artificial and playful ones such as these) gave us insights into exchange that we had never gained from observation. The point that struck us most forcibly was how difficult these exchanges were to carry off, a difficulty that was exaggerated, but not created, by our foreignness. Logically these exchanges were not terribly complicated. But in practice, working under the pressure of time and trying to manage a large number of fragile social relationships, they were incredibly difficult, frustrating and intellectually absorbing, as we believe they were for Ponams themselves.

A NOTE ON GENDER

Feminists have made the accusation that anthropologists claim to write about "people", but are really talking about "men" only, leaving women, women's work and women's perspective obscured. This book has the opposite flaw. Its subject is kinship and exchange, and we write about "people", but the real protagonists of this story are women (WT&E: 55–61). On Ponam both men and women participated in exchange, and participated on more or less equal terms (and we have written the text very carefully to make this point, using "he and she" repeatedly and tediously to stress that activities can be carried out by both men and women; the word "he" always refers to men alone and never to people in general). But women dominated the spheres of exchange and kinship, a fact that everyone on Ponam openly acknowledged.

Women knew genealogies, remembered the stories of marriages, births and deaths of previous generations, and men relied on their knowledge unashamedly. Women initiated almost all the minor day-to-day gift transactions that provided the framework of debt and obligation on which major exchanges were constructed. Women made or purchased most of the goods and cooked most of the food given in exchange. Women took charge of most of the minor gift prestations, organising gifts in both their own and their husbands' names, and also could redistribute what their husbands received, though usually a couple would discuss this together. Couples discussed major prestations and decided on them jointly, though more often than not it was the woman who actually carried them out. Exchanges were attended primarily by women, and some minor affairs were attended exclusively by women. The men who were centrally involved in any exchange would attend it and participate in its organisation, except for the most minor occasions. And on important occasions, such as brideprice payments, even men who were not closely involved in the affair would attend, and take a real and active interest in what went on during the course of the exchange and in what happened to the goods that they gave and received. But in general, most men left most of the work of exchange to their wives, and were content to do so.

In short, kinship and exchange were women's work. They constructed it, they took most of the pleasure, the glory and the shame of it. Men stood or fell by the work of their wives, and no man would consider taking part in exchange without the consultation, and if possible the support, of his wife.

This is a remarkable inversion of the usual state of affairs in Papua New Guinea, where the dominant picture has long been that of the Highlands. There women are relegated to a politically-inferior domestic sphere and struggle valiantly to gain recognition for the labour that they invest in the exchanges that redound to the glory of their husbands (e.g. Brown & Buchbinder 1976; Josephides 1985; M. Strathern 1972; but see M. Strathern 1988). Ponam women too were relegated to the domestic sphere, and largely excluded from public political life, but this domestic sphere included the world of exchange and thus gave them dominance in it.

Women's world was the world of the domestic household, *om*, while men's world was that of the men's house, *kamal*. Real property — land, sea, and fishing rights — was inherited and managed by the men of these *kamals*, and women were largely (though not entirely) debarred from owning and managing property in their own names. Men devoted most of their time to the management of this property, work that involved primarily the tasks of fishing, and of concocting, conducting and settling disputes about property ownership.

While a man was engaged in these male affairs of property and the *kamal*, his household was managed by his wife, sister or daughter. She spent most of her time at home. She cooked, cleaned, cared for children, fed and looked after his elderly relatives, and heard the stories and histories of the old and dying. She conducted the petty giving and receiving that were so much a part of village life. It was she who had control of the family's household, or movable, property, and perhaps most important, it was she who was expected to manage the family budget. At least in principle, a man's valuables, including his money, were managed by his wife, just as any real property she might inherit was managed by him.

It was her role as manager of the household that gave a woman a position of such importance in exchange, for exchanges, with a few relatively minor exceptions, were the business of households and kin rather than the business of property-owning *kamals*. Men, of course, were members of households and had kin, and this gave them a real and undeniable interest in the affairs of kinship and exchange. But the household was not the centre of a man's world; his primary role in life lay elsewhere.

A NOTE ON ORTHOGRAPHY AND TRANSLATION

Ponams were a literate people. Everyone born after about 1940 had been educated in English, and many of those born earlier were literate in Pidgin. Reading and writing were an important part of the daily lives of most people. For the most part they read and wrote in English or Pidgin, rather than in the vernacular. However, people were able to write in Ponam when they chose, and there was considerable consensus about a correct Ponam orthography. The main ambiguities in spelling arose with some of those sounds not found in the English and Pidgin orthographies on which Ponams based their own. The prenasalised "b", for example, was written variously as "mbr", "br" or simply "b". Here we spell Ponam words as Ponams conventionally did, though where variant spellings were common we choose the one that seems most like English. The only exception to this is names of places outside Ponam Island. There we use official Papua New Guinea names.

Unfortunately, Ponam orthography is not very informative to English speakers, and it is beyond our competence to provide an analysis that would make it so. But since it is most unlikely that anyone who reads this will be called on to speak Ponam, the issue is not very significant. One orthographic note is useful, however. With only a few exceptions we have used a dash to indicate where we have omitted the intimate possessive suffixes that would be distracting to the reader. We write, for example, *lowa-* (cognate) rather than *lowak* (my cognate), *lowam* (your [sing.] cognate), *lowan* (his or her cognate), and so on. The exceptions to this are a few kin terms where the common form of address did not use the possessive suffix. The most important of these are *tama* (father), *tine* (mother) and *asi* ("FZ").

When anthropologists were all more or less in agreement that kinship was about clans and lineages and relationships such as descent, filiation or siblingship, they could agree that although translation was a problem in principle, it was reasonable, and necessary for the sake of scholarship, to make the compromise of translating vernacular terms into their nearest anthropological equivalents. With the modern interest in indigenous meanings, however, such correspondences become unacceptable (see Schneider 1981*a* for examples of the abuse these can elicit). Although an emphasis on indigenous terms may be desirable, ethnographies larded with endless strings of untranslated foreign words are almost unreadable. In this text we try to avoid this. Ponam words that can be translated plausibly into English are given a standard translation, which is then used consistently throughout the text. These terms are explained in more detail in the glossary. Terms that we think cannot be translated reasonably into English are kept in Ponam; however we have tried to reduce the number of these terms to a minimum.

A NOTE ON THE ETHNOGRAPHIC PAST TENSE

The convention endures in anthropology of writing in the present tense about events and institutions that one observed in the past. This convention gives ethnography a peculiar timeless air, and is sometimes actually deceptive. We have chosen instead to write entirely in the past tense, about Ponam as it was when we were there. Ponam has changed in dramatic and interesting ways over the course of this century, was changing even as we knew it, and will continue to change in the future. Nothing, be it significant or trivial, that we describe here is immune to this process.

A NOTE ON MONEY

Since it became independent in 1975, Papua New Guinea's currency has been the kina (indicated by "K"), consisting of 100 toea (indicated by "t"). At the time of the main period of fieldwork in 1979, the kina was worth approximately £0.66, $US1.30 and $A1.20. The kina fluctuated widely over the later period of research, between then and late 1986. Because of this, we have not converted the kina into any other currency in this book. When we refer to money prior to independence, we use either the currency circulating at the time or the currency used in the source of the information we report.

Acknowledgements

This book is based on Achsah Carrier's doctoral thesis, 'The structure and processes of kinship: a study of kinship and exchange on Ponam Island, Manus Province, Papua New Guinea, 1920–1980.' It was written while she was a research student at University College London, under the supervision first of Andrew Strathern and then of Daniel Miller. James Carrier had primary responsibility for the revising of the thesis to turn it into the present volume (particularly the introduction and conclusion) and for preparing camera-ready copy. That thesis was based on fieldwork done by both authors on Ponam Island, and so inevitably entailed a degree of collaboration, as has all the writing coming out of that fieldwork. In the field and after, we developed an informal division of labour. James Carrier was concerned primarily with economics, Achsah Carrier was concerned primarily with kinship and exchange, realms that overlap a great deal, particularly on Ponam.

Portions of this book rely on earlier work dealing with Ponam Island. The most important of these are: Achsah Carrier and James Carrier, 'Brigadoon, or; Musical comedy and the persistence of tradition in Melanesian ethnography.' *Oceania* 57 (1987): 271–293; James Carrier and Achsah Carrier, 'Every picture tells a story: visual alternatives to oral tradition in Ponam society.' *Oral Tradition* 5, special issue on the South Pacific, Ruth Finnegan and Margaret Orbell (eds), (1990): 354–375, 'A Manus centenary: production, kinship and exchange in the Admiralty Islands', *American Ethnologist* 12 (1985): 505–522. We acknowledge permission to reprint portions of these papers granted to us by the copyright holders, and we note that their permission does not extend to permission to reprint those passages elsewhere. Portions of 'Brigadoon' are included by permission of the editors of *Oceania*; portions of 'Every picture tells a story' are included by permission of the editors of *Oral Tradition*; portions of 'A Manus centenary' are included by permission of the American Anthropological Association.

In addition, we tried out many of our ideas on colleagues at seminars, particularly at the Department of Anthropology and Sociology of the University of Papua New Guinea, where both of us taught for seven years, but also at the Department of Anthropology at University College London, the University of Sydney and the University of Virginia. We must content ourselves with a blanket acknowledgement of the helpful comments made at those seminars.

The research on which this book is based relied on help from many others. We are grateful to David Lancy, then Principal Research Officer of the Papua New Guinea Ministry of Education, for encouraging us to make Ponam our field site. The University of London Central Research Fund gave financial assistance to Achsah Carrier during our initial period of fieldwork. The University of Papua New Guinea Research Committee gave financial assistance to James Carrier during our return visits to Ponam in 1981, 1982, 1983 and 1986. The governments of Papua New Guinea and Manus Province gave permission to carry out the research, and the Australian Archives and the Papua New Guinea Archives helped us with documents and the permission to cite them. Also we owe thanks to V.E. King, who kindly allowed us permission to make use of the information in his 'The end of an era: aspects of the history of the Admiralty Islands 1898–1908' (King 1978). His labours in the records of German firms and administrations made our task of discovering Manus history much easier. We want to thank the people of the Manus Provincial Government and Secretariat for their permission to do the research and for their help. Daniel Miller and Andrew Strathern deserve thanks for the insights they provided as they supervised Achsah Carrier's thesis.

Our decision to rewrite Achsah Carrier's thesis was sparked by Nicholas Thomas. Because of his historical orientation (e.g. Thomas 1989) and because his concern with the structural and synchronic nature of much Pacific anthropology matched our own, he was enthusiastic about the thesis, encouraged us to revise it and provided helpful suggestions about how we might do so. Indeed, re-reading his work as we revise this one has reminded us of the many, striking points of convergence between the two. We owe him thanks for inducing us to rework a set of ideas that seemed to have fallen on stony ground. We hope the result has not disappointed him.

In addition, Bruce Knauft made helpful comments on the introduction and conclusion to this book, for which we are grateful.

Although this book is about the people who live on Ponam Island, we owe a great debt to the Ponams living in Port Moresby who befriended us during our seven years there and who were always ready to talk about their home, especially Mr and Mrs T. Kakaw, Mr and Mrs C. Korai, Mr and Mrs F. Misso, Mr and Mrs J. Paliau and Mr and Mrs P. Songo.

To the Ponams on Ponam Island, we have dedicated this book.

Approaching Ponam society

Ponam is a lovely place in a lovely setting. It is a small island off the north-central coast of Manus Island in the Admiralty Islands, the main part of Manus Province, Papua New Guinea. As Ponam is a small island, so Manus is a small province, the smallest in the country by far, with a resident population of 25,844 in 1980 (Papua New Guinea 1980). It is an island province, about 270 kilometres north-northeast of the coast of Madang Province, the nearest place on the New Guinea mainland, and about the same distance west of New Hanover, the closest large island in the Bismarck Archipelago. The core of the province is the large island of Manus and the smaller island of Los Negros, the two barely separated by a narrow, winding passage. This core, the Manus mainland, is surrounded by small islands, especially to the southeast and north (see map 1, at the end of this chapter).

Manus is distant from the economic and political centres of Papua New Guinea and without any substantial source of income of its own. In 1980, at about the time of our most extensive period of fieldwork, there was no industrial production, and commercial agriculture consisted largely of copra with some cocoa. There was no commercial fishing, but provincial waters had been used by overseas fishing firms for baitfish, which generated some royalty income (Otto 1989). This lack of local commercial production was reflected in the fact that around 1980, only five percent of provincial government revenues came from provincial sources, the rest coming from national government grants (Titus 1980: 29). Equally, only ten percent of all the money coming into the province was in return for goods produced there (Lansdell 1981: fig. 3). Thus, both individuals and the provincial government depended on sources of money located outside Manus (*WT&E*: 87).

Nonetheless, Manus was well-served and relatively wealthy. Appendix 1 uses a number of social indicators to compare the Manus Census District (it was so small that, unlike other provinces, it contained only one census district) with districts that include provincial capitals in the two neighbouring island provinces, Kavieng District (New Ireland Province) and Rabaul District (East New Britain Province), and with the national maximum and minimum for each indicator. The data show that Manus was comparable with Kavieng and Rabaul in many ways, particularly in the provision and use of education services, where they approached or equalled the national maximum on all variables.

1

Ponam itself is a sand cay, about three kilometres long and varying between 200 and 400 metres wide. It lies about 5 kilometres off the Manus mainland, and is surrounded by a huge but not terribly fertile coral reef. The island is of naturally low fertility, like other sand cays, but this was exacerbated when much of it was covered with concrete and used as an airstrip in World War II. This infertility was not really of much concern to Ponams, however, for they were, and always had been, sea people and not gardeners. 'We're Navy', they said, 'not Army'.

Most of the ties between resident islanders and other Manus people were concentrated within their electorate, Tulu-Ponam, which was established in 1979 and had a resident population of 920 (Papua New Guinea 1980). This consisted of the villages of Aran, Lehuwa, Ponam, Saha, Tulu I and Tulu II, and the Bundralis Catholic Mission station. These are in map 2, of north-central Manus, which shows Ponam Island, its surrounding reef, and nearby important villages. (This map also is placed at the end of the introduction.)

Though linked to the other villages of the electorate in important ways, Ponam had its own village court, aid post, church and two-class primary school, and so was largely self-contained. In 1979 the island had about 300 residents in 70 households, and 200 migrants. By 1986 the resident population had increased to about 335 in 78 households. These people were all clustered into one village near the western end of the island.

While Ponam was small and relatively self-contained, it had a number of internal divisions. We will describe these largely as they existed at the time of fieldwork; the history of many of them is described in the body of this book and in *Wage, trade, and exchange in Melanesia*.

Kinship was the basis of the main divisions. The most visible was the set of 14 named patrilineal property-owning groups, which Ponams called *kamal*s (male[1]). These had genealogies of from four to seven generations of ancestors, and were divided into sublineages and sub-sublineages, though these subdivisions had no generic name. Everyone born of a Ponam father inherited a *kamal* membership, but a woman who married gave up her natal *kamal* membership and became a member of her husband's *kamal* and took on full rights to use his agnatic group property.

Ponam also had *ken si*s (one origin). These were cognatic stocks, descended from each islander who had children. Stocks were most important in ceremonial exchange, as exchange goods circulated in terms of the stocks descended from ancestral relatives of those involved in the exchange. Stocks did not own property. Any real property owned by a stock's apical ancestor

---

[1] We provide brief glosses for Ponam terms in the text. More detailed discussions of many terms are in the glossary.

passed to the patrilineal property-owning group descended from him or her, which was the agnatic core of the stock. However, although stock members who were not in the agnatic core did not own rights in that real property, they had special claims on it. Ponam values encouraged the core group to help their fellow stock members by granting them ready access to the group's real property.

In addition, Ponam was divided into moieties, though these were not marriage classes or corporate groups. These were Tolau (North, the northern half of the island) and Kum (South, the southern half of the island), defined by bisecting the island with the line of the central village street. Each *kamal* was identified as being in one moiety or the other, usually based on the location of its first men's house. Individuals took their moiety membership from that of their *kamal*, so that physical residence and moiety membership were distinct, though these did coincide for almost all people. While moiety membership was important, it was so primarily when the island as a whole was acting in relation to some outside body. The government (first colonial and later provincial) was such a body, and community work assignments carried out in response to government orders were usually divided along moiety lines.

Another spatial division, less significant in 1980 than moieties, was the island's districts: Tonuf on the east, Lahai in the middle, Ponam on the west. Originally, islanders said, there was petty warfare between districts, and To-nuf people had a distinct language. However, nineteenth-century warfare destroyed all Lahai *kamal*s, so that "Lahai" became primarily a term for a part of the island, though kinship links through deceased Lahais remained important. That warfare also killed most Tonuf agnates. Only two Tonuf *kamal*s survived, and their members sought shelter with relatives in Ponam *kamal*s, though they kept their distinct Tonuf *kamal* identity and real property. At the time of fieldwork, members of these two *kamal*s continued to live in Ponam village, but maintained their distinct district identity, which was of greatest practical importance in fishing (*WT&E*: 103–106, 112). Although members occasionally talked of moving back to their ancestral site, they were deterred by the thought of the isolation the move would entail.

The last significant division that reflected the pre-colonial social order was based on matriclan membership, each islander inheriting a set of substance taboos from his or her mother. There were nine totemic matriclans, and while each prohibited some fish and other foods, no set of prohibitions seemed so extensive as to cause real inconvenience. While *kamal*s were the realm of the jural identity and property rights of Ponams, matriclans were responsible for the substance or being of individual islanders, overseeing their life-crisis rituals and aspects of their health. Ponams agreed that, at least in principle, a couple from the same matriclan would have an easier time of it, needing to observe only one set of taboos, but like moieties, matriclans appear to have had no impact on marriage patterns.

In addition to these pre-colonial groups based on kinship and geography, there were a number of more modern groups and institutions on Ponam, which cross-cut these older ones (*WT&E*: 43–48).

First is Nai, the young women's club. While it was founded in the 1960s to improve the health and welfare primarily of married women, it quickly became a single-women's club, whose members sewed, made handicrafts, played sports, performed dances for provincial celebrations and participated with other women's clubs in the province under the general oversight of the central Lorengau Women's Council.

Second is Posus, which began as a young men's club but gained a number of mature members. These included single women or widows, who used their membership to secure help from club members with heavy labour. Also, Posus performed heavy work for hire, including house-building or transporting large logs from the mainland. Many islanders thought that hiring Posus was cheaper and easier than organising relatives to perform these tasks, feeding them and keeping peace with them. Posus also supported several sports teams and a guitar band, which occasionally participated in provincial competitions.

Third were the island's two factions, one led by the village councillor. Although these factions were modern, the split between them reflected enduring tensions between *kamals*. In its current form, the split began in 1972, a result of Ponam resistance to the council government system the Australians were imposing, and more particularly the power of council government to fix poll taxes. As a result, one young Ponam man was inspired by the Tolai Mataungan Association, and he founded an association modelled on and named after it. Though he hoped Ponam's Mataungan Association would become a force for political change and economic development, it became simply an island party in opposition to the councillor, who, members felt, had not acted properly during the tax dispute. By the time of fieldwork, the Association had become something simpler, the island's third club, one for adults. Like Nai and Posus, it wanted to found a business and develop the island. But, like Nai and Posus, it could not devise a suitable project or raise the money to start one. (In 1985 the club was wound up and its assets distributed to its members.) Just as the Mataungan Association was concerned with development, so was the village councillor, and consequently the village government. In his official position, he got government assistance to build an aid post, water tanks and a teacher's house. These were not what Ponams saw as development (J. Carrier 1988: 58–59), but islanders did receive construction wages, as well as the benefit of the projects themselves.

There were two other significant modern institutions, the church and the school. The church played no marked political role, but Catholicism was important to people. In particular, it provided one key set of explanations for illness and misfortune (A. Carrier 1989). The church had a catechist who led services and a church leader who ran the practical side of church affairs and mediated a number of personal quarrels. There was also a committee that managed church funds. The two school bodies were the Board of Management, in charge of non-academic school business, and the Parents and Citizens Association, which mediated between parents and the school and raised funds.

Islanders lived in households, and much of their day-to-day activity was geared to household life. Household members had many productive responsibilities. Men had primary responsibility for fishing, which meant also making and repairing much of their own fishing equipment, most notably canoes. They were supposed to catch enough to feed their families and provide a surplus for market, but some left much of this work to their wives. Men also were responsible for building. Islanders said that a man should not marry until he had built a house and made a canoe and a sail, all things necessary for a household to survive. A household should have at least two canoes, a small one for inside the reef and a large one for sailing in open waters, and a large family could be expected to have several. Canoes and houses needed continual repair and eventual replacement: canoes lasted between three and ten years, houses between ten and fifteen. In addition, men cleaned their *kamal*'s men's house, tidied its grounds, cut the firewood burnt there and cooked the fish eaten there. Women did a significant amount of fishing and had primary responsibility for maintaining the household: cutting firewood, gathering coconuts, looking after children, cooking, doing laundry, sewing and cleaning. As women usually had high standards and large households, they worked hard at their tasks, many claiming that they worked harder than men. In addition, women were the ones who made valuables given in exchange: woven bags, skirts, armlets, beadwork and shell money.

As we have indicated, Ponams grew some coconut palms, and they planted small quantities of leafy greens, squash and bananas for household consumption. However, Ponams were island people, and saw their main productive activities as involving the sea, rather than the land. They had an elaborate system of fishing that used a range of different technologies and was embedded in a complex system of marine tenure. There were distinct and overlapping systems of rights to use different fishing techniques, to fish in different areas of the island's waters and to catch different species of fish (*WT&E*: 96–113). Fish were rarely used in exchange between islanders, and most of what they caught was intended for domestic consumption, though some was used in local trade.

This trade centred on two local markets that Ponams shared with different groups of mainland Manus villagers, one located at the Bundralis mission station and one at Tulu village (*WT&E*: 146–151). The markets were weekly affairs, under the joint control of pairs of island and mainland patrilineal groups that were supposed to ensure orderly and fair trading. Because of changes brought about by colonisation, especially since World War II, mainland villagers had a decreasing need for Ponam fish, while islanders had a continuing need for mainland starch, especially sago flour and taro, as well as vegetable produce in general and betel nut and leaf. As a consequence of this imbalance in need, these markets were fragile, tensions were common, and one or the other would close for a shorter or longer period of time.

In addition to these local markets, Ponams used their fish in transactions with their trade partners, or *kawas* (*WT&E*: 153–156). However, as the terms of market trade had changed following colonisation, so had relations with trade partners. By 1980, islanders were as likely to trade cash or cash goods as fish. However, they were no longer dependent on their trade partners for manufactured goods, as foreign imports had almost totally replaced local manufacturing by 1950 (*WT&E*: 80–88). Even so, trade partnerships remained important. They were a source of some key raw materials, especially wood and thatch for housing and logs for canoes. As well, islanders drew on trade partners when they wanted large quantities of food for exchanges, though by the 1970s many islanders who were responsible for the very largest exchange contributions were turning to stores in Lorengau for their supplies. At the other extreme, islanders bought many, minor daily necessities from one of the island's trade stores, which carried a range of staples, most especially kerosene, tobacco, sugar, tea, tinned meat and fish, rice and biscuits (*WT&E*: 134–142).

Their deteriorating position within the Manus economy meant that Ponams faced a growing need for money to buy both imported and local goods. The main way that islanders, and indeed most Manus villagers, met this need at the time of fieldwork was through a system of education, migration and remittance. Ponams had access to formal schooling since the 1920s and to English-language schooling since the early 1950s, including an English-language primary school on Ponam itself. And they took advantage of this access. Effectively all Ponams who were between 21 and 40 years of age in 1980 had completed primary school, and the mean education of men and women aged 21 to 30 was between two and three years of secondary school (*WT&E*: table 16, 17). This education paid practical dividends. In 1980, two Ponams in five were living elsewhere in Papua New Guinea either as workers or their dependents, while for the province as a whole 18.7 percent were migrants (Walsh 1983: 79), the second highest rate in the country. Further, at the time of fieldwork 92 percent of Ponam adult males had migrated at one time or another, while 57 percent were migrant at the time. Ponam women migrated less, but 45 percent of adult women had ever migrated, and 28 percent were migrant at the time, though women generally migrated as dependents of employed Ponams rather than as employees themselves (*WT&E*: table 14).

Not only did many Ponams migrate to other parts of the country in search of work, they managed to secure jobs of high status that paid well, as did Manus migrants more generally. Ponams appear especially fortunate in this regard. Around 1980 Ponams occupied positions of ordained Catholic priest, National Librarian, Secretary of Education, Chief Engineer of the National Broadcasting Commission and one of the two regional supervisors of the Office of Post and Telecommunications. As these examples suggest, at the end of 1979 Ponam migrants were overwhelmingly in skilled or white-collar jobs, with only one migrant man in 12 (and only about one employed woman in six) in un-skilled or subsistence labour (*WT&E*: table 15). Because of this, migrants could save and remit to Ponam significant amounts of money, which filled the gap between what resident islanders earned (about K5000 annually) and what they spent (about K25,000 annually). In addition, migrants sent home large quanti-ties of purchased goods, everything from outboard motors and fishing lines to pressure lamps and clothing. And again, this pattern was common in Manus. According to a provincial estimate, in 1980 migrants remitted about K1.2 million to the province, about K46 for each resident (Lansdell 1981: Fig. 3).

While migrants sent back money and objects in many different ways under many different circumstances, the most visible and persistent was as contributions to ceremonial exchanges of different sorts. This is doubtless one reason why ceremonial exchange took up a great deal of people's time, involved the circulation of a great deal of wealth, and was so was frequent and time-consuming. During our continuous period of fieldwork, between 1 December 1978 and 1 January 1980, the average resident adult Ponam spent 76 days involved in important exchanges and the total value of the goods circulated through these exchanges was about K55,000 (*WT&E*: table 21). In addition, during this period Ponams held nine public parties modelled on traditional exchange, to celebrate New Year's Day, Independence Day and other holidays, the opening of public buildings, the arrival of important visitors and other occasions of general importance. These brought the total number of days devoted to exchange to 85 and the total cost to a bit over K55,000.

Beside these major events, each Ponam also participated regularly in minor exchanges involving fewer people. These smaller exchanges were held to mark personal events, such as the completion of a canoe, net or sail, the harvesting of first fruits from an important tree, an unusually large catch of fish, the curing of an illness, the settling of an argument, and so on. Although these exchanges involved fewer people, they followed the same general pattern as the larger ones, and were just as time-consuming for those involved. Most people participated in exchanges of this sort about ten times during the period of fieldwork, and while it was not possible to get precise figures for the amount of money spent on these exchanges, it was almost certain to exceed K5000.

In summary, then, the average adult Ponam was involved in formal exchange of one sort or another on about 95 days of the 390 day period for which we have good continuous information, and the island spent something in the neighbourhood of K60,000 on exchange during that time. Converting this to annual figures, the average Ponam adult was involved in an exchange on 89 days, or about one day in every four, and Ponams collectively spent something over K55,000 on exchange. It should be obvious, then, that exchange was of overwhelming social and economic importance.

Neither of us intended to study kinship and exchange when we went to Ponam: Achsah Carrier intended to study indigenous mathematics and James Carrier intended to study responses to introduced formal schooling. But we were drawn to kinship and exchange regardless of our intentions. They were too important socially and economically for us to ignore, as well as too intriguing, exciting and exasperating. Ponams were drawn to them in just the same way. They were proud of their island, their culture and their traditions, but we sometimes felt that exchange and the complications of kinship that it necessarily involved was the one element of their culture about which they were particularly ambivalent. It provided people with endless worry and anguish and embarrassment and inevitably led to arguments between kin, even between kin who loved one another. Achsah Carrier's father once said to her, in one of his few outbursts of emotional intensity, 'I can't imagine why you came to study this stuff. I hate it. It drives me crazy. I would never do it if I didn't have to.' But he had to. And everyone else had to, those who loved the excitement of it and those who were tormented by it. To write about Ponam, we have to write about kinship and exchange.

APPROACHING KINSHIP AND EXCHANGE

We said in the Preface that our presentation of Ponam kinship and exchange revolves around structural and processual perspectives. Indeed, this book is as much an exploration of these perspectives as it is of Ponam society, and we have oriented our presentation in terms of these perspectives. This is because they are important and recurring themes in Oceanic anthropology, and we want to trace them out here. But the object of this history is not the teleological one of tracing the growth of a theory, of providing, as it were, its pedigree. Instead, we present this history with two ends in view. First and most immediately, structure and process are complex notions. They appear in various guises, and recounting that history will help explain what they mean by showing some of their manifestations. Second, this history will help justify our use of these approaches and the tension between them in the rest of this book. There are other ways of summarising the history that concerns us, and some of those ways have been expounded and defended already (e.g. Ortner 1984[2]). We thus feel under some obligation to defend our choice. This history is intended to show the persistence and intractability of the themes of structure and process. And while concerns with structure and process are not necessarily contradictory, this history shows that they do not make easy bedfellows; those with an interest in one tend to ignore the other.

These perspectives have been given many definitions, explicit and implicit, over the years. We will start with definitions taken from work in the 1950s, Meyer Fortes's for a definition of structure and Raymond Firth's for a definition of process. Because this book is in large part concerned with history — Ponam's history and anthropology's history — it seems appropriate to choose historically-hallowed work from two men who were key figures in the development of kinship studies in Oceania after World War II, a development that entailed changing notions of how society ought to be conceived.

In 1953, Fortes wrote that the structural perspective sees society as 'a social system [that] can be apprehended as a unity made up of parts and processes that are linked to one another by a limited number of principles of wide validity' (1953: 39). Thus he was concerned with the way that parts of a system fit together in a generalisable order, a concern that can apply in the study of social organisation, ideas, history and a range of other aspects of social life. Firth, on the other hand, was more interested in the study of what he called social organisation, or what we call more generally "process". In 1954 he wrote that social organisation 'refers to concrete social activity.... It is the processes of [the] ordering of action and of relations in reference to given social ends, in terms of adjustments resulting from the exercise of choices by members of the society' (1964 [1954]: 45).

The history we present here is the history of the ebb and flow of these two approaches, and we want to characterise that history briefly before we recount it. The first part of this history, running from the 1950s to around 1970, revolves around a central structuralist question: Is there a logical structure that is isomorphic with the structure of real social groups? Put in other words,

---

2 Ortner's review of anthropological theory since the 1960s contrasts those writers who focused on meaning and identity with those who focused on group relations. But as we show, studies of groups and meanings in Melanesia had far more in common than she suggested. Neither was concerned with the processes of human action.

words that presume a structuralist orientation: What are the 'limited number of principles of wide validity' that determine social organisation and people's actions? The classic structuralist answer to this question was: The principles of unilineal descent. However, in Oceania this classic answer was challenged by those we call processualists. They denied that any such unambiguous principles existed. Ultimately, they argued, contingency and choice, as they were embodied and made visible in the processes of social life, were the source of the organisation of societies. Ethnographers pursued this debate in terms of two different but related issues: the nature of descent groups and of kindreds in Oceania. The processualists won. They succeeded in showing that while societies were organised in terms of groups, these groups could not be explained satisfactorily in terms of unambiguous principles of descent and cognation, or indeed any other structural principle in social life. Instead, choice and the vagaries of circumstance were crucial in shaping the social structure that the analyst saw.

The second part of this history describes the reaction to that processualist victory. That reaction was not the abandonment of structure or the thorough incorporation of process. Instead, it was a retreat to structures of a different sort, described and analysed with little regard for process. In other words, the processualists really lost. One line of retreat was to the study of exchange. If organising principles did not exist in descent, the argument seems to have been, we must look for them elsewhere. The second line of retreat was to the study of culture. The argument here seems to have been that, if people's notions of descent and all the rest do not explain social organisation, then let us divorce culture from society and pursue cultural categories as structures to be investigated and explained in terms of their own organising principles.[3]

This plot line, even more than the history it summarises, is simplistic. Both ignore the subtleties of the arguments they summarise and tend to essentialise processual and structural approaches. Partly this is a result of the need to condense the much longer and more detailed historical description from which this is drawn (i.e., A. Carrier 1984, 1987: chap. 1, 2). Equally, what we present here is itself something of a structuralist history, because it ignores the range of social and practical (i.e. processual) factors that have shaped what counts

---

[3] This retreat to the structural study of culture was hardly unique to Melanesian ethnography. In a passage that anticipates several of the points we shall make in the course of this book, André Béteille (1990: 490) argues that a similar change occurred in Indian studies at about the same time. He says that scholars began to redefine 'the whole field of sociology as the sociology of ideas. ... [T]his meant a slow ... shift from the "fieldview" to the "bookview" of society, culminating in the assignment of a privileged position to traditional "structure" over contemporary "reality".'

as interesting anthropology.[4] These factors range from the personalities of individual anthropologists to the growing significance of American researchers and institutions, with their more cultural orientation, at the expense of the British, with their more social orientation. And of course they include changes within academic fashion and Pacific societies themselves. Even so, this plot line will serve to clarify the history that follows, as that history will serve to clarify the description of Ponam kinship and exchange that follows it.[5]

STRUCTURE

During the 1950s and 1960s analyses of kinship in Oceania were framed in terms of, or in opposition to, the African lineage model, particularly Meyer Fortes's (1953) formulation of it in 'The structure of unilineal descent groups'. In his view, unilineal societies were structured on a genealogical frame by the replication and nesting of like units based on descent. He said these lineages 'exist to unite persons for common social purposes and interests by identifying them exclusively and unequivocally with one another' (Fortes 1959: 208). The key to descent in these societies was *unilineal* descent, because only through it could persons be precisely and incontrovertibly fixed into unambiguous corporate kinship groups (1953: 30): 'local ties do not appear to give rise to structural bonds in and of themselves' (1953: 36). Further, lineage structure was pervasive: indigenous concepts, ritual, religion and indeed 'all levels of organisation' followed the lineage model (1953: 29). And this model made sense in Melanesia. Trobriand clans, like Mae Enga descent groups, yielded to structuralist description.

However, as the 1950s progressed this model came under attack. A key paper explaining the nature of that attack was David Schneider's 'Some muddles in the models'. There Schneider identified an important premise underlying Fortes's model when he said that unilineal structure depends on members 'having no compromising allegiance ... outside the group' (1965: 49), that such a structure requires that groups be based on the given-ness of

---

[4] Thus, the structuralist orientation appears to resonate with a prevailing tendency in Melanesian anthropology to produce totallising and essentialistic descriptions of particular societies or regions. The ethnography of a particular society, in other words, generally has consisted of describing the structures of the society; or, more recently, the culture. More processualist writers, on the other hand, seem to have been more open to seeing the societies they studied not as distinct entities, but as places where processes of different sorts were played out in different ways. This is only a tendency, however, and we point to it only tentatively.

[5] This history is recapitulated by Keesing (1987a) in terms of his own changing approach to Kwaio social organisation in the Solomon Islands. We omit this from discussion here because his paper is a retrospective reflection on the issues that concern us, rather than a part of the debates of the time.

genealogical connectedness and not the mutability of local ties. But this requirement created trouble for Pacific ethnographers, who confronted large, corporate, bilateral, ancestor-focused groups. In these systems, individuals would belong, by the logic of descent alone, to more than one group, whose membership would overlap and be ambiguous (1965: 61). Schneider (1965: 63) used the conflict between these groups and lineage theory to argue that Fortes's model was wrong:

> The muddled part of that model is the notion that somehow the segment is not only a conceptual segment, but also in some way a physically distinct and concrete segment. For it is only with a segment so conceived that choice of membership, and frequent changes of membership, and multiple membership, may create ... ambiguity.

The problem that Schneider identified was important, for it revolved not just around ethnographic anomalies, but around different views of the nature of society. For structuralists, the conceptual and concrete segments *had* to be isomorphic if writers were to explain the concrete behaviour of actual people in terms of descent rules. If concrete segments were not isomorphic with the conceptual segments that the rules were intended to explain, then the rules could not explain concrete behaviour. In other words, Fortes was not defending simply a type of society, but a type of sociology, one in which concrete human behaviour was determined by clear, unambiguous rules. He was defending, in other words, structuralism, that form of sociology in which the logic and order that analysis can abstract from society are also inherent in it. And in the debate that followed, analysts of "cognatic descent groups" in the Pacific resolved the problem not by establishing cognatic descent groups as a new type of society that could be understood with structuralist sociology, but by articulating a new type of sociology with which they could be understood.

Much of the ethnography on Oceanic kinship in this period revolved around this issue. Thus, for example, in 1955 Ward Goodenough argued that a key feature of Oceanic kinship was the cognatic descent group. Such groups lacked the crucial feature of unilineality, the ability to form discrete, unambiguous social groups. Instead, said Goodenough, membership was restricted to those of the founder's descendants who acted in a way that met some specified criteria in addition to that of cognatic descent, such as establishing residence. In the years following, writers attempted to reconcile groups like this with descent models, arguing, for instance, that they could be explained as the functional equivalent of unilineal descent groups or as a kind of logical extension of them (e.g. Davenport 1959; Mitchell 1963; Murdock 1960). However, these writers failed to grasp, or at least failed to comment on, the significance of the fact that the descent category and the descent group were not the same. Under Fortes's model, the category of people generated by the application of the descent rule was, and had to be, the same as the people who were in the descent group. However, these cognatic descent groups, the actual groups of people on the ground, were formed at least in part by people's actions, by social process, whether that action was establishing residence on descent-group land, performing labour, or whatever.

Raymond Firth, one of the more important and sensitive Pacific ethnographers, was instrumental in exposing the depth of this problem. In his 1957 paper, 'A note on descent groups in Polynesia,' he attempted to reconcile Polynesian descent groups with Fortesian lineage structures, and found it necessary to consider an issue that did not arise in the lineage model, the role of individual choice in the constitution of descent groups, and thus the role of contingent, non-structural factors in determining group structure. What he said of descent-group segmentation characterises his recognition of the importance of contingency in shaping social structure: 'segmentation in any social structure is not an automatic process but is related to the available resources' (1968 [1957]: 222–223). Here Firth makes explicit the point, which seems at issue throughout his paper, that social group formation was not purely determined by social-structural principles, but was conditioned by other factors.

Firth's work illustrates how the concept of cognatic descent, and the consequent attempts to define cognatic descent groups and to discover the structural principles in terms of which they operated, posed a challenge to structural models of group formation. If descent group membership was not determined by a single structural principle, that of genealogical descent, but instead was affected by individual choice, then the theoretical, descent-based category would not match the actual group. If this were so, then the total social structure that the Fortesian analyst sought to observe from the outside would not be an embodiment of the principles of social organisation and so could not be used to deduce those principles. Instead, that structure would be the consequence of numerous individual decisions, which could not be explained from the outside in terms of structural principles as Fortes had done. Instead, it would be understandable only from the point of view of individual egos and the contingencies they faced.

The other challenge to Fortesian structuralism developed from the debate about kindreds. This, too, led to a reconsideration of the concept of group and to the development of a theoretically-significant distinction between social groups and conceptual categories. It was agreed after the publication of Goodenough's article that kindreds were different from descent groups. Because kindreds were ego-focused rather than ancestor-focused, they could not be used as the basis of corporate groups. But if they could not be corporate groups, what could they be, and how could they be incorporated into the model of society provided by unilineal descent theory?

The discussion of kindreds revolved around three questions (cf. Keesing 1966: 346). First, were kindreds categories or groups? Or, what was the relationship between cultural categories and social groups, between the theoretical and operational organisation of society? Second, how were kindreds internally structured? Did they include affines, were they symmetrical or skewed, was their composition affected by non-genealogical factors? What kinds of principles could be used to form a kin group? Third, could kindreds coexist with unilineal descent groups? Could more than one principle of social organisation or categorisation be used within the same domain of social life, and what were the theoretical implications of choice between principles? And running through all of these was the crucial question, was social structure the determining factor in the process of social life, or an epiphenomenon of it?

One answer to these questions was Derek Freeman's 1960 Curl Bequest Prize Essay, 'On the concept of the kindred', a defence of structuralism and an attack on the challenges to it emerging in the Pacific studies of cognatic descent. Freeman agreed that kindreds were the equivalent of unilineal descent groups, but skirted over the issue of precisely how cognatic categories were trans- formed into cognatic groups. Others, however, rejected a structuralist approach. They saw cognation as a cultural element that could not, in itself, shape how people organised themselves or how they acted. One of the first such descriptions of kindreds was Robert Pehrson's description of Northern Lapp kin groups. Pehrson was a processualist who did not elicit a set of rules or principles that created bilateral organisation. Instead, he set himself the task of analysing the factors that led individuals or sibling sets to ally with one reindeer-hunting band out of the many with whom they had kin connections. And he found that genealogical connectedness in itself did not explain these alliances: a number of other factors were necessary. Pehrson, then, stressed the importance of understanding the process of group formation for understanding the organisation of bilateral societies.

In 1962 Ward Goodenough took Pehrson's paper as the starting point for his analysis of kindreds and local group formation among the Lakalai of what is now West New Britain Province in Papua New Guinea. This was one of the first explicit attempts in Oceania to look at kinship from the point of view of ego and local organisation rather than from the total social system. Echoing Pehrson, he argued that groups composed of kin need not have kinship as their determining principle. He used this approach in his analysis of Lakalai local groups, and he argued that Lakalai residential groups, though made up of people who were kin to each other, could be understood only as sets of people brought together by individual ties of friendship, clientship or mutual interest.

As we have shown, the Oceanic bilateral society, either of cognatic descent groups or of kindreds, challenged the Fortesian model. The pertinent

kin categories necessarily overlapped, and individuals were not unambiguously placed in social groups by the operation of structural descent principles
on their 'irreducible genealogical connections, the given relations of actual connectedness' (Fortes 1969: 52). Consequently, the organisation of individuals on
the ground could not be made isomorphic with kin categories or the ideological
domain of social life generally except by sleight of hand. Individual action
intervened. When residence, kinship, political allegiance, property ownership
and so forth were not isomorphic, how were they related? And if they were not
unambiguously aligned, but were brought together only as individuals choose
for their own best advantage, how could the genealogical structure be determ-
inate? What, then, was Fortes's 'point of view of the total social system', other
than the point of view of the ethnographer summing up the activities of
numerous egos, activities that created the epiphenomenal appearance of a
social structure, but did not determine it and were not determined by it?

This was the end of the slippery slope down which Fortesian structuralism was led by the concepts of cognatic descent and bilateral organisation. It
could not be avoided, but had to be confronted. The first Pacific ethnographer
to do this was Harold Scheffler, and his book *Choiseul Island social structure*
marked a turning point in Pacific ethnography.[6] It provided the first fully-
formed non-structural model of social organisation in Oceania, focusing
attention not on the formal properties of structures, but on the processes of
individual action and on the problem of the relation between ideology and
practice, or, as that distinction was framed by Scheffler and those like him,
between culture and society.

PROCESS

Cognatic descent was a dilemma because lineage theory said that the
ideational and practical domains of social life are isomorphic. Scheffler dis-
posed of the dilemma by saying they need not be. He drew a radical distinction
between culture (ideas, norms and cultural constructs) and society (social processes and individual actions), and said there was no particular reason for them
to be the same. His demolition of the structural model was thorough. He based
his definition of groups not on Maine's analysis of the corporation, but on
Goffman's ethnomethodology; he approached groups not as the consequence of
social-structural rules or principles, but as the consequence of how actors
organised themselves and how they understood that organisation (Scheffler

---

[6] Scheffler later changed his mind about the issue of descent and argued that
Fortes was correct (e.g. 1986): there are genuine, logical, structural constraints
that shape the forms that society may take, and the concept of "cognatic descent"
does not describe any of those forms. This shift of position merely further illustrates the intractability of these issues.

1965: 43). Likewise, he argued that social structure was only a model, whether of actors or anthropologists, that may feed into social processes as an element of rhetoric, but no more. Scheffler thus provided a kind of Processualist Manifesto: Structure is but a simulacrum animated by process. Or, 'Continuity or stability of a "total" system, once demonstrated, is a datum for study and must be seen as the adventitious by-product of multiple transactions rather than a postulated or assumed inherent dynamic of social systems' (1965: 292).

At the same time that Scheffler was cutting through the tangles of cognatic kinship, a new and more disquieting challenge to the Fortesian model was emerging. It was disquieting because it sprang from Fortesians' home ground, agnation. Societies of the New Guinea Highlands were large, acephalous and ideologically agnatic, as were classic African patrilineal societies. But demographic analysis showed that Highlands groups were not organised in the way that African ones were supposed to be.

In 1962 John Barnes published a survey of hitherto rather piecemeal research and crystallised the problem of these supposedly agnatic Highlands lineage societies. He picked out three areas in which they seemed to diverge particularly from the African type. First, if descent groups use descent as the only membership criterion, then 'it is hard to discover descent groups' (1962: 6) in the Highlands, where groups usually had shallow, weak genealogies and contained many non-agnates. Second, unlike the African paradigm, Highlands societies had considerable optation and multiple group membership, individual choice and initiative (1962: 6). And finally, group segmentation did not follow the "chronic" structurally-determined African pattern but seemed to be "catastrophic" and "arbitrary" (1962: 9). The activities of individuals and the factors that conditioned individual choice seemed more important than genealogical principles.

As summarised later by Marie de Lepervanche (1967–1968), in the Highlands, structuring rules were less important than the processes of exchange, production, warfare and especially leadership. Kinship was a cultural or ideological phenomenon, whose significance in the processes of social organisation was not clear. An early instance of this in the ethnographic literature was the Bena Bena. They thought of themselves in classic patrilineal terms but did not behave that way, and even converted group members who were not agnates into agnates from time to time. L.L. Langness (1967 [1964]: 144) stressed the obvious point: 'What this means ... is that the sheer fact of residence in a Bena Bena group can and does determine kinship'. This was a profound challenge to the core Fortesian concept of kinship, genealogical and biological. In these societies, genealogical descent was not always sufficient or necessary for membership in a descent category, and even though descent existed as a principle of classification, membership in a descent category was not always sufficient (as in Africa) or necessary (as in the Pacific) for membership in a descent group.

The obvious question arose: What was descent in the Highlands for?

De Lepervanche, drawing on Scheffler, argued that the discrepancy between agnatic ideology and practice reflected ethnographers' failure to see what people really meant by descent. For the Highlands, descent was 'a way of talking about groups' (1967–1968: 181) whose actual constitution was determined by other social processes, it was not a principle of recruitment, organisation or segmentation (see also A. Strathern 1973, 1979b). Inherent in her argument was not merely that genealogical descent did not determine membership in descent *groups*, but that it did not determine membership in descent *categories* either.

This line of research in the Highlands brought the processual demolition of structural theory to its extreme. Fortesian social structure was anchored in reality at two points: it derived from the biological reality of kinship, and it determined real social relations between kin. Research in the Pacific cut the link with social practice, research in the Highlands cut the link with biology.

But this work was not simply destructive. In their efforts to correct the errors of the Fortesian model, researchers developed a new model that was, in large measure, an inversion of the old. The structural model saw the facts of human biology as the basis of a social structure that governed individual action. On the other hand, processualists discarded kinship as an ordering principle and took the individual actor as the starting point. People did not act because of structural rules, but in order to fulfil their interests within a world of material constraints, and the apparent orderliness of social life was only epiphenomenal. Actors may have comprehended and justified the world they created through notions that looked like kinship, but this was not the kinship of Fortesian biological and genealogical connectedness. Instead, it was a cultural notion, and there was no one-to-one correlation between it and the physical universe or the social order. Kinship, like any other cultural concept, did influence action, but only as an element of rhetoric used in the pursuit of individual goals. But when they undercut kinship in this way, anthropologists denied themselves the classic foundation on which institutions of politics, religion and so on were built. As a result, the entire framework came tumbling down. We were left not with "society" but with collections of individuals struggling for self-interest. Whatever the validity of these processual arguments, they brought many anthropologists to an impasse. They cut the social out of social anthropology and left people searching for another prefix.

Processualists attacked structuralism at its weakest point, where structure, or its rules and norms, intersects with individual action. Being unable to find a link between apparent social order, ideology and individual action, theorists determined that they should be rigourously separated. Each was to be studied independently and on its own terms. But declaring social order to be epiphenomenal did not make that order disappear, did not resolve the problem that structural theory addressed: How it is that diverse people with diverse interests manage, even imperfectly, to achieve a common culture and organisation that endure over time (and that may be remarkably like the common culture and organisation of a distant set of people with whom they have no contact)? By denying the existence of overarching structures, processualists could provide no explanation for the regularities of human social organisation. By defining structure as epiphenomenal or by limiting it to the realm of culture, processualists seemed to have defined away anthropology's subject matter, and located the essential causes of human social arrangements in someone else's discipline; in ecology, demography or psychology (but, curiously, not history).

Perhaps as a consequence, these processualist arguments were challenged by new structuralist arguments almost before they were fully formed. Interestingly, however, the conflict was silent, exponents of the two styles competing but rarely arguing openly against one another. Neo-structuralists did not attack processualists, but instead tried to formulate arguments against descent theory that would be superior to those of the processualists, that would provide economical, wholly anthropological, answers to processual problems.

Many anthropologists writing on Papua New Guinea in the 1970s came to argue that exchange should replace descent. They drew on Lévi-Strauss and Mauss, which gave their work a peculiar, anachronistic air, locked into ancient debate about descent and alliance theory, and thus out of step with the Marxist theorising that was important elsewhere. Researchers suggested that by using the correct exchange-based model, the discrepancy between ideology and practice would disappear. But in doing so they ignored exchange practices. Instead, they pursued the logic of people's ideas and exchange structures, not the census material and quantitative data that were used to undercut Fortesian structuralism in the 1960s and the early 1970s. In other words, they felt it was no longer necessary to deal with the practical processes of politics and group formation, and it became possible once again to pursue social anthropology at the level of structure rather than process.

STRUCTURE

One of the first important new-style Highlands ethnographies was Roy Wagner's *The curse of Souw*, published in 1967. He argued that the descent theorists erred in assuming that social groups were both defined and inter-related according to principles of agnation and patrilineal descent. Because of this error, ethnographers mistakenly tried to explain groups not composed exclusively of agnates by proposing the radical separation of ideology and behaviour. Ideology and behaviour merely *appeared* to diverge, Wagner argued, because the biases of descent theory made it impossible to understand kinship ideology correctly. Wagner sought to rectify this with his description of Daribi kinship theory, one which contained 'a principle of exchange which is capable of forming units on its own terms, although it necessarily interacts with the principle of consanguinity' (1967: 231). This invocation of a Daribi "principle of exchange" to explain the presence of non-agnates in "agnatic" groups quietly marked the reimposition of structure on a key area where processualists had attacked the earlier descent models. Accounts based on individualistic social processes or political alliance, warfare, and so on, were replaced by a model whose logical properties were intended to account for empirical observation.

Although exchange was prominent in *The curse of Souw*, it was Anthony Forge in 1972 who was the first to argue explicitly that exchange rather than descent was the central structuring principle in Melanesian societies: 'in terms of both ideology and practice[,] rules of descent and the groups formed in their name take second place to the principles of exchange' (1972: 539). (In this paper Forge also raised the issues of gender and affinal relations that were to become increasingly significant through the 1970s and 1980s as more researchers begin to investigate exchange and kinship as a system of meanings.) Similarly, in 1973, Erik Schwimmer portrayed exchange as the key to understanding Orokaiva group composition and action. But unlike most other writers, he attempted to combine structural and processual concerns. Instead of accepting a "principle of reciprocity" as self-generating and self-explanatory, Schwimmer rooted the phenomenon of exchange in its cultural meanings, in the Orokaiva conceptualisation of the complementarity of donor and recipient as mediated by the object exchanged, for it was only through this that one could approach the question of how exchange was begun and why it continued (1973: 4).

While Schwimmer leavened his structuralism with attention to process, others appeared to think that exchange structure was the key to social structure, that 'exchange ... can provide a model for the shape and form of society over time' (Mcdowell 1980: 66), that it 'orders all social relations between groups and individuals' (Feil 1980: 297). This view became so widespread that, by the middle of the 1980s, one influential writer could casually state, 'exchange itself is the central dynamic' of Melanesian social organisation (Whitehead 1986: 80), without even feeling the need to argue the point. For some, this concern with exchange meant a return to Lévi-Straussian structuralism, as writers tried to piece together the logic of systems of restricted marriage exchange (e.g. Feil 1980; Kelly 1974; J. Weiner 1979, 1982). But when they abandoned descent, these writers and others like them did not abandon two key features of Fortesian structuralism. Their focus remained the total social system; they construed and investigated the logics of social order and ideology independently of the processes by which individuals acted out or used them. This appears strikingly in Paula Rubel and Abraham Rosman's *Your own pigs you may not eat*. They investigated kinship, residence, marriage, affinal exchange and leadership in thirteen societies, and concluded: 'The structure of ceremonial exchange also organizes behavior in other cultural domains, which is why it can be singled out as the dominant structure' (1978: 320).

Interestingly, Marxist theory, pivotal in much of anthropology in the 1970s, was not a notable part of this re-emergence of structure. Even Maurice Godelier, influential elsewhere, was almost completely ignored by those who wrote about Melanesian kinship and exchange (see the *Social Science Citation Index*, 1976–1980). Only in the 1980s did Marxist ideas begin to appear in significant ways, and even then they were more the structural Marxism of Althusser than the processual Marxism of E.P. Thompson. The prime Marxist appearance was in the assertion that exchange and kinship were only two elements of a triad, the third being production. Marxists opposed material production with kinship and its associated relations, reconceptualised as social reproduction, the two realms being linked through exchange.

While some anthropologists influenced by Marx's ideas focused primarily on the objective structure of Melanesian societies and exchange practices (e.g. Gregory 1982; Modjeska 1982), others sought to incorporate indigenous meanings in their models. For example, in his analysis of Muyuw society in Milne Bay, Frederick Damon argued that *kula* valuables encapsulated and mediated relations of both exchange and production, different terms and meanings being assigned to the valuables to indicate which sort of relationship they represented. As *kitoum*, valuables were individually-owned products of labour that could be exchanged in various ways. As *mwal/veigun*, they circulated between enchained *kula* partners, linking men and making their names. The logic of the system, for Damon, was contained in these two conceptions of valuables: 'Ultimately the contradiction in the kula ring is not between two modes of circulation, generalized and restricted [as Lévi-Straussian analysis would suggest], but between the circulation process of *mwals* and *veiguns* and the production process whereby *kitoums* get their significance' (1980: 286, emphasis omitted).[7] Similarly, Maurice Godelier (1986), Lisette Josephides (1985) and Andrew Strathern (1979a) linked social structure, production, exchange and indigenous beliefs. For them, however, the key structural element is gender inequality, and the key elements of belief are those that define and devalue the place of women in production, whether of valuables or of human beings.

---

[7] Damon (1983) extended his argument about the importance of production for exchange by looking at affinal exchange. We deal with this briefly in chapter 3.

A concern with social reproduction and meaning came together clearly in Annette Weiner's analysis of kinship and exchange on the Trobriand Islands, in Milne Bay, though hers is hardly a Marxist model. She argued that rituals of kinship and exchange were concerned not just with human reproduction, but also with the important and closely-related reproduction of material and cosmological phenomena. Marriage exchange, in other words, entails not merely the exchange of women and their reproductive potential, but also the reproduction of "elements of value", 'human beings, social relations, cosmological phenomena such as ancestors, and resources such as land' (1980: 71). Therefore, understanding exchange requires understanding the way people conceived of the processes of production and reproduction of both people and objects; that is, how they understood the processes that exchange was intended, at least in part, to control (1980: 72). From this perspective she criticised what she saw as the classic theory of exchange. She said first that it led to a focus on discrete transactions rather than on long-term relations between exchanging parties. Second, it implied that the purpose of giving was to put the recipient in the giver's debt rather than to achieve a far more complicated control over the process of social reproduction itself. Third was her intuitive point that it could not account for the ritual, intellectual and political complexity of ceremonial exchange.

> [I]t seems appropriate to raise the question of whether or not the enormous energy, preoccupation, and ritual extravagance found, for example, in Melanesian societies, can be reduced to mere sets of linear "gift" and "counter-gift" situations. Do elaborate and well-articulated exchange systems function only to insure, for example, that a man replaces his sister with another man's sister, or that the tradition of the exchange of an armshell for a necklace previously given is perpetuated? (1980: 73)[8]

The concern with kinship as meaning reaches its apogee in those who adhere to David Schneider's conception of anthropology's task as the cultural analysis of meanings. This conception reduces the study of kinship and social organisation to the study of how people define relationships, and so excludes most of the interests of the anthropologists of earlier decades, as well as the Marxist interest in exploitation and false consciousness (e.g. M. Strathern 1988). One of the best-known Melanesianist of this group is Roy Wagner, whose complex view of meaning is best illustrated, rather than described.

---

[8] However, this criticism applies equally to the arguments of Weiner herself and others who seek to explain exchange in terms of ideological systems. Why should the reproduction of what appear to be rather abstract "elements of value" excite such interest in villages? Analyses of cultural systems are important, but by no means sufficient, and bring us back again to the question of the relation between ideas and actions that was at the core of the descent controversy.

The traditional approach to kinship studies, established by Louis Henry Morgan, has been to assume that cultures fit themselves into a regime of "natural kinship" given by the "facts" of genealogy, by organizing a set of social roles that develop it into a system of institutions, rights, and marriage practices... . An analogic approach, by contrast, begins with the centrality of relationship — the fact that all modes of "relating" are basically analogous — and asks how the differentiation of kinds of relationships, imposed by culture, controls the flow of analogy among them. ... Analogic kinship is a matter of maintaining a morally appropriate flow by balancing similarity against differentiation, keeping generation from turning into degeneration, as it were (1986: 34).

Wagner clearly does not think of himself as a structuralist. Certainly he is not in, for example, a Lévi-Straussian manner. Yet from our perspective he is one. He is concerned with the creation of models of people's conceptions of the nature of relationships, models whose logical orderliness is illustrated by the fact that, as he presents them, they seem always to take the form of regular octahedra; and he explicitly ignores 'the practical and normative issues of how meaning is linked to social action' (Wagner 1986: 124).

In his review of the state of kinship studies in anthropology, John Barnes (1980: 301–302) criticised their highly structural, symbolic nature at that time, and called for a renewed processualism. This has still not happened in Papua New Guinea.

MUDDLES IN THE MODELS

We have not presented this brief review of some of the history of writings on kinship and exchange in Melanesia simply in a fit of self-indulgence. Rather, we have done so to illustrate what seems hard for some anthropologists to grasp: a central problem that concerned Fortes, lineage theorists, their processual critics and the latter-day structuralists and cultural anthropologists has not gone away.

This problem first appeared when the Fortesian descent model moved to Oceania, and the essence of the ensuing controversy was outlined by David Schneider twenty-five years ago: 'the muddled part of that model is the notion that somehow the [descent] segment is not only a conceptual segment, but also in some way a physically distinct and concrete segment' (1965: 63). In other words, Fortesians held that it was necessary for people's rules and people's behaviour to overlap. The difficulties of accommodating descent rules to the actual formation of social groups led to the downfall of structural-functional descent theory, but not structural theory itself. Instead, it led to the proposition that culture (ideology) and society (practice) should be radically distinguished. Anthropologists have spent their time since then investigating ideology, exchange and a whole range of different topics. However, though they may continue to celebrate the overthrow of Fortesian structural-functionalism and may continue to see Barnes's 'African models in the New Guinea Highlands' as the beginning of the end of the old approach, generally they have continued to use the same kind of logical, structural premises that had underlain the Fortesian research of the 1950s.

Anthropologists of Melanesia do not remember what the battle with Fortesian descent models was about.[9] They have forgotten the reason for the downfall of descent theory, or they mis-perceive it as the failure of Fortesians to produce an accurate model of kinship ideology. However, the controversy was not purely about whether exchange or descent was the source of the more fruitful explanations of Melanesian societies. Instead, there was another issue, the one we have pursued here. This was concerned with the adequacy of structural models for anthropology. The antagonists here were not Fortesian descent advocates and exchange advocates, but structuralists and processualists. The structuralist victory that we have described allows researchers in the 1980s to assume that the structures that they discern within the cultures they study are adequate foci of analysis. Anthropologists of Melanesia no longer seem to feel compelled to study actual behaviour in the way that many Highlands processualists did, no longer seem to feel compelled to pry into the relation between the systems of meanings that were being uncovered and people's actions, no longer seem to feel compelled to compare the logic of their models with the social worlds they confront.

Few anthropologists would deny the importance of both structure and process as ways of approaching the societies they describe. Equally, we are not the only Melanesian anthropologists to attend to the distinction between structure and process either in their own work or in regional ethnography.[10] But even though this issue has attracted occasional, and perhaps growing, interest, it is not a part of the discipline's main understanding of either the region or its own history; relatively few have made the effort to take both structure and process seriously in their ethnographies or to address the relationship between the two in their analyses in the way that we do in this book.[11]

---

[9] This forgetting was brought home to us when one senior anthropologist (not otherwise associated with this project) who read a draft of our discussion of processualist arguments remarked: 'I had forgotten we used to write about that.'

[10] Some more, and less, obvious examples include Gewertz (1983: esp. 221–222), Knauft (1990), LiPuma (1983; 1988) and O'Hanlon (1989: esp. chap. 7). Of course other examples could be found.

[11] This is true outside of Melanesia as well. In her Distinguished American Ethnological Society Lecture of 1987, Sally Falk Moore made many telling criticisms of structural approaches. However, she then proceeded to reject such approaches wholesale, and so failed to see the need to take both structure and process into

Just as the problem of structure and process is not peculiar to Melanesian studies, so it is not peculiar to anthropology. Outside of modern anthropology it appears in Marx's distinction between class-in-itself (class in structural terms) and class-for-itself (class in processual terms); in Weber's concern for how and under what conditions people's class location (structure) affects their actions (process). More recently, E.P. Thompson (1968) has argued against a purely structural model of class in the analysis of English history, and Anthony Giddens (1977) has attempted to bridge the gap between structure and process with his theory of structuration.

We do not claim that our description of Ponam kinship and exchange will settle this broad and persistent issue. However, in exploring these perspectives explicitly in this ethnography we hope to show that the ascendant structuralist concern with meaning is as mis-guided as were the processualist attacks on lineage theory. Neither allows an adequate understanding of Ponam society, where these views are not alternatives, but complements. Attention both to symbolic and social structures and to actual decisions and choices are essential to understanding the operation of kinship and exchange.

Both cause and consequence of modern anthropology's common failure to deal with this central problem is the failure to introduce a genuine historical dimension into its work, a dimension that helps clarify the place of contingency and circumstance in influencing people's actions and the social regularities that those actions help generate. We are not arguing that history is an anthropological panacea, just as we are not arguing that all anthropologists of Melanesia have ignored it (e.g. Feil 1982; Gewertz 1983; A. Strathern 1982).[12] Certainly history is a pursuit as full of danger for the unwary as is anthropology, and it can become a source of structure just as determinant as biological connectedness was for Fortes (J. Carrier 1987a). We do argue, however, that anthropological descriptions and analyses of kinship and exchange, and much else, in Melanesian societies would be better if researchers attempted to discover how people's actions and societies' orders were affected by events and changing circumstance both within and beyond the village. These factors constrain and liberate individuals just as they impinge on social structure in different ways. To understand kinship and exchange in Papua New Guinea one must incorporate these changing circumstances. For Ponam, as for many other places in the

account. The most forceful modern counter-statement from within anthropology is probably Pierre Bourdieu's *Outline of a theory of practice*.

[12] It is interesting that there appears to be a growing interest in the past among Melanesian anthropologists, but one that is concerned with prehistory and evolution (e.g. Feil 1987). It is appropriate to our argument that this sort of history tends to be highly structured, as well as being thoroughly divorced from processes in modern Melanesian societies.

country, changing circumstance has meant changes that reflect colonisation and independence. These changing external forces, and the ways that islanders have responded and adapted to them, are central to the analysis we undertake.

THE APPROACH OF THIS BOOK

We have sketched out the changing fortunes of the two different perspectives that we call "structural" and "processual". Our concern with these perspectives shapes this book, and the frame of comparison we use is constituted by these two approaches rather than by the body of work on kinship and exchange in Melanesia. We make no systematic effort to relate Ponam practices to what is described for other societies in Papua New Guinea.

The different parts of this book are explorations of structure and process, played out not in abstract theoretical terms of the sort that we have used in this historical sketch, but in the more concrete terms of ethnography. Thus, the first two chapters form a pair, investigating the overall system of Ponam kinship from contrasting structural and processual perspectives. Chapter 1 describes the organisation of kinship groups that we saw in the 1980s. It emphasises the importance for Ponams of formal genealogical reckoning and largely descent-based kinship. Chapter 2 shows that this structure, however real it may have been at the time, could not be understood adequately if one approached it only in structuralist terms. Instead, it is necessary to attend to process, in this case the vicissitudes of history and people's efforts to cope with their changing circumstances. We show that the rigidly genealogical system we saw in the 1980s was one that emerged as a consequence of changes in the Manus economy. And this basic point applies more broadly, not just to areas of kinship, but also to Ponam life in general.

The next pair of chapters looks at exchange in the same contrasting ways. Chapter 3 describes the formal rules of Ponam exchange, intelligible only given a prior understanding of kinship. We describe both the reciprocal logic of individual exchanges and the cyclical logic of the system of exchange as a whole. As we show, Ponam exchange has an elegant and compelling structural logic similar to that described in some other parts of Papua New Guinea. However, as our historical discussion in chapter 4 shows, this structural logic did not exist alone and self-supporting. Instead, the logic apparent in the exchanges of the 1980s had not endured for many generations. It was a product of circumstance and can be understood adequately only in terms of the circumstances in which it existed.

These first two pairs of chapters show the shortcomings of a purely structural approach, one that attends only to the formal properties of systems of kinship and exchange. In each, a structural model is presented, and then undercut by showing the importance of process, and especially historical process. Our purpose in this book, however, is not to denigrate structure, except insofar as structural approaches have dominated recent Melanesian anthropology, as we have argued in this introduction. The final section of this book, chapters, 5, 6 and 7, corrects this imbalance. These chapters explore the issues that concern us from the opposite viewpoint. First, they are not concerned with overall structures and cycles and historical forces of the sort we describe in the first four chapters. Instead, they are concerned with what people do in exchange and how they think about it, doings and thinkings that embody, express and recreate Ponam kinship and exchange week by week and year by year. Second, they do not set up the notion of structure only to knock it down with process. Instead, they are concerned to show that people's daily, practical kinship and exchange activities are profoundly shaped by the rules and structures that people see around them and represent and recreate in those activities. Chapters 5 and 6 describe the way that Ponams objectified the structure of kinship during the displays of gifts made in ceremonial exchange and the way that this logic thereby achieved a constraining reality independent of the will or motives of individuals. Chapter 7 describes how individuals operated within that logic, using it or falling victim to it as circumstances dictated.

The ethnography we present and the way we organise that presentation will make clear that understanding Ponam society requires attention to both structure and process, for neither stands alone.

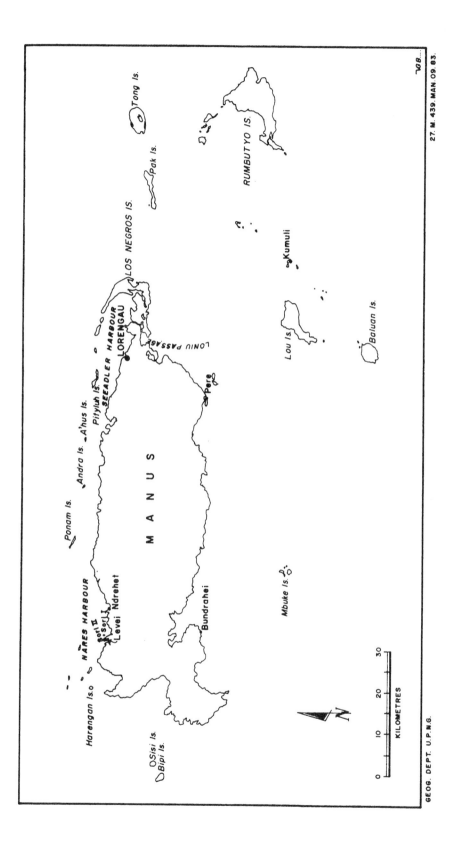

Map 1   *Manus*

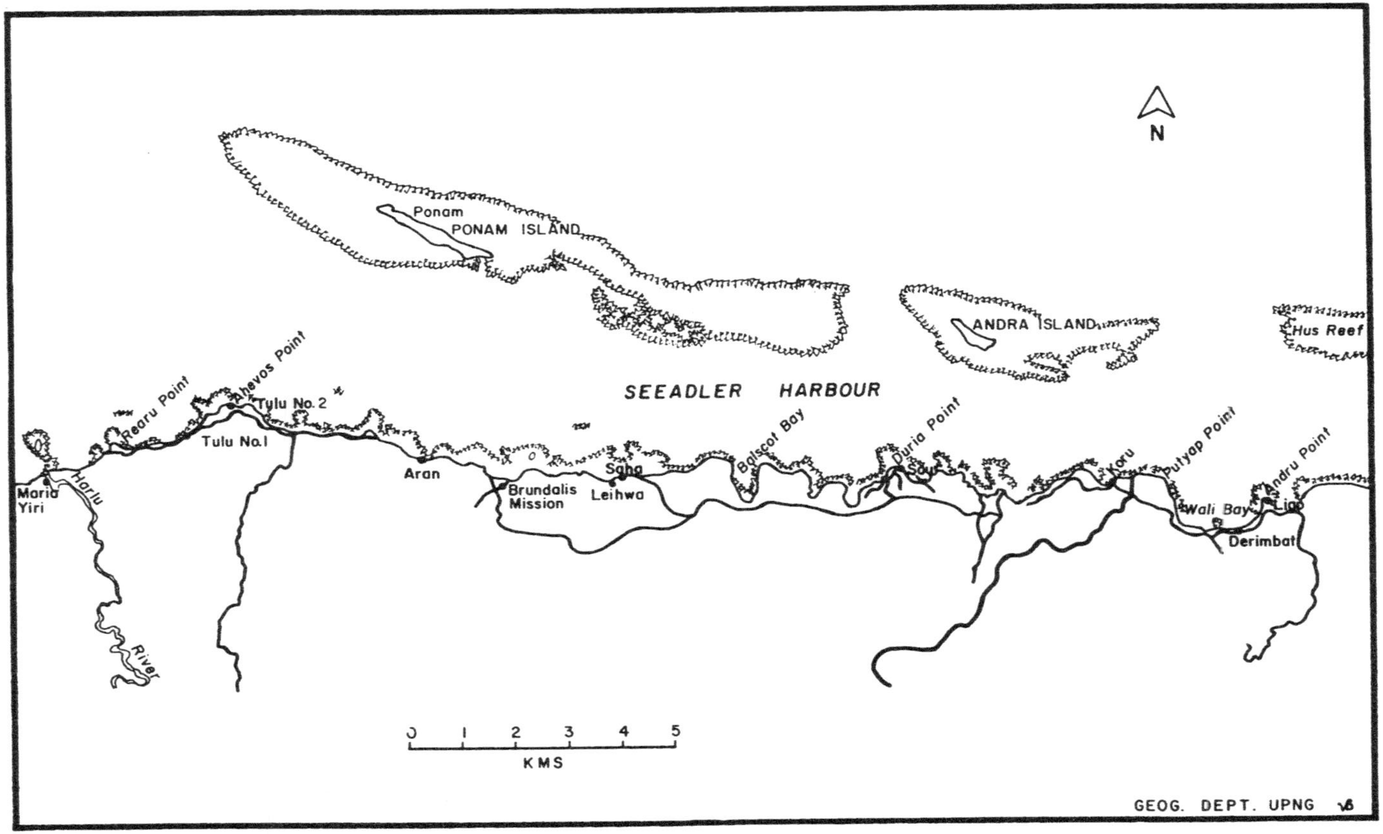

Map 2   *North-Central Manus*

CHAPTER ONE

The organisation
of Ponam kinship

In many ways, the Ponam that we saw would have been instantly recognisable to Meyer Fortes. In much of their daily interactions, islanders talked about and acted toward each other in terms of their kin relationships. The men who went in the cool of the early morning to clear the ground around a stand of palms explained their presence by describing how they were related to each other. The women who chatted and tended the fire during the long, slow process of cooking coconut cream down to oil explained themselves in the same way. The child who was urged to fetch water, and be polite about it, was told to do so 'for your aunt', not 'for Julia' or even 'for Aunt Julia'. The man who stayed behind and sprinkled powdered lime and admonitions, after the mourners had taken the coffin to the graveside service, explained that he was of the class of relative the dead woman's spirit would respect and heed, when he told her to quit the village she knew and loved and go to the cemetery with her body.

When the interactions involved real property or activities affected by ceremonial exchange, people's relations to the kin groups that owned the property or that were involved in the exchange were added to kin relations among individuals. And because so much around Ponam was real property, and because Ponam exchange was so frequent, these groups and relations were a constant part of everyday activities. The men who went angling at night with pressure lamps were careful to go only where they had the right, which meant the waters owned by their patrilineages. The group of men and women who cut down the casuarina tree and chopped it up explained that they were relatives of the groom, cutting firewood for the marriage. Of course this was heightened in more formal circumstances. After less than a month on Ponam, we went to a feast to celebrate the raising of a men's house. Watching forty or more people working, eating and talking, we asked who was there. The reply was three names: long-dead children of the clan founder; one, moreover, a woman who had died single and childless.

We could not begin to understand Ponam, either as a set of interacting people or as a structured whole, until we began to understand Ponam kinship. That is why we start with a discussion of kinship terms, groups and categories. What we describe is not a system we have constructed for the purposes of analysis, but an indigenous system central to Ponams' understanding of their social organisation. Because it is focused on the meaning of terms, this description presents an idealised picture of the proper relations between categories. Ponams were fully aware that people did not always conform to this pattern. But, by and large, they believed that the island would be a better place if people did (*WT&E*: 48–52). And regardless of whether or not people always acted in accord with this model, it was a significant influence on their actions and on their understanding of the actions of others.

PONAMS' RELATIVES: KINSHIP FROM THE EGO FOCUS

As is the case in most Oceanic languages, Ponam kin terms normally take the intimate possessives form, and thus necessarily have an ego-focused orientation. The same is true of the terms for the two broad categories into which Ponam speakers divided kin, *lowa-* and *marike-*, cognates and affines. (We define Ponam kin terms as well as we are able in appendix 2.)

We translate the term *lowa-* as "cognate" or "kindred". *Lowa-* included any person related to ego through either parent. Thus, ego's siblings and their children, his or her patrilateral and matrilateral parallel and cross kin, of all ages and generations, were all *lowa-*. However, ego's own children and their descendants were not. In principle, *lowa-* could be traced as far as human memory allowed, and anyone to whom ego could trace a cognatic link, no matter how distant or obscure, could be addressed as a cognate and treated accordingly.

Ponams very much preferred to marry within the island, and recognised that as a result of this all islanders were *lowa-* to each other. Most people could provide numerous details of their exact relationships to others, and a variety of kin terms by which they could appropriately address any other. Thus, the most common response to the question, 'What do you call So-and-so?' was 'Through what kin link, through my father or my mother or someone else?' The term used for a linking kinsman or kinswoman was *sal*, "road". Kin terminology identified a given Other as a certain class of relative, and this was important for understanding how people thought of and acted toward each other. However, Ego also had to know the genealogical details of the relationship, which included the names of the various linking relatives, for these determined the way in which individuals should participate in ceremonial exchange. Most Ponams also recognised that they were probably distantly related to most other Manus, though in many cases the details of these relationships had been forgotten, for they were not used so frequently.

Ponams' theories of conception were compatible with this cognatic vision of the kin universe. A child was said to be equally formed by the contributions of maternal blood and paternal semen. People explicitly denied that blood and semen contributed separately to the formation of the child's body; that, for example, the semen formed bones and the blood formed flesh. Ponams expected that children would look like both parents, though in varying degrees, and found pleasure in pointing out the development of recognisable features.

The question of whether biological, genealogical kinship really is or is not at the heart of all "kinship" systems is a venerable one, but apparently not on its last legs (e.g. Fox 1989; Schneider 1981*b*). So, it is appropriate to describe Ponams' position on it. First, for them genealogical connectedness, the fact of being born of a particular father and mother, did make a person a cognate (*lowa-*) to those his or her parents called a cognate regardless of any subsequent action. Thus, for example, the father of an illegitimate child was and remained that child's *tama* (father), and hence a cognate, regardless of whether or not he chose to marry the child's mother or to acknowledge his paternity in any other way. However, cognatic relationships could be created in other ways. The illegitimate child's mother's husband was also its *tama* and his kin were also cognates. Further, people who treated one another as cognates and declared themselves as such were seen as cognates and expected to remain so. However, in recent times Ponams did not create kinship this way within the island. Instead, such relationships were created between Ponams and outsiders, particularly friends that Ponams had made at work and at school.

Thus, the kin terms discussed in this section could be used between people linked genealogically in the appropriate way, but could also be used for those who chose to act in the manner prescribed for those so linked. The issue of whether they were "really" kin or simply acting like kin was simply not relevant in Ponam thought. It is important to make this point here, for this openness in creating relationships did not obtain in all spheres of Ponam kinship, most notably the sphere of patrilineal property-owning groups, *kamals*.

As in other Manus languages (Mead 1934: esp. 338–352), Ponam terminology for cognates followed a Crow system. Though there have been objections to the notion of a distinctive Crow–Omaha terminology (esp. R. H. Barnes 1976), Ponams did have the four elements of the classic Crow–Omaha complex: exogamous unilineal descent groups, dispersed affinal alliance, a strong emphasis on maintaining alliance between groups once linked by marriage, and a concept of tribal completeness. But Ponam is unusual because its most prominent unilineal descent groups were patrilineal rather than matrilineal, which is standard among Crow systems.

The basic principles in Ponam terminology were these. Men and women used the same terms for patrilateral cross-kin, but different terms for matrilateral cross-kin. For both men and women parallel cousins were classed with siblings; FZCs and FZDCs were classed with father and fathers' sister; and FZSCs were classed with siblings. For men, mothers' brothers were classed with

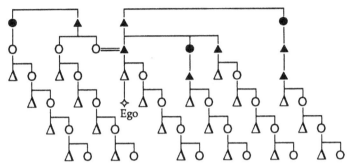

Figure 1   Tamatu: *some of ego's* asis *and* tamas

Note: Solid figures are linking kin and are not themselves ego's *tamatu*.
Note: Here and in all subsequent figures, the symbol ✧ is used for a person whose sex is immaterial.

sisters' children; and MBCs were classed with own children. For women, MBCs, brothers' children and sons' children were all classed together. (Detailed diagrams of Ponam cognatic kin terms and Crow equations are in A. Carrier 1987: appendices 2 & 3.)

Within *lowa-*, Ponams distinguished one particularly important category of kin, *tamatu*. This included all of the relatives whom ego called *asi* and *tama*; that is, all of the women ego's father called sister (*naropiso-*) or mother (*tine*) and all of the men ego's father called brother (*nato-*). *Tamatu* was not a possessive, and in fact the suffix *tu* had no significance in Ponam. However, the term is obviously cognate with other Austronesian languages in which this suffix is used to form the possessive (e.g. Motu, *tamagu*: "my father", which in Ponam would be *tamak*). Except for the solid figures, all of the people shown of figure 1 are *tamatu* to ego, and the figure shows how extensive this class of relatives is. In addition to its genealogical designation, the relationship between ego and his or her *tamatu* was also called *mbrutile-*, a term connoting particularly the affectionate joking relationship that was supposed to hold between these kin rather than the more formal, unequal relationship connoted by the terms *asi* and *tama*.

*Tamatu*s had special ritual obligations to and powers over ego. They had the power to bless with strength (*ken dof paton*) and to curse (*tenen*). As a part of the ritual of blessing, they danced (*han*) for their kin who called them *tamatu*, prayed (*njames*) to the ancestors and invoked formulaic blessings, the most common of which was 'May my faults remain mine, and my virtues be yours' (*Pono arak sala'an ki se arak; pono arak masin ki le aram*). The inversion of this blessing, 'May my virtues remain mine, and my faults be yours', was the most potent possible curse, bringing with it insanity, promiscuity, sterility and other disasters. It could be removed easily, however, if the *tamatu* who made the curse chose to do so.

Because they had these powers, *tamatus* had the special authority and obligation to supervise ego's moral behaviour and to intervene in, and even enforce settlement of, his or her disputes. No one else, with the possible exception of magistrates and officers of the Church, had this right. Ponams incorporated the authority of *tamatus* into the rituals of the Catholic Church. Thus a boy's godparents and the members of his wedding party were chosen from his *tamas*, and a girl's godmothers and members of her wedding party were chosen from her *asis*. These *tamatus* henceforth had an intensified obligation to supervise religious upbringing and to act as marriage counsellors.

In addition to this general supervision of moral welfare, *tamatus* also provided ritual blessings on occasions of life crisis. The two most important of these were ego's first return to Ponam after a long voyage (this was usually during childhood) and ego's burial (these are described in chapter 4). The *tamatus* were given responsibility for the burial because they, with their special powers of blessing and cursing, were the only ones capable of restraining the probably malevolent and certainly reluctant ghost.

Although Ponam terms for cognates were in daily use and known to everyone, Ponam affinal terms were rarely used and were not known by most of those born since World War II. These younger people commonly referred to all their affines by the Pidgin term "tambu", or by the Ponam term *marike-*, which apparently had applied originally only to a certain class of affines. Our reconstructions of affinal terminology through interviews with older people are somewhat contradictory: different people often gave different terms for the same genealogical relationships. Without being able to hear these terms used in natural circumstances it is difficult to discover the reasons for these variations. In spite of these difficulties, we can lay out what appear to be some basic features of affinal terminology. (The most plausible reconstructions of affinal terms are diagramed in A. Carrier 1987: appendix 4.)

First, the same sets of terms were used for spouse's kin, ego's children's affines, and maternal and paternal cognates' affines. For example, a woman used the same term, *njana-*, for her husband's mother, husband's brother's wife, son's wife and sister's son's wife. The relations differentiated most carefully were those between inter-marrying sibling sets. Three different terms were used for these. There was also a single distinct term for spouse's *asis* and for those who called spouse *asi*. The rest of spouse's kin and immediate affines (e.g. MBW) were all classed together. Distant affines not covered by these terms (e.g. BWM or MBWF) were also classed together.

Second, affinal terminology was modified to take age into account in a way that was not done with cognatic terminology. Oceanic languages commonly make terminological distinctions between older and younger siblings (Marshall 1984). Ponams did not do this, but they did distinguish between the affines of elder and younger cross-sex siblings. A woman called her younger sister's husband and her husband's older brother by affinal terms, but called her older sister's husband "father" (*tama*), and her husband's young brother "child" (*naro-*). Similarly a man called his younger brother's wife and his wife's older sister by affinal terms, but called his older brother's wife "mother" (*tine*) and his wife's younger sister "child".

Following a similar principle, a person addressed all of his or her spouse's junior kin by the cognatic terms used by that spouse. There was no special affinal term for those whom ego's spouse addressed as "child" (*naro-*) or "grandchild" (*abu*). Instead, ego took over the term used by his or her spouse. However, when the distortions of generations obliged ego to address an affine who was an elder or peer by the term suitable for an inferior (e.g. "child"), the formal term "ancestor" (*tombru-*) was usually used instead. These terms were extended to a sibling's spouse's other kin if the relationship was close and friendly. A boy who called his older brother's wife "mother" might also call his older brother's wife's brother "mother's brother". And when that boy reached manhood, his son might call the older brother's wife "father's mother".

This substitution of cognatic terms for affinal ones had a practical importance. Affines who addressed each other by cognatic terms did not have to follow the etiquette of avoidance (*fili'i*) that normally separated cross-sex affines. Indeed, the explanation Ponams gave for this usage was that it would be difficult and inappropriate for people greatly different in age (as in younger brother and much-older-brother's wife) to avoid one another, particularly when one affine had a quasi-parental role toward the other. Unless a shift in terminology permitted them to act as cognates, cross-sex affines were required to avoid one another in ways that made it very difficult for them to live together in a single household. They could meet and speak together, but in a rather formal manner, and they were often uncomfortable in one another's presence, especially when they were young. They could not eat together or chew betel nut together. They could not touch one another's bedding, wash one another's clothes, or sleep in one another's presence. Generally, women were expected to avoid men, to leave them alone to sleep or eat in peace. But if a woman did not do so, avoidance etiquette forbade a man to remind her of her error.

Ponams generally believed that this etiquette of avoidance was less carefully followed than before, and some suspected that eventually it would be abandoned altogether. Once, they said, these rules were followed strictly throughout the life of a marriage. But in the 1980s they tended to wear off as the marriage endured, and some young couples never took them up. The behaviour of these young people, particularly young brides, was the subject of much gossip but little else, for this etiquette had no sanctions behind it. Breach of the rules did not cause sickness or any other misfortune.

The last aspect of kinship from the ego focus that we describe is sibling-ship. Some have argued that ideas about siblingship are extremely important in Oceanic people's conceptions of kinship, even more important than ideas of descent, around which anthropological analyses have traditionally been framed. Thus, in his introduction to a collection on the topic, Mac Marshall (1981: 10) says: 'Both siblingship *and* descent are involved in the conceptual organization of social groups, but siblingship usually takes precedence'. Siblingship was certainly of great importance on Ponam, but it should not be separated from or considered independently of ideas of descent. The essential element of the relationship between siblings was that they provided the roads linking other groups. In the first generation they linked their two sets of affines; in later generations they linked their two sets of descendants. The relationship between siblings in the present was always shaped by the knowledge that they were establishing in prospect the relationship between those who would follow after. Thus it is fruitless to dissociate these concepts or set them in opposition to one another.

PONAM'S KIN GROUPS:
KINSHIP FROM THE ANCESTOR FOCUS

Margaret Mead (1934: 310) argued that Pere kinship had much in common with that of the Western Pacific, especially Tonga, Samoa and Fiji. These same similarities were apparent in Ponam kinship, which had a number of features that are common in Micronesian and Polynesian societies. The predominant features of Ponam kinship organisation were these. Islanders recognised non-localised totemic matrilineages. They recognised localised, property-owning patrilineal groups that were the basis of political organisation and ranking and that were divided into moieties. They recognised numerous overlapping cognatic groups. Finally, they distinguished between the descend-ants of brothers and the descendants of sisters, with the latter having ritual powers over the former, the members of the agnatic groups from which they were dispossessed.

MATRILINEAL GROUPS

Each Ponam inherited from his or her mother a set of totem animals and plants, food taboos and ritual obligations, and there were nine totemic groups represented on Ponam. The word for totem itself, *kowun*, was sometimes extended to the entire group of people who avoided the same totem, but gener-ally Ponams referred to totemic groups by their own particular names, or by the name of one or another of their prominent totems. For the sake of convenience we use *kowun* to refer to these groups and their totems. Ponams said that they did not know the true origin of totems. They asserted that totems were not ancestors in any literal sense, though some said that "other people" thought they were. The first human beings were created by God and henceforth born of women, not from animals. Although they were reasonably confident about what had not happened, they were not sure just how the ancestors had acquired their totemic obligations. Some people suggested, however, that some early ancestors had simply decided that this would be a good idea and had made it so. (This idea, that people voluntarily thought up and enacted important aspects of Ponam social organisation and practice, is a recurring one. We will have occasion to refer to it again.)

Ponam's *kowun*s were not unique to the island, but were Manus-wide, with members in many different villages and many different language groups. Further, not all Manus *kowun*s had members on Ponam, and the *kowun*s represented on Ponam could change. New *kowun*s could be brought to the island if outside women from different *kowun*s married onto Ponam and bore children there, and several *kowun*s were known to have been brought to the island that way. *Kowun*s could also die out on Ponam, as one seemed destined to do.

In 1979 the *kowun* Piri had only two living members, an elderly widow and her middle-aged son. After the widow died in 1981 her son's life was in constant jeopardy, for there was no one to cure him of totemic pollution or perform totemic rituals for him. There were other members of his *kowun* elsewhere in Manus, but they were so distantly related that there was doubt about whether or not their prayers could cure him. Fortunately there were only two species that were really dangerous for him, dugong and pandanus. Pandanus was easy enough to avoid, but when Ponams killed a dugong, as they did once or twice a year, he would flee the island for a month or more to avoid pollution from its blood, which seeped into the ground and the water and contaminated them both.

This Piri was afraid that contact with one of his totems might be fatal because he had no matrilineal kin to cure him, but most people were not so concerned. Generally totemic pollution was thought to cause degenerative afflictions rather than fatal ones. Cataracts, tooth decay, deafness and skin eruptions were all commonly attributed to contact with a totem, or even to indirect contact, such as taking lime from a stick used by someone who did not avoid your own totems, eating from a dish in which one had been served, or breathing the steam from a pot in which one was cooking. Although there were many possible sources of contact with a totem, most people did not follow rigorously all the restrictions needed to avoid all contact. Instead, they followed the elementary precautions of refusing to eat it or have it served in their households, and went to seek the help of a senior *kowun* woman if they noticed a totemic affliction developing. The problem with this common strategy was, however, that the results of totemic pollution sometimes did not become obvious until the disease was well advanced and no longer curable. As a result, old people all suffered the consequences of their careless youth.

When new and still curable, totemic illnesses were treated by a senior woman of the sufferer's immediate matrilineage, usually his or her mother, mother's mother or one of their sisters. Treatment was simple. The senior woman called out the names of matrilineage ancestors, whose power was thereby embodied in a piece of ginger, or perhaps aromatic bark. The sufferer then rubbed this on the afflicted part and expected a cure to take place within a few days. This cure could even be carried out by post, and urban Ponams frequently had cause to write home for a piece of ginger.

*Kowun*s were also particularly important for dealing with matters of women's gynaecological health and fertility. A woman could call on a senior member of her *kowun* to invoke matrilineage ancestors and the power of their *kowun* in order to cure menstrual problems and barrenness, and in order to prevent pregnancy.

Women dominated totemic ritual and curing, so that the *kowun*s were matriarchal as well as matrilineal. Men were involved only as sufferers and in rituals that required public speaking, a role normally reserved only for men. Other work was conducted exclusively by women, who addressed their prayers to women. Men were not formally excluded from *kowun* work or forbidden to know about it, but their presence was simply superfluous because, as men, they lacked the power to conduct rituals or curing effectively.

The inverse was true of many of the male rituals and activities associated with fishing. Women were not forbidden access male knowledge; they simply lacked the power to act on it, so it did not matter what they knew. Unlike people in many parts of Papua New Guinea, Ponams did not put a great deal of emphasis on knowledge and secrecy as a source of power. The most important forms of ritual and spiritual power derived largely from social status, particularly those of senior *kowun* members and *tamatu*, and were thus innate and not transferable. Those Ponams who were seen to have exceptional power and influence in their society were not thought to have acquired it from their ritual and secret knowledge. Instead, they got it from their detailed knowledge of kinship, custom and etiquette — knowledge that was available to all, but only at the cost of time, effort and tedious attention to the words of the old.

In addition to day-to-day concern with matters of pollution and health, *kowun*s also performed rituals for their members on occasions of life crisis: on first returning to the island from a distant place, at a woman's marriage, on the birth of a woman's first child, after the death of a man's or woman's spouse. Ponams carried out these totemic rituals at the same time that they held prestations to individuals' *tamatu*s, though conceptually the two sets of events were distinct. These rituals generally involved some form of seclusion, the invocation of matrilineage ancestresses, and emergence from seclusion to wash in the sea. An important feature of these rituals is that maternal kin, these maternal *kowun*s, were not paid for their work. This set them off from a person's *tamatus*, who were always paid with gifts of valuables for the blessings and care they gave (often on the same occasion as *kowun* rituals), as we describe later.

As matrilineages, the *kowun*s maintained no links with the descendants of male members, and they played no part in ceremonial exchange, in the political or economic life of the community, or indeed in any activity that would have required them to act as a group in relation to any other group. Individuals who were members of the same *kowun* did exchange with one another and could become political and economic allies and friends, but when they did so they invoked their cognatic relationship, rather than their matrilineal relationship as *kowun*. As one might expect from this, *kowun*s played no part in marriage. People did not forbid or encourage marriage within the *kowun*. It was considered wrong to marry any close cognate, whether a member of the same *kowun* or not, and a distant member of the same *kowun* was a more acceptable partner than a closer relative who was not. Some people even said that a member of one's own *kowun* was the best partner, because domestic management was much easier if the household had only one set of totems to avoid. This was a bit of a joke, however, and no one would actually choose a partner on those trivial grounds.

Because they were found throughout Manus, *kowun*s had the potential to form the basis of an integrated region-wide religious institution. Theodore Schwartz (1963: 70) says that prior to colonisation totemic groups did have some inter-ethnic significance. They provided a system of safe conduct for trade among warring or hostile villages, particularly on the mainland. At least in modern times, however, Ponams did not seem to have been linked to other communities in this way. They did not attempt to maintain ties to people from other areas with whom they shared totems and, as described above, there were serious doubts about whether distantly-related members of a *kowun* had the power to cure totemic pollution or perform appropriate rituals for one another.

PATRILINEAL GROUPS

The single large village in which all Ponams lived was organised as a series of named and clearly demarcated hamlets. Map 3 shows the village and its hamlets in 1979. Most hamlets were associated with a men's house, called *kamal* (male), which usually stood in its centre. Ideally, all of the households in a hamlet were headed by men, single women or widows who were from that hamlet's men's house. These men's-house groups were called *kamal*s, as were the men's houses themselves. They were exogamous corporate, patrilineal,

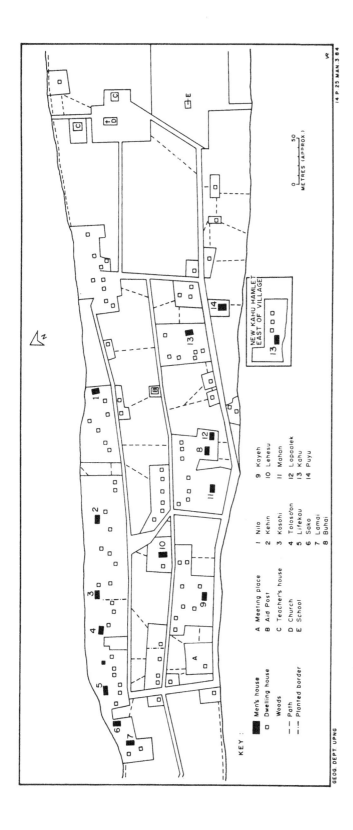

KEY:

■	Men's house
□	Dwelling house
	Woods
——	Path
———	Planted border

A Meeting place
B Aid Post
C Teacher's house
D Church
E School

1 Nilo
2 Kehin
3 Kosohi
4 Toloso'on
5 Lifekou
6 Soko
7 Lamai
8 Buhai

9 Kayeh
10 Lehesu
11 Mahan
12 Lopaalek
13 Kahu
14 Puyu

NEW KAHU HAMLET
EAST OF VILLAGE

N

0   50
METRES (APPROX.)

14 P 25 MAN.3 84

VR

Map 3   *Ponam village, December 1979*

property-owning groups and, from Ponams' point of view, these were the most important groups on the island. Almost all Ponams were said to be "from" one or another of these men's houses, or inversely, the men's house was said to be his or hers (*I paro kamal Nilo*: He/she is from Kamal Nilo; *Kamal aran Nilo*: His/her *kamal* is Nilo).[1]

As with *kowun*s, Ponams did not give these patrilineal groups a divine or mystical origin, but claimed to be ignorant of their true beginnings. They speculated, however, that *kamal*s were begun when the ancestors first decided that property should be inherited through men only. In the past land was thought to have been equally divided among sons and daughters, but this caused many problems, for land was broken up too minutely and no one knew what belonged to whom. So the ancestors decided that women, who moved on marriage and could use their husband's property, should not inherit, while men, who stayed with their fathers, should inherit. Out of this, they speculated, the institution of *kamal* was born. It is both interesting and typical of Ponam thought that their explanation, however speculative, of the origin of what they recognised as their most important institution is a sociological explanation, not a religious one. *Kamal*s were social institutions created by real, though nameless, human beings in order to solve a social problem (see J. Carrier 1987a).

The nameless ancestors who first began the institution of *kamal* lived well before the earliest ancestors whose names were remembered. And most patrilineages bore the names of ancestors who were not the earliest known Ponams, or even the earliest known people in that descent line. Instead, Ponam patrilineages bore the name of the ancestor who built for his heirs a men's house, or *kamal*. In most cases these apical ancestors lived four or five generations prior to the current adult generation.

All of the people who were from a particular men's house formed a single group that could, and sometimes did, bear three different names. These were, the name of the man who founded their first men's house, the name of the site on which that founder built their first men's house, and sometimes the name of the site on which their men's house currently stood (no *kamal* buildings remained on their original sites). For the sake of clarity we shall use "*kamal*" for this group and "men's house" for the *kamal* building, though Ponams did not make this distinction. Map 3 shows the location of men's houses on Ponam at the time of fieldwork.

---

[1] The handful of exceptions were those men and single women whose fathers were not Ponams. Such people routinely were closely but informally affiliated with the *kamal* of a close cognate (e.g. mother) or affine (e.g. wife), though as we describe later in this chapter and illustrate in chapter 7, close affiliation was not the same as membership.

These fourteen *kamal*s were classed into two geographic moieties. The island was divided lengthwise down the middle into Tolau, the North, and Kum, the South. Each *kamal* was classified as being in the north or south according to the site of its ancestral property. The Kum *kamal*s and Tolau *kamal*s formed distinct social categories, important for a number of purposes, and activated on occasion into groups. These moieties were not marriage classes. Their main use was for the organisation of islanders whenever they wished to act as members of the political unit Ponam, rather than as members of particular kin categories. Thus, village maintenance, entertaining visiting dignitaries, commercial fishing projects, and other work considered to be of benefit to the community as a whole was divided among Kum and Tolau.[2]

In addition to being known by the name of their founding ancestors, *kamal*s were also known by site names, by the names of the places on which current or previous men's houses had stood. We use ancestral names here because they are simpler, not because this reflects a Ponam preference. If anything, islanders preferred to use site names. This slight preference for site names reflects the fact that the key feature of a *kamal* is that it was a property-owning group — a community bound together largely by its members' common interest in the founder's property: land, sea and fishing techniques.

The fact that land ownership was crucial for the constitution of a *kamal* is apparent in people's descriptions of the formation of new *kamal*s. In order to found a new *kamal* a man needed to have both sons and land. Having only one without the other was not enough. Consequently, new *kamal*s could only be founded by members of existing *kamal*s; that is, by members of groups that already owned Ponam land. New *kamal*s could not be established by immigrants. People said that Ponam was probably first settled by immigrants from the mainland who moved on to uninhabited land, and in the case of Kamal Kahu, people knew the name of the immigrant and knew which was his part of the mainland. But this sort of move had long since been impossible, because all of the island land was owned and not transferable. Thus, for example, there was one family on Ponam that had descended from a turn-of-the-century immigrant, Maka from Tulu. Although this group contained an agnatic core genealogically identical to the membership of a *kamal*, it had no men's house,

---

2 During the course of fieldwork this division became more and more pronounced. By the time we left Papua New Guinea in 1986 it seemed both logical and possible that the village would be divided into two distinct political units. This change was all the more likely in view of the fact that, if approved by the provincial government authorities, it would allow Ponams to have two representatives in the Local Government Assembly of the Pomotu electorate (one of 15 such electorates in Manus), rather than the single member allowed when this new form of local government was established in 1984 (Pokawin 1983).

was not a *kamal*, and could not become one, because it had no land on which to build a men's house or which could be transmitted in the patriline. It was this men's house and the transmission of property that was necessary to transform a set of kin into a *kamal*, a corporate entity.

Although *kamal*s were property-owning groups, they were also clearly kinship groups, for rights to property and thus rights to *kamal* membership could only be acquired through patrilineal inheritance. Only a man's legitimate children had absolute rights to a share of his property (though they endlessly disputed the division of these shares), and only his sons transmitted this right to their own children in turn. The children of a man's daughters, even if those children were illegitimate and without fathers to look after them, had no property rights. They depended on the good will of their mother's brother's children. Adopted children had, at best, ambiguous rights, and were always in danger of being evicted by true agnates. It was impossible to gain full rights in a *kamal* or *kamal* property by the manipulation of non-genealogical substance of the sort described for some societies in the Highlands of Papua New Guinea (e.g. A. Strathern 1973). One might live on *kamal* land, eat fish from *kamal* waters and work for *kamal* members for a lifetime without becoming a *kamal* member or achieving such rights for one's children.

This rigidity in the construction of *kamal*s contrasts with the fluidity of "kinship" described in the previous section of this chapter. People may have been able to become *lowa-* to one another either through birth or through action, but *kamal* membership was not so flexible. A man may have been *tama* (father) to the illegitimate son his wife brought to their marriage, just as he was *tama* to his own son born afterwards. But it was the son of the marriage who was a true *kamal* member and had rights to his father's property, while the illegitimate son could enjoy these privileges only on the sufferance of his legitimate brothers.

A *kamal*'s property included island land, areas of reef and sea, and the right to use certain fishing techniques (*WT&E*: 48–55, 103–118). Some *kamal*s owned the rights to lead and manage markets with particular mainland communities. Many *kamal*s also owned property such as the right to decorate their canoes or sails in particular ways. However, *kamal*s did not own mystical property. They did not own myths, names, ancestors, magical rites or spells, or any other similar forms of intangible property.

Kamal land was not centrally managed. No single person was responsible for allocating rights to *kamal* members each year or each generation. Instead, each child inherited a share of his father's property and managed it himself. However, the *kamal* had a reversionary interest in this property, which should return to the nearest agnate in default of male heirs. Fishing rights tended to be more centrally managed, however. Rights in land, sea, and fishing techniques passed from a father to his sons or, barring sons, to his nearest agnates. These rights could only be alienated if they were given as compensation (*anof*) in order, for example, to redress wrongful injury or to compensate allies for wartime losses. Land given in compensation became the absolute property of the recipient and his *kamal*. Its ownership did not entitle the recipient to membership in the donor's *kamal*.

Single women had the right to use their father's property but could not pass the right on to their children. Once married, a woman gained rights in her husband's property and lost rights in her father's, including the right to transmit it to her sons. People made it quite explicit that when a woman married she ceased to be a member of her father's *kamal* and became a member of her husband's instead.[3] Although a married daughter and her children could not acquire full rights in her father's property, they could acquire limited rights by gift, as could other people. A man could give (*polangai*) land to someone other than a son, for example a sister, daughter, sister's son, daughter's husband or father's sister, but this gift could not be absolute. It was a gift of use rights only and the giver's heirs maintained in perpetuity the right to reclaim the property and any improvements made to it at any time and without compensation. The fact that this right was not easy to secure in practice, as Ponams themselves were aware, did not lessen its significance in principle (*WT&E*: 48–53).

Although women belonged to *kamal*s and had rights to *kamal* property, as men did, their status and significance was clearly secondary to that of men. *Kamal* affairs, the management of *kamal* property and the public, political dimensions of life that went with it, were definitely male affairs. Women did not usually participate in this male business unless they belonged to *kamal*s or patrilineages that had no men, or unless they were acting as guardians for their minor, fatherless children.

The political governance of the community was also largely a male affair and the business of *kamal*s. Another term for *kamal* was *poho-kol*, "voice of the place", and ideally a *kamal*'s leader, or *lapan*, represented his people in all political affairs. People declared, for example, that political decisions ideally should be made in meetings of *lapan*s, a procedure they claimed was traditional. In fact the village was governed by elected officials through community meetings, and only a few *lapan*s had real authority and influence over their agnates. Even so,

---

3 In our initial census, undertaken in our first weeks on Ponam, we asked the *kamal* membership of both husbands and wives. On the first day, people gave the husband's *kamal* as the name of the wife's *kamal*. We explained that we wanted the wife's natal *kamal*. Ponam was a small village, we were a topic of conversation, and word got around quickly. From the second day of our census, people gave us wives' natal *kamal*s, reinforcing our presuppositions about the unalterable, substantial nature of *kamal* identity, and making it that much harder to understand the jural nature of *kamal* membership.

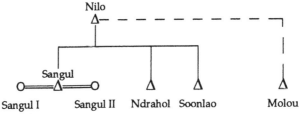

Figure 2   *The five companies of Kamal Nilo*

Note: The broken line indicates the uncertain connection between Nilo and Molou.

this ideal persisted and was important. And certainly the idea that public, political affairs were male affairs remained largely unchallenged. Women rarely spoke in public or took an active or explicit role in public affairs. This does not mean, however, that women were relegated to an insignificant position in village affairs, either in their own minds or in the minds of men. They had important, active roles to play, but these were not roles associated with property and public politics.

Because full property rights were inherited inevitably and exclusively in the male line, a *kamal* included all of, and no more than, its founder's patrilineal descendants. Consequently, *kamal*s looked like classic anthropological patrilineal descent groups (though we avoid this term because it does not carry the connotation of property ownership that was essential to the constitution of *kamal*s). Further, the internal organisation of *kamal*s was very much like that prescribed by segmentary lineage theory. Large *kamal*s were clearly divided into named sublineages descended from the founder's sons and their different wives. These had no indigenous generic name. Instead, a sublineage was referred to by the name of its focal ancestor, just as a *kamal* took the name of its founding ancestor. However, Ponams had adopted a useful term for this type of group from English or Pidgin. They called it a "company" (or *kampani*, though we use the English form here), business corporation. The genealogy of Kamal Nilo, shown in figure 2, illustrates the structure of *kamal*s. (We accepted Ponam genealogies at face value unless there were obvious reasons not to do so. But in any event, for the purposes of this book the real historical accuracy of these genealogies is not significant.)

The story accompanying this genealogy is brief. After murdering his brother, Nilo fled from Kamal Toloso'on and built a men's house of his own on a site called Apan. Nilo had three sons of his own: Sangul, Ndrahol and Soonlao. He also cared for a man named Molou, whose origin was obscure. Ndrahol, Soonlao and Molou each had one wife. Sangul had two, the first from Ponam and the second from the mainland. From these men and their wives descended the five ranked sublineages, or companies, of Kamal Nilo.

The first-ranked company was that descended from Sangul's first wife. This group was known variously as Sangul I, Sangul Mbroso (Island Sangul) and Sangul Salin (Right Sangul). The second-ranked company in Kamal Nilo was descended from Sangul's second wife and was known as Sangul II, Sangul Usia (Mainland Sangul) and Sangul Kamau (Left Sangul). The sons of first and second wives were conventionally distinguished as "right" and "left", and the descendants of the first always had precedence. The companies descended from Ndrahol and Soonlao were ranked third and forth, in the order of their birth. Molou, the non-agnatic company, ranked fifth.

This hierarchy of companies was important as it determined rights of leadership in the *kamal*. The senior company had the right to use the men's-house front door (*sal pe hau*) on ceremonial occasions. Associated with this, it was this company that provided the *kamal's* leader or *lapan*, a position inherited by primogeniture. The second company, Sangul II, used the men's-house back door (*sal ka'uf*) and provided assistance to the *lapan*. Other junior companies used the building's side door and provided, as it were, the chorus. Although the company descended from Molou had been associated with Nilo for many generations, it had never acquired a status equivalent to the others, and in principle at least, it never could. Molous were, and would remain, dependents.[4]

The four companies descended from Nilo himself were *mak malangan*, "the upper bed", and had precedence over the descendants of Molou, who were *mara mak ahin*, "the lower bed". We heard two explanations for the terms. The first, from younger and more idealistic men, was that true *kamal* members slept on the higher beds so that they would be ever ready to leap to the defense of their dependents. The second, from older men, was that the dependents slept on the floor because they were labourers for the true agnates, and were supposed to keep working through the night stoking the men's-house fires.

In the past, powerful *kamal*s constantly attracted and accumulated dependents, through adopting either individuals or entire, though weak, *kamal*s. By the 1980s, however, adoption and patronage of this sort had ceased. No *kamal* appears to have accepted patronage from another since World War II. In fact, the inter-war period had seen a great shaking out of *kamal*s, with many *mara mak ahin* (lower bed) lines dying out, running away, or rebuilding men's houses of their own. Molou was one of the last of the *mara mak ahin* companies to remain attached to its patron.

---

[4] They could, of course, attempt to assert their independence. In 1985, the Molou lineage appeared to try this. Their compound was separate from the main Kamal Nilo compound (it was the cleared area to the east of the Nilo men's house in map 3), and Molous designated a large building in their compound as a men's house. However, other Ponams appear to have been unimpressed. (This is discussed in chapter 5.)

Not only was the adoption of *kamal*s rare after World War II, but so was the adoption of individuals. Ponams did not trade their children about as expressions of, or in order to create, bonds of sentiment between kin. One important reason for this was that adopted children were perceived to have rights to their adoptive father's property and *kamal* that were ambiguous at best, and true parents were reluctant to foist this uncomfortable position on their children without good reason. Thus, children were only given in adoption to childless couples, those unlikely to produce any rivals to the child's claims. Moreover, boys were unlikely to be given to anyone other than a close agnate. Girls, who were expected to have no claims on parental property in the long run, might be given outside the *kamal*. Furthermore, it was considered impossible for any man to change *kamal* membership or for any woman to do so except on marriage. A man might, as a result of disputes with *kamal*-mates, choose to work more often with another *kamal* than that of his father, but this choice did not affect his legal rights in his own *kamal*, did not give him rights in the *kamal* with which he chose to work and did not make him a dependent in it.

This abandonment of the system of adoption and patronage is a significant one that is described in more detail in the next chapter, for it marks a shift over the course of this century from a genealogically fluid and highly political system of constructing *kamal*s to a system that was rigidly genealogical and took little account of political expediency.

COGNATIC GROUPS

*Kowun*s and *kamal*s were institutions with specific purposes, one ritual and the other largely, though not entirely, the management of property and political affairs. Although their members were kin (*lowa-*) and although genealogical connectedness was an essential element of their constitution, this kinship did not seem to be their essential or defining feature. This was the case particularly with *kamal*s, where agnates without property could not constitute themselves as a *kamal*. Ponams did, however, identify kinship itself, the fact of being related to others, as being of considerable significance. Previously we described one of the important terms describing the fact of being related this way, *lowa-*, an ego-focused term translated as "cognate" or "kindred". By definition all those who belonged to one *kamal* or one *kowun* were *lowa-* to one another. In addition to this ego-focused term, Ponams also had a way of talking about the relation among cognates as perceived from the ancestor-focus.

All those who shared a common ancestor, male or female, through any combination of male or female links, were said to be *ken si* (one origin). The image used to describe this was that of a clam shell, with its two distinct halves joined into one at the base (*ken*). Used adjectivally in this way the term was virtually equivalent to *lowa-*. Thus, the sentence *Olo ken si*, "They two have one origin", was almost synonymous with *Olo lowa-olo*, "They two are cognates." The term *ken si* could also be used nominally, however, to refer to a set of people who descended (*rif*, to arrive) from a common ancestor. We generally will translate *ken si* as "cognatic stock". Each cognatic stock was known by the name of its male or female apex, and its members could be referred to collectively by that name. This apical ancestor was the *sal* or "road" who linked all of the stock's members together. In and of itself, the term *ken si* did not specify in what way descendants were connected to their common ancestor or the depth of that connection. Thus, two siblings were *ken si* by virtue of their common mother and their common father. Members of a *kamal* were *ken si* by virtue of their common descent from their founder. And so were those who shared a totem, by virtue of their common matrilineal ancestor, whether known or simply presumed.

Every Ponam who was remembered and known to have living descendants was the apex of a cognatic stock that bore his or her name, and every living Ponam belonged to the stocks of numerous ancestors. Consequently, there was a vast number of partially-overlapping and potentially-conflicting cognatic stocks. Sometimes a person was expected to join with mother's father's descendants, sometimes with father's mother's descendants, sometimes with father's father's descendants, and so on. This raises the old problem of the 1950s: How were these groups organised and how did they cope with the problems of multiple membership and the conflicting obligations of their members? As we said in the Introduction, anthropologists of the 1950s tried to refute Fortes's arguments against the concept of cognatic descent by describing a number of the different ways that cognatic descent was used in the Pacific to create practical social groups. Most of these involved restricting membership in some way by making descent only one of the criteria for group membership. For example, membership might be limited to descendants who also inherited or who chose to live on the descent group's land. By restricting membership in these ways cognatic groups could overcome some of the organisational problems that would arise if individuals were members of many different descent groups and had conflicting obligations to them.

Ponam's stocks did not operate in any of these ways, however. On the contrary, multiple membership and multiple participation were obligatory. Instead of resolving the problem of forming cognatic groups by restricting membership, Ponams resolved it by restricting the roles that these stocks played in island life. *Ken sis* were not corporate groups, nor were they permanently active. They coalesced as groups only in order to assist their individual members with ceremonial exchange or other projects. Thus, although every individual was a member of a great number of stocks, it was rare for more than a few of those to be active as groups demanding participation at one time.

Usually it was not difficult to act as a member of several stocks at the same time, because participation involved bringing gifts or help with labour, and a person could help several different groups in this way at the same time. Thus, *ken sis* provided the structure in terms of which the members of a kindred could organise to work together. They provided, as it were, the structure of island kinship, the structure of relations among individuals, but not the structure of island politics or the structure of relations among groups.[5]

Although women were peripheral members of *kamals*, and only peripherally involved in *kamal* affairs, they were centrally involved in all *ken sis*. In fact, the business of organising the stock's affairs was generally dominated by women. Women were peripheral to *kamals* because *kamal* property was inherited through and by men, and women were considered to have no lasting interest in it. Married women were also debarred in practice from *kamal* affairs by the fact that their obligation to avoid their husband's brothers required them to stay away from the men's house where the business of the *kamal* in which they had rights was conducted. However, women were central to *ken sis* for similar practical and structural reasons. Stock business was conducted in houses, not men's houses, and women's place was in the home. Their place in the home kept women in touch with old people and their knowledge of history and genealogy, and in touch with the networks of informal gift exchange and of contributions to formal ceremonial exchanges. These networks of obligation among households were the main business of *ken sis*. There were also important structural reasons for women's importance in stocks, however, because the construction of stocks and the relations among them revolved around women, women as out-marrying sisters.

THE STRUCTURE OF STOCKS

Ken sis were cognatic in that they could be focused on ancestors of either sex and they included descendants through either sex. However, they were not amorphously cognatic. On the contrary, they were rigourously structured as sets of inter-nesting patrilines and had a strong patrilineal bias. Each woman who married and had children became the founder of a patrilineal descent line that bore her name. Her descendants through males would make up a segment of her husband's *kamal*, a company that would act in his name. But they would also form the core of a group that bore her name and that would mobilise in order to assist her brother's patrilineal descendants. This relationship was specially recognised and named. The descendants of a brother were *lau ara*

---

[5] The relationship between *kamals* and cognatic stocks on Ponam resembles in many ways the relationship between *sem* and *twem* that Rena Lederman (1986) describes in Mendi, in the Highlands, though Ponam cognatic stocks were structured very differently from Mendi *twem*.

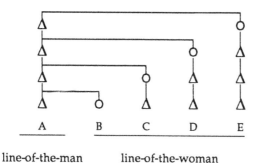

line-of-the-man   line-of-the-woman

Figure 3   *Line-of-the-man and line-of-the-woman*

kamal ("men of the male"; more loosely, line of the man) to the descendants of a sister, while the descendants of a sister were *lau ara parif* ("men of the female", line of the woman) to the descendants of a brother. Figure 3 shows this relationship.

The ties between a line-of-the-man and its corresponding line-of-the-woman were close and were expected to remain so over many generations. Members of the patriline A in figure 3 would expect to be remembered and helped by members of patriline E, just as they would expect help from their own sister, B (but not in such quantities). They would continue to expect help through ensuing generations, until eventually the two groups inter-married, and a new line-of-the-man/line-of-the-woman relationship began.

Ideally, line-of-the-woman and line-of-the-man ought never to marry, because such marriages were impractical. The explanation people gave for this was that such marriages converted a helpful ally, who could be relied on for assistance with affinal exchange and other projects, into an affine to whom marriage payments were owed. This ideal of avoiding marriage with line-of-the-woman conflicted, however, with the strong preference for island endogamy, and a compromise was necessary. Thus, people agreed that it was reasonable for a member of a line-of-the-man to marry into the most distantly related of the line-of-the-woman lineages that contributed to his or her family in exchange. But it was not reasonable to marry into the more closely related line-of-the-woman lineages. Young people did not always stick to this injunction, any more than they married exclusively within the village, but marrying too close to home and too far away were both considered recipes for trouble.

Relations between line-of-the-man and line-of-the-woman lines were not symmetrical. The line-of-the-woman assisted its corresponding line-of-the-man with ceremonial exchange and with labour, but usually did not recruit this kind of assistance in return. Thus, in figure 3, A would get help from his sister B, and from lineages C, D, and E. A would give to B and to C in order to assist them with exchange, but would be unlikely to give to members of lineages D or E.

This bias in favour of assistance to those descended from brothers appeared more generally in Ponam. Thus, obligations in exchange between the descendants of sisters were relatively unimportant. One would normally help one's mother's sister's child directly as MZC. However, if a MMZDC needed help, one would be likely to give through some other connection rather than through this one. On the other hand, obligations in exchange between people of the same *kamal*, who are the descendants of brothers, resembled the obligations that the line-of-the-woman had to its line-of-the-man. The descendants of brothers gave to one another in exactly the same way and in about the same amounts as the descendants of sisters gave to the descendants of brothers. However, *kamal*-mates should never marry, no matter how great the distance between them, and thus relations of obligation within the *kamal* should be permanently reciprocal and should never end.

As described so far, line-of-the-woman was a patrilineage descended from a woman, and it mobilised in order to give assistance to the patrilineage descended from that woman's brother. This is a simplification, however. It is true that the woman's patrilineal descendants formed the core of line-of-the-woman and provided its leadership. However, all of a woman's descendants, the entire cognatic stock bearing her name, could participate. They did so, however, through a series of line-of-the-man and line-of-the-woman relationships of their own.

Figure 4 shows this. Lineage A, on the left of the figure, is line-of-the-man to the descendants of its out-marrying sisters. However, the lineages descended from women are themselves internally structured, being composed of inter-nested line-of-the-woman and line-of-the-man lineages. Thus, the group labelled BI-1 is descended through men from a sister who married out of lineage A, and BI-1 will assist their line-of-the-man, lineage A, whenever A has work to do. But BI-1 will be assisted in turn by its own line-of-the-woman, BI-2, and by a higher order line-of-the-woman lineage, BII. BII is in turn divided into line-of-the-woman and line-of-the-man lineages, BII-1 and BII-2. Thus, when help is being given to A, the various groups that are line-of-the-woman to BI-1 will come together at the house of a senior BI-1 member to plan their actions, and will go as a body to present their assistance to A. From the point of view of outsiders, they will act as B, a single group, one *ken si*, despite their internal segmentation.

One important element in the relationship between a line-of-the-man and a line-of-the-woman was that members of the line-of-the-woman were also *tamatu* to some members of the corresponding line-of-the-man. Thus, in figure 4, the living adult members of BI are likely to be *tamatu* to the living adult members of Lineage A. (The discussion here refers to tendencies rather than certainties, for generational skewing in real paired lines-of-the-man and lines-

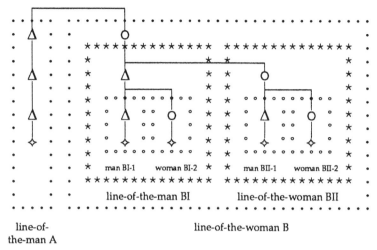

line-of-
the-man A

line-of-the-woman B

Figure 4   *Relations between line-of-the-man and line-of-the-woman*

of-the-woman can alter the situation.) Thus, although line-of-the-woman regul-arly helped line-of-the-man in exchange without receiving equivalent returns in their own exchanges, their contributions were not merely those of subservient partners. As *tamatu*, members of the line-of-the-woman usually had a very strong say in the affairs of their corresponding line-of-the-man.

The relations between a line-of-the-woman and a line-of-the-man existed, in a sense, quite independently of the institution of *kamal*. A man helped and received help from his FZC and his FFZSC on all kinds of occasions — in work, in exchange, in times of sickness or difficulty — without the issue of *kamal* membership ever being raised. Many of the affairs of daily life were the busi-ness of cognates and kin, and did not require the invocation of *kamal*s or *kamal* membership. Thus, one can imagine that Ponam kinship could exist without *kamal*s. The inverse, however, was not true. *Kamal*s and their companies could do very little without calling on those related to them as line-of-the-woman. For example, the major project undertaken by a *kamal*, the building of a new men's house, always required the support and assistance of those in related lines-of-the-woman, both materially, as they contributed money and labour, and ritu-ally, as the descendants of sisters came to dance for the new men's house, to bless it and its members.

*Kamal*s were essentially outward-looking groups, and the line-of-the-woman associated with them were their roads to the wider world. In this, *kamal*s were different from the matrilineal totemic *kowun*s. These groups were purely inward looking, concerned only with the health and fertility of their members, and they had no relationships with any other group of any kind. Thus the institutions of line-of-the-woman and line-of-the-man were never invoked by or on behalf of *kowun*s.

KINSHIP AND THE ROLE OF WOMEN IN EXCHANGE

In creating the three different ways of structuring social groups described in this chapter, Ponams defined gender responsibilities in a way that
permitted, even necessitated, the very prominent role that women took in
ceremonial exchange. To describe matters very simply, in one realm women
dominated, in another men dominated and in yet a third, men and women each
had important responsibilities, so that men and women could interact on terms
of relative structural equality (*WT&E*: 55–61).

The realm of the matrilineal *kowun* was the realm dominated by females,
though it was important to both men and women. This realm was concerned
with the physical substance, growth and health of its members, inward-looking
and independent of marriage, politics and kin relations outside its own boundaries. The realm of the patrilineal *kamal* was the quintessentially male realm of
the men's house, though it is important to remember that women were affected
by *kamal* activities and that they had an important role to play in the maintenance of the *kamal* of which they were members. This realm was concerned with
the material wealth and well-being of its members, outward-looking, dependent on politics, marriage and kin relations outside its boundaries. If we
restricted our attention only to these two sorts of groups, we could fit Ponam
into the model that sees Melanesian gender in terms of complementarity of
interest, orientation and even substance (see, e.g., the papers in M. Strathern
1987). However, *kowun* and *kamal* were not all there was on Ponam. Standing in
a sense between these two, was the realm of *lowa-* and *ken si*, based on the
household. This was a realm in which men and women each had critical and, in
many ways, indistinguishable roles to play. Being based on the household, it
was dominated by women as wives, though as will become apparent, this
domination was fortuitous in some ways, the consequence of historical circumstance. This realm thus was distinct from the matrilineage, dominated by
women as women, as it was distinct from the men's house, dominated by men
as men. This was the realm of groups that had no object other than that of
helping their members, and thus were concerned quintessentially with circulation, with the exchange and distribution of gifts that kept the rest of the social
universe ticking over.

Ponam thus lay between the poles that appear to define the presentation
of women in Melanesian societies. Ponam women were not simply subord-
inates in a world dominated by men, a world in which they sought to exercise
what power they could cobble together by virtue of their positions as producers
of wealth that men distributed (e.g. Josephides 1985) or by virtue of their
positions as intermediaries between their male kin (e.g. M. Strathern 1972). At
the same time, Ponam women, at least in the areas of kinship and exchange,

could not be characterised primarily in terms of a distinct position and set of interests, either a set of ritual concerns and relations that were formally their own (e.g. Godelier 1986) or a less formal but still pervasive set of personal relations and obligations that marked off their separate sphere and interests (e.g. Errington & Gewertz 1987a). Certainly Ponam women were subordinate to men in important ways, just as they did control important ritual activities and did have important webs of personal relations and obligations to each other. But in addition, women had an important position in exchange, and the importance of exchange itself meant that the influence of women in that realm pervaded many areas of Ponam life.[6]

To a degree, one can account for their importance by looking at the structural position of women in Ponam exchange. Exchanges normally took place between individuals (or sets of siblings) who recruited contributions from and made distributions to kindreds, which in turn were composed of *ken sis* linked to the leaders through men and through women. These *ken sis* themselves were composed of inter-nested line-of-the-woman and line-of-the-man lineages, in which the descendants of brothers depended on sisters and their descendants economically, as indeed they did ritually as well. Women, as out-marrying sisters, thus had a pivotal role to play. But even though Ponam women had this important structural position and role in exchange, the evidence from societies elsewhere in Papua New Guinea (e.g. Josephides 1985; M. Strathern 1972) is that women commonly occupy this pivotal mediating position without thereby gaining the relative independence and publicly-prominent role in exchange that Ponam women had. Something more is needed to show why Ponam women were able to use their in-between position as they did. To anticipate some of what we say in the following chapters, women gained their prominence at least in part because of the decay of the male-dominated world of commercial exchange, *lapan* politics and *kamals*. With the decline of this sphere of life, the locus of exchange shifted from the world of the men's house to the world of the domestic house.

At heart, important forms of exchange on Ponam in 1980 revolved around transactions between households. We will explain how this is so in later chapters; here we can only assert the fact. These households were constituted of husband and wife, who were obliged to exchange with and through each other in order to exchange with their affines and to participate in exchange more generally. But this was not merely a polite fiction that masked a reality in which men exchanged with their brothers-in-law and women served as passive

---

[6] To a degree, this resembles the situation of Mendi women that is described in Lederman (1989), though the picture she presents is somewhat simpler and characterised more by conflict than was the case with Ponam.

links between them. Instead, husband and wife jointly controlled their household wealth, as manifest in the fact that when a man was absent from Ponam, it was his wife, and not his brothers, who acted in his name and managed his personal property. Husband and wife stood or fell together as a household in their exchange dealings, each relying on the other in crucial ways. And finally, this is manifest in the fact that a Ponam husband and wife could not divorce each other, could not add a second spouse, and could not even remarry on the death of the spouse.

This illustrates that one cannot prejudge the meaning of domestic or private spheres or the role of women in these spheres. Marilyn Strathern (1984a) has argued that the Western denigration of domesticity motivates Western anthropologists to try to define the roles of the women we study in a way that moves them out of the domestic sphere and into the light of public politics, the realm that we value more highly. But the domestic sphere elsewhere is by no means always confined to its Western boundaries. On Ponam in the 1980s it encompassed household management and ceremonial exchange, and by this unusual convergence it gave women an unusual role to play. Because, at the time of fieldwork, exchange was a largely domestic institution, women were influential by virtue of their prominent role in the domestic sphere. Indeed, men said that women were important in exchange precisely *because* they stayed at home.

This interesting state of affairs was, however, new and not old, the result of changes in the power and significance of *kamal*s that took place over the course of this century, largely as a consequence of the economic changes brought about by colonisation. We describe these in the next chapter, and that description will show the partiality of the very structured picture of kin relations presented in this chapter and of the very structured sketch of gender relations we have just presented. This structure was created out of circumstances, out of historical processes. Consequently, Ponam kin relations and structures, whose logic is described in this chapter, cannot be understood in terms of their logic alone. They must be understood in terms of the practical environment in which people acted and the structures they brought to it.

CHAPTER TWO

Colonial history and changes in *kamal*s

The previous chapter described the Ponam kin groups that were particularly important in the 1980s. But it did so in formal ways. It described rules, principles and structures of organisation, but made little effort to convey a sense of how these groups operated and what the implications were of the structures that they defined, made little effort to look at these groups in processual terms. This chapter corrects that structural orientation by looking in a more processual way at one kind of group, the *kamal*.

The processes of concern here are historical.[1] This chapter will show what *kamal*s were like and what their importance was in the early part of this century. It then describes how their economic context changed with colonisation and independence, and how this affected the role *kamal*s played in island life, and indeed the way they were formed. In particular, this chapter looks at the element of *kamal*s that most fits the classic structural lineage model, their agnatic composition.[2] In the 1980s, as we have said, *kamal*s were strictly agnatic. They did not absorb sisters' children, refugees, immigrants or others. Ponam stories of the past, however, made it very clear that *kamal*s were much less rigid in the past, more like the *kamal*s Margaret Mead had described in the 1920s and more like Highlands clans as they were described in the 1960s and 1970s. They were focused on leaders who recruited not only agnates, but anyone else who would make the leader and his *kamal* strong. And much of the activity of *kamal* leaders centred on ceremonial exchange, the domination of which gave them

---

[1] This chapter parallels the historical discussion contained in chapter 2 of *Wage, trade, and exchange*. However, though they both describe Ponam history in the last hundred years, they do so from different perspectives and for different purposes. While some repetition is unavoidable we have reduced it so far as possible, consistent with the need to make this discussion self-contained, and we refer the reader to our other book on Ponam for additional detail.

[2] At several points we also contrast the changes in *kamal*s and the largely male relations they entailed, with the changes in the organisation of domestic households and the position of women. However, we did not study changes in household relations and the largely female realm of cognatic kinship in anything like the same depth that we studied the changes in *kamal*s. The *kamal*s, after all, were outward-looking, political and male, and had a much greater historical visibility.

the power to recruit and hold *kamal* members. Over the years of this century, however, this completely changed.

This description of *kamal*s from the perspective of history gives an understanding of their structure and composition in the 1980s that is very different from the preceding chapter's synchronic description. In many ways it seems that the ideology underlying *kamal*s, their logical structure, has remained relatively constant over the years. However, the practical significance of that logic changed almost completely as people applied it in the changing political and economic circumstances of this century. The history provided here is thus intended not to refute or discredit the investigation of structure, such as we presented in the preceding chapter, but to illustrate its partiality.

EARLY COLONIAL PONAM

Like the other islands off the north coast of Manus, Ponam is small and infertile, and people seem never to have grown more than coconuts, casuarina, and occasional fruit trees. Instead, they survived by trading produce from the sea and from their large and profitable reef, about 18 km long and covering about 45 sq km. Ponam was not uniquely unproductive, but was much like other coral islands, and only somewhat better off than the south-coast lagoon villages such as Pere, where Margaret Mead worked. Mead's description (1968 [1956]: 70) of what she called the economic treadmill of Pere in 1928 could have applied equally well to Ponam in the early years of this century.

> This Manus way of life ... [was the product of] a highly commercial society, of a people who pitted unremitting labor, supported by a driving and relentless religious system, against the poverty and uncertainty of an existence in which they owned nothing and had no skills, except those of the rough shipwright and carpenter, the fisherman and the navigating trader. ... [T]he logs for the houseposts and canoes, the leaves for thatching shingles, the rubber nut for caulking, the materials for grass skirts, the bark for fish-line and bark cloth G-strings for the men, the pots and baskets and coconut shell containers, and the starchy foods sago and taro, which formed their staples — all these came from the land. By unflagging diligence, by long, chilly and dangerous voyages, by all-night fishing to catch a handful of fish to take to market at dawn, and by a complex economic system in which every man was caught in a chain of obligations such that each debt paid plunged him into a new indebtedness, they prospered.

This driving competition was led on Ponam, as in Pere, by *lapan*s, the rich industrious men who could pull together the members of their *kamal*, their agnates and dependents, into a unified body of labourers (and in the early days, warriors), and could build alliances with other *lapan*s through the judicious marriages of their siblings, children and dependents. *Lapan*s achieved and demonstrated their pre-eminence by their ability to sponsor major prestations, particularly the large, competitive inter-community prestations called *lapan* and the feasts associated with the building of a new men's house. But a man's ability to do this depended on his ability to control the flow of wealth, to control property and to control the endless round of exchanges in which he and his dependents were inevitably involved.

In the early part of this century there were nine independent *kamals* on Ponam: Kehin, Sako, Nilo, Toloso'on, Kosohi, Kayeh, Mahan, Lopaalek and Lehesu. Most of these were patrons to one or more smaller, dependent *kamals*, including the five other *kamals* still in existence in the 1980s and a number of others that had disappeared by then. They also contained a variety of individuals, sometimes disaffected men from other Ponam *kamals*, but more often refugees and immigrants from elsewhere.

Not all *kamals* were equal. In the 1980s most Ponams acknowledged that the *lapan* of the North *kamal*, Kehin, had been Lapa-Ponam, the leader of all Ponam, and they acknowledged Kehin as the leading *kamal*. The only ones to dispute this claim were members of Kamal Nilo (another North *kamal*), whose *lapan* was acknowledged by others to have been the war leader for the island. The pre-eminent South *kamals* were Kayeh and Mahan, and Kayeh was said to have been the island-wide leader in arranging peace settlements. The *lapans* of Nilo and Kayeh also owned two of the markets Ponams attended, which probably contributed to their importance. Because *kamals* and their *lapans* were so clearly sustained by their economic activities, in order to understand them it is necessary to understand the economic climate of the time.

THE REGIONAL ECONOMY IN EARLY COLONIAL TIMES

The pre- and early-colonial Manus economy has been described by Theodore Schwartz in his paper, 'Systems of areal integration', and what he says generally accords with what Ponams described. What both these sources indicate is that Manus was a region of villages linked and shaped by complex networks of trade and exchange, some over long distances. Such networks were, of course, a feature of many areas of what is now Papua New Guinea. The most renown of these is the *kula* trade system in what is now Milne Bay Province (Malinowski 1922; Leach & Leach 1983), but important systems existed as well in the Gulf of Papua among people of the southern New Guinea coast (Seligmann 1910) and the Vitiaz Straits on the north coast (Harding 1967), as well as among inland villages (Hughes 1977).

Manus was characterised by an extremely elaborate system of ownership in which land, sea, production rights and trading rights were owned by the region's numerous local patrilineal groups. This created an extensive division of production between villages and meant that control over people was the key to control over production, both because people were labour power and because people had rights to use property. Complementing this division of production was a system of circulation that distributed local products through the villages of the region. Circulation took place primarily through ceremonial exchange between kin and through kin-based trade partnerships, and thus control over people was also the key to control over circulation. Judicious adoption, patronage and marriage arrangements were keys to wealth and political power.

Through the division of production Manus was integrated into an economic whole, for every village relied on products produced in villages elsewhere for ceremonial goods, manufactured items and even staples (*WT&E*: 67–68). At one pole were the villages built in lagoons or on small infertile islands such as Ponam, whose residents specialised in transport and marine products. At the other pole were villages of mainland Manus, with extensive land resources but in most cases no access to the sea. In between were people from the large islands, especially in the southeast, who had both gardens and reefs (see map 1, of Manus, page 27).

This ecological division into agricultural and fishing societies was maintained by the endemic warfare between mainland groups and their island and off-shore counterparts, especially when either group tried to colonise the coastal strip. This made it difficult for any group to have access to both soil and sea (though some did, e.g. Kuluah 1977). However, just as war divided villages, so it united them, for one common objective of warfare was to take captives. Many of these were eaten or sold to be eaten elsewhere, but sometimes women and children were kept and married into their captors' villages or sent off in marriage elsewhere. Successful marriages were legitimated by marriage prestations and formed the basis for new trade and exchange relations between the two communities.

Ponams relied on both ecological and monopoly specialisation. Like all island and lagoon dwellers, they grew no crops but instead produced seafood in demand on the mainland. Within the Ponam community there was also an extremely complex division of ownership. Fishing techniques, species of fish, and areas of reef and sea were all separately owned by *kamals* or companies (*WT&E*: 103–113). Ponams produced a limited range of manufactures for their own use: tools, canoes, armlets and household goods, all made with raw materials imported from the mainland. And they provided one particularly important specialty valued throughout Manus, shell money (strings of tiny polished white discs made from *Imbricaria punctata*) (J. Carrier 1987b: 155–156).

The items that Ponam and other villages produced circulated throughout the region and were important in every community. Consequently, even though they were politically independent, Manus villages were economically interdependent. The most important ways in which goods circulated were markets, trade partnerships, and ceremonial exchange.

Markets for the exchange of produce between mainlanders and island or lagoon dwellers were held at four- or five-day intervals in sites all around the coast of mainland Manus. The early markets Ponams described sound very much like those Mead (1930) reported observing in 1928, and were probably much like those of pre-colonial times as well. Island sea food and mainland vegetables were the most common market items, but raw materials and manufactures also could be traded.

The markets Ponams attended and the villages with which they shared these markets changed from time to time (especially as markets were a popular site for an ambush) but were always located on the mainland opposite Ponam. Like every other valued resource, the markets were owned by *kamals*. Each of the markets was owned jointly by one Ponam and one mainland *kamal*, whose *lapans* were responsible for supervising it. They maintained peace, ensured that trading was fair and set the rate of exchange for fish and sago. The market owners did not collect market tax or derive any immediate reward for ownership, but they did have the authority to close the market altogether if they wished, an authority that gave these *lapans* influence over both fellow villagers and market partners. Only members of the owners' villages had the right to attend the market: others were admitted only if accompanying relatives from those villages. But trade took place freely between all those who had the right to attend, and was not limited to kin.

Ponams also traded with *kawas*, a Manus-wide term that can be glossed roughly as "trade partner", a kinsman or kinswoman who lived in another community and with whom one had a long-term trading relationship. As Ponams remembered it, partners could exchange goods directly at rates agreed upon by discussion, but the relationship also routinely involved long-term, large-scale obligations. Having *kawas* in different regions of Manus made it possible to trade for the products of those regions for, at least before the 1920s, it was unsafe to visit where one did not have kin. Unlike markets, which were used primarily to obtain food and materials for daily living, *kawas* were used primarily to obtain raw materials such as canoe logs and building timber, and to obtain the large quantities of the specialist products needed for exchange. Ceremonial exchange required a considerable amount of inter-village trade, even when it took place between co-villagers, because the exchanges required gifts produced in many of the different villages throughout the region.

The ceremonial exchanges that Ponams participated in can be roughly divided into three types, in order of their prestige and frequency. First were the major competitive inter-community exchanges sponsored by village *lapans*; second were the exchanges and feasts held by *kamals* in order to commemorate the building of a new men's house; and third were the numerous forms of exchange between individuals marking stages in individuals' lives or marriages.

The major inter-community exchanges, appropriately enough called "*lapan*", could only be sponsored by a village's *lapan*, which in the case of Ponam meant the *lapan* of Kamal Kehin. This was an explicitly-competitive occasion, in which the sponsor's aim was to defeat the *lapan*s of other villages by giving more than they could ever give to him in any subsequent *lapan*. These exchanges were held infrequently by any one community, for it was most unlikely that any *lapan* would sponsor such an exchange more than once in his lifetime, and not every *lapan* was capable of sponsoring one. Further, these exchanges could only be held by the leading *lapan*s of communities, not by lesser men. However, the lesser *lapan*s of Ponam also had a major ceremony of their own, the feast held to commemorate the building of a new men's house, a feast called *kana pe hau*, "the feast of the door".

Pigs were the central item in these feasts, and a *lapan* could not build a new men's house unless he could rely on his kin to provide twenty or thirty for the feast. This work began when the *lapan* called together his agnates and those who were line-of-the-woman to his *kamal*, and assigned them the work of finding building materials for the men's house. When the materials were prepared, the building began. All the men and women of the community could participate and all had to be fed while they worked. When the building was complete, the feast of the door began.

For a month or more there would be dancing and feasting at the men's house every night. The slit gongs rang out through the village, and could be heard even on the mainland, calling people to bring pigs for the men's house. Eventually, when the *lapan* felt that people were ready with their pigs, he marked the day for the main feast. All of the *kamal* members, their affines and descendants of out-marrying women were expected to bring pigs. Pork was given to *kamal* agnates, affines and other relatives, all of whom should have contributed, but it was also given to the other *kamal*s of the community in a major distribution called *sahai*. This distribution legitimated a group's status as a *kamal*. After this the senior men of each *kamal* went into the new men's house to eat pork. The sponsoring *lapan* killed extra pigs for this, and hoped to kill more than the men could possibly eat, even though they might stay there for a week or more.

This feast of the door was what, in a sense, defined a *kamal*. Groups without considerable wealth and enterprising *lapan*s could not hold such a feast, could not build a real men's house, and were likely to be forced into a position of dependence on another *kamal*. Since a men's house could not be made to endure for more than about twenty years, even with careful rebuilding, *kamal*s were under constant pressure to revalidate their status, and it is likely that one or another of the island's *kamal*s was always preparing for the building of a new men's house.

The third important form of ceremonial exchange was that of life-cycle and marriage exchanges, and their basic principles seem to have been common throughout Manus. In general, most of the important exchanges revolved around marriage and the life crises of its children. They were often held at birth, initiation, betrothal, marriage, pregnancy and death. Most of these prestations on Ponam were made by one individual to another, though gifts were accumulated from and distributed to a range of kin, so that large numbers of people could participate in every exchange. These exchanges were sponsored by individuals and families, not by *kamal*s and *lapan*s. Nonetheless, *lapan*s tended to dominate these through their use of patronage, as they dominated other exchanges.

The structure of these forms of exchange was not inherently competitive, as will become apparent in our description of them in chapter 3. Affines did not compete to give ever larger and more impressive gifts through the life of a marriage and the lives of its children. But they were made competitive when they were dominated by *lapan*s, as each *lapan* attempted to make the best possible display for his dependents. This air of competition was particularly prominent when two *lapan*s had arranged the marriage of a number of their dependents, as was likely given the then-current preference for the continued exchange of brides between *kamal*s.

The important features of the Manus economy in the early part of this century were, thus, these. Production was specialised, and each community depended on many others for the goods needed for survival and particularly for ceremonial exchange. Production rights were owned by patrilineal groups. The circulation of goods took place through kin- or *kamal*-based links, in markets, in *kawas* trade and in ceremonial exchange. Consequently, economic success and political prestige fell to those who could manage trade intelligently and who could control the people through whom they could find rights of access to production and circulation, as well as labour. On Ponam, those who could do this were *lapan*s, the leaders of *kamal*s.

Women were certainly significant in this era as producers, as marriage property, and probably also as powers behind thrones and as hands that rocked cradles, but the domestic household that women ruled did not have the significance at this time that it gained later, and women's lives were very much restricted. However, the economic changes of this century brought the gradual but sure devaluation of Manus property, and the devaluation of the *kamal*s that owned it and the *lapan*s who controlled it. As the significance of *kamal*s decreased, so the significance of households and the women who dominated them increased proportionately.

KAMALS AND LAPANS

How did *lapans* and *kamals* operate? How did *lapans* acquire influence over people, make their *kamals* cohesive and strong, and manage to dominate trade and exchange? In *Kinship in the Admiralty Islands*, Margaret Mead described the way that important men in Pere village manipulated the system of kinship in order to achieve the most success in ceremonial exchange. Because Ponam kinship was traditionally managed in much the same way, it is worth reporting Mead's findings in some detail.

PERE

Three types of kinship groups were particularly important in Pere. One was patrilineal property-owning descent groups, which were divided into two hereditary classes, the elite ruling *lapan* and the commoner labouring *lau*. It was expected that 'the *lapan* takes care of the economic needs of the *lau*, and the *lau* works for the *lapan*' (Mead 1934: 336). In addition to the patrilineal clans, there were matrilineal totemic groups that regulated ritual life. Third was what she called a "mixed descent group", which combined these two principles of patriliny and matriliny and united the descendants of a sister and the descendants of a brother. The prescribed marriage rule held that marriage should take place 'between the children of two male cross-cousins or of two cross-cousins who are father's sister's daughter and mother's brother's son to each other' (1934: 228). For the marriage to be legitimate, the cross-cousin descended from the sister should arrange the marriage by demanding his cross-cousin's daughter as a bride for his son. This rule would have been easier to obey if Peres allowed the children of classificatory cross-cousins to marry, but they did not do so: legitimacy went only to the children of true cross-cousins. However, this rule was not totally restrictive, for Peres did allow the marriage of the children of cross-cousins linked through adoption as well as those linked through blood.

Even though many people would contribute to it, the expense of bride-price could only be met by men who were reasonably wealthy and who had the skills and contacts necessary to manipulate a complex network of trade partnerships and thereby ensure that the numerous items required to make the payment arrived from all the distant corners of Manus in the requisite quantities on the appointed day. A poor man who wanted to arrange the marriage of his son had to seek out a financier-patron. By financing a boy's marriage, a patron could become his "father", and take a father's position at the centre of the series of affinal exchanges. Not only did young men seek patrons, but wealthy men sought to take on boys and girls as dependents specifically so that they would be able to establish relationships of affinal exchange with other wealthy men by arranging the betrothal of these dependents. Through adoption and patronage the system of affinal exchange became an elite system of competitive exchange for prestige.

The practice of adoption and patronage fuelled competition between leaders in other ways as well. For instance, by becoming a father or patron, the financier could take over, or at least take advantage of, a child's rights of production and existing kin connections (both *kawas* and kin within the village). Equally, a client was obliged to work for his patron or "father" to pay off the debt of his marriage payments: to catch fish for him, market for him and visit his trade partners with goods. This kind of economic domination extended over women as well. During childbirth and the months immediately after, a woman was looked after by her "brother", who would carry out certain exchanges for her. In return for this, the woman gave her "brother" shell money and other lesser valuables she produced (1934: 258–259).

Astute leaders used marriage and adoption in all of these ways. In creating adopted clients, they were able to gain control over central elements of the economic system: labour, productive techniques and the commercial activities that sprang from the division of production. Thus, *lapans* in Pere manipulated the kinship-based system of economic control in several ways: by financing exchange they created new kin relations that gave them control of resources, production, and commercial activity mediated by trade partnerships. Affinal exchange, and marriage more generally, was important in all three areas, so that production, circulation, exchange and kinship were all intertwined. The human link between these different realms was the *lapan*, who sought control over each realm to secure control over the others.

This picture presented a real problem for Mead, however, because it contradicted in a number of important ways the ideas then being developed by Radcliffe-Brown and later formulated as segmentary lineage theory, particularly the idea that the genealogical relations of kinship provided the structure for political and economic organisation in primitive societies (Mead 1934: 337). Pere certainly had a system of kinship rules and ideas that could have provided a framework for political organisation. However, the system did not work this way, for genealogical relations were constantly subverted through adoption in pursuit of exchange wealth. Thus, in Pere Mead saw a contradiction between the structure and practice of kinship which, like the Highlands ethnographers so many years later, she resolved by elevating kinship to the level of what, in those innocent days, she called "thought".

Mead said that because the genealogical rules of inheritance, authority and marriage were incompatible with the Peres' competitive economy, they were all endlessly circumvented.

> The Manus kinship system with its prescribed marriage forms, if followed carefully, would at best prevent the Manus from the exercise of discretion

in forming marital alliances. Furthermore, it assumes a democratic equality between individuals which is foreign to the Manus individualism.... . The Manus have made the affinal exchange system a pivotal point in their culture; in order to do this, it has been necessary to eliminate the binding forms of purely blood ties (1934: 316).

The two mechanisms that allowed this were adoption and patronage. Through these, children could acquire new parents and a new clan affiliation, and through these new parents, they could acquire numerous new sets of cross-cousins (without ever giving up those previously accumulated) and numerous new opportunities for making marriage arrangements. By adopting children, then, a patron acquired many new opportunities for match-making, while still conforming to the rules of the marriage system.

> The result is that a few aggressive initiating men finance half the marriages in the community which splits up into three distinct classes which have very little to do with the *lapan, lau* distinctions. These classes are rich and powerful economic entrepreneurs, the dependent relatives of these men, and men who are poor and obscure, but who are not dependent on others. The entrepreneurs finance the marriages of their dependents and their dependent's children, and in return their dependents fish for them.... . Upon the skeletons provided by the kinship system rich and enterprising men are thus able to build up a dependency who will fish for them and serve them in their middle years (1934: 328).

As a result, kin relationships that formally appeared to be genealogical, practically seemed to have no genealogical content at all. Kin terms were used not to describe genealogical relations, but relations of exchange and finance. However, Mead said that the idea of genealogical connectedness continued to be of great importance. She concluded,

> It may be questioned why I consider it legitimate to speak of a structure which is so flagrantly disregarded and reorganized. I do this because the Manus themselves conceive their system formally, ideologically, without making explicit allowance for the continual contravention.... . It is ... a system by which power is wielded in terms of a kinship system which is no longer dominant in practice, but only in thought (1934: 336–337).

PONAM

Like Peres, Ponams distinguished *lapan*s and *lau*s, elite and ordinary. On Ponam, however, the term *lapan* referred not to entire *kamal*s, but to the individual leaders of *kamal*s, a position inherited by primogeniture. As a practical matter, the eldest sons of eldest sons were not always capable of playing the role of *lapan* and might be displaced by others. However, these genealogically-senior men had the advantage of authority in claiming leadership.

As in Pere, Ponam *lapan*s achieved prominence and control of their *kamal*s though their ability to dominate exchanges and feasting. And also as in

Pere, they did this by controlling and dominating other men and women and thereby achieving power over their labour, production rights, trade links and marriage prospects. We have described already how a *kamal*'s independence depended on its wealth and its ability to sponsor men's-house–raising feasts, but it also depended on its members' continuing ability to finance the lesser exchanges of marriage.

Ponam men and women needed wealth in order to marry. Boys from poor families often could not marry because they could not finance the large prestations with which marriage began. Girls from poor families often could not marry because their families could not meet the continuing obligations of prestation and return prestation that a groom's family expected. The wealth needed for marriage prestations was accumulated through contributions from siblings and parents' siblings, especially the father's. Those from small *kamal*s with few men and few out-marrying sisters were unlikely to be able to accumulate marriage prestations on their own. In order to marry, these children, and their parents, became dependents of other men who financed their marriages in return for the right to arrange the marriage, receive and distribute incoming prestations, manage the dependent's property and direct the dependent's labour as they would the labour of any other child. These stark economic terms are ours, they are not the way Ponams in the 1980s described these relationships. They said instead that the patron offered help and support to those who could not help themselves. He became a father and expected no more from the dependent than he would from any other child. This may well have been true, but it is also clear that fathers expected, and seem to have received, almost absolute service and obedience from their children.

According to Mead's description, patrons in Pere took in dependents and children from almost anywhere, from brothers, sisters and wives, from distant relatives and even from those who were no kin at all, and the children of each clan ended up being distributed through most of the other village clans. In the end, clans became almost entirely political constructions rather than genealogical ones. However, patronage does not seem to have operated quite so widely on Ponam.

The wealthy men of a *kamal* generally took only certain people as their dependents: orphans of the *kamal*, the children of poor *kamal* men, their own younger siblings. They rarely took on dependents from another *kamal* if that *kamal* had any wealthy men remaining in it. So long as a *kamal* could support itself, it did so. But when it became so small or so poor that it could not do so, then the entire *kamal* became the children and grandchildren of a patron *kamal*'s *lapan*. The dependent *kamal* was thenceforth "below" (*paha-*) its patron, its members slept on the lower beds (*mara mak ahin*). Wealthy men also could take in an individual, or a whole family, from another community without being patron to the immigrant's entire *kamal*. These dependents were usually war captives, refugees from warfare elsewhere, or *kawas* of various kinds who ran away to Ponam to escape from troubles or to seek new fortunes.

The patron arranged and financed the marriages of his dependents and their children. Significantly, he never arranged for these dependents to marry into his own *kamal*, for this procedure would have defeated the entire purpose of the operation. The object was not to bind the dependent to his *kamal* and increase its numbers and strength that way, but to use the dependent to forge exchange links with others, for it was in managing exchange that *lapans* and *kamals* found strength.

Both Mead and Reo Fortune (1935) located the main sanction behind the Pere *lapans'* domination of their kin and dependents in illness brought by ancestral ghosts who punished disobedience and defaulting on debts. These ghosts were also important on Ponam for the same reason. But Ponam *lapans* also sought to secure their position through sorcery, the control of malevolent spirits (*njam kowau*) who would both protect the *lapans'* property and punish those who disobeyed them.

It appears then that Ponam's *lapans* and *kamals* of the early 20th century were rather different from those of later years. The recent *kamals* were genealogical affairs, with almost no practice of adoption or patronage, and no apparent interest in such a thing. And with the exception of a few significant individuals, *lapans* appeared relatively unimportant. Certainly there was no rush of people to claim that status, and no clamour to overset rightful *lapans* who seemed uninterested in their positions. While the idea of *lapan*-ship remained important to people, few actually wanted to do anything about it. Furthermore, although *kamals* remained pre-eminent in village ideology, their practical significance was at least equalled by the household's, which certainly appeared to be of greater significance in the realm of ceremonial exchange.

Fifty or sixty years before, however, things seemed different. *Lapans* had active roles to play in exchange and, just shortly earlier, in warfare as well. And they were actively involved in constructing exchange and marriage links by accumulating dependents, financing marriages and absorbing refugees. These dependents were not totally absorbed, for it is obvious that many people's origins were remembered and they have since broken away again, but at the time, at least, they acted as members of their patron's *kamals* and were important ingredients of a *lapan's* success.

The power of *lapans* depended on their ability to manipulate property and property rights through their control over people, and their ability to control people through the debts they incurred by financing exchanges with their wealth. The history of this century, however, has been the history of the disintegration of the Manus regional economy, the destruction of the value of *kamal* property and the dethroning of *lapans*. Unable to control wealth, they lost their power to attract dependents, as indeed those who had once been their dependents ceased to need them. Consequently, *kamals* gradually ceased to be political-economic confederations, and became in fact the agnatic groups that they had long been ideologically. We need to explain how this happened.

EARLY COLONIAL HISTORY

Regular contact with Europeans began in Manus during the 1870s, when the area became a commercial source of pearl shell, tortoise shell and beche-de-mer, and by the time of German annexation in 1884, most Manus were familiar with European goods, if not with Europeans themselves.

Relations between Manus and Europeans were tense and often violent during this early period, as Manus people attacked the colonisers and the Germans responded with frequent punitive raids. This also was a time of increased warfare among Manus, exacerbated, Schwartz suggested (1963: 87), by the Administration's attempts at pacification, as well as by the fact that some groups were able to capture guns and use them to wipe out old enemies and venture long distances in search of booty. The south coast Titan-speaking Manus (the language group to which Pere belonged, and which gave the province its name) were particularly militant at this time, and King (1978: 76) suggested that this was because they were trying to prevent the German traders from taking over their historic position as middle-men and carriers. Despite this warfare, Europeans continued to visit Manus to trade.

Although Ponams never came into direct conflict with the Germans, they were caught up in the fighting with other Manus. During the 19th century, probably during the very early phase of colonisation, Ponam was invaded by people from the south coast, and most of those living in the eastern district of the island, Tonuf, were killed or forced to flee to the west. Later, in 1900, Ponam was invaded again, by south coast Titan speakers who had captured guns and swept up around eastern Manus and along the chain of islands off the northeast and north-central coast (King 1978: 73–74). At this time Ponams were also involved in renewed fighting with their mainland market partners, the Tulu people, as well as with people of Sori island to the west, though they did not use guns.

Although the European record shows clearly that Ponams saw Europeans at least sporadically before 1900, this was not what Ponams remembered. For them, colonisation began dramatically with a storm and a shipwreck that brought Isokide Komine to the island for the first time. He was a Japanese trader who had first begun working in the Bismarck Archipelago in 1902 (J. Carrier 1987a: 114–116). In 1906 Komine returned to Ponam and bought the uninhabited eastern two-thirds of the island and its accompanying reef to use as a plantation. Ponams said that it was probably bought with trade goods, but do not remember what he paid or to whom he paid it. Nor do people remember there being conflicts over the purchase, probably, they said, because that part of the island was still uninhabited.

In this same year, 1906, people from Manus first began to sign labour contracts. Ponams said that almost all men who became adults after the arrival of Komine signed at least one three-year labour contract. These initial contracts were usually for plantation labour, which was universally unpopular. After their first contract men sought to work instead as domestics, boatmen, and best of all policemen, and those who could not get these better jobs usually went home rather than sign on again.

These young contract labourers were a source of wealth and influence for their fathers and patrons, for recruiters paid bounties to young men's relatives in order to secure permission to recruit them. Gillian Sankoff (1985: 105–106), in her analysis of the Queensland labour trade, suggested that payments such as these were not thought of as bounties, bribes or payments suggesting sale into slavery, but were more like brideprice payments, the exchange of gifts allowing the transfer of labour. The last living Ponam to have been recruited during this early period, probably about 1914, made a similar analogy, though not in the beneficent sense that Sankoff implied. Joseph Karin asserted that fathers forced their unwilling sons into labour contracts in order to get wealth out of the Europeans, just as they forced their unwilling daughters into marriage in order to get wealth out of their affines.

Not only were fathers able to earn wealth from their sons' departures, but they were usually able to appropriate what the sons brought home on their return as well. By arranging and financing marriages for the absentees, they presented a ready-made network of debts to be repaid on return. This system was not foolproof, however. Colonisation offered men an escape they had never had before; they could avoid these obligations simply by staying away, by signing on for second and third contracts. And ultimately labour migration was to make young men independent of their seniors.

Although German control was established through force, the Administration seems to have interfered very little in village affairs. Between 1915 and 1921 the Australians, who replaced the Germans, were nominal rulers, but had no time to spare for the administration of such a distant and unprofitable district as Manus, and the most notable European presence in the region during this time was that of the German missionaries, whom the Australians had allowed to remain.

The first mission to settle in Manus was the German Catholic order, the Missionaries of the Sacred Heart (see Hempenstall 1975). In 1913 they went to

Papitalai in eastern Manus but had no success. In 1916 they moved to Bundralis on the north-central coast opposite Ponam (Kelly n.d.: 16). Like most of their neighbours, Ponams were suspicious of the missionaries at first. They worked intermittently on the mission plantation at Bundralis, which seemed no different from any other, but wanted nothing to do with the Church. Eventually, however, they were attracted to the school begun by Father Borchardt in 1918, and by the mid-1920s many children from Ponam and other north coast villages were enroled. The first Ponam child to attend school was Lapan Kuluah Jaf, later baptised Marcus. His father was Kuluah Jaf Sangul, the *lapan* of Kamal Nilo, the island's fight leader and a notorious sorcerer. He was also an astute man who recognised the value of literacy, Christianity, and connections with the mission. Sending his son to school was apparently a trial, and a few years after this he himself accepted baptism, renounced sorcery, and persuaded others to renounce it as well.[3] This step opened the way for Ponams' wholesale conversion to Catholicism.

One of the first significant acts of the new Australian administration was to seize the German-owned plantations and sell them to Australian ex-servicemen. The Ponam plantation, which Komine had bought for a German firm, went to a man named McEvoy (Patrol Report [hereafter "PR"]: February 1949). Like Komine, he seems to have got on well with people. He employed Ponams intermittently to work on his plantation, bought the trochus they collected, ran a trade store at which he allowed extended credit, and used his ship to import sago from elsewhere in Manus, particularly during the northwest monsoon season when Ponams found it difficult to sail. All in all he seems to have been a friendly and unpretentious man whose presence allowed people to earn an income from land that they did not particularly need themselves, with a plantation they would not have been allowed to manage in any case.

The Australians slowly began to build a structure of administration and control. They introduced health programmes, regular censuses and patrols, the adjudication of disputes and so forth. Also, they recognised and reappointed as luluais the men who had been appointed by the Germans (PR 6 of 1952/53). In Ponam's case this meant they reappointed Kuluah Kaso, the *lapan* of Kamal Kehin. They continued this policy of appointing Kehin luluais until they finally forced Ponams to vote for a councillor in the early 1970s. It is difficult now to determine how holding the office of luluai influenced the role of Lapa-Ponam. Kehins certainly claimed that their *lapan* always held considerable power on the island, but others, particularly from the competing Kamal Nilo, suggested that

---

[3] We heard of Kuluah Jaf often, because the house we used in 1979 was hard by the place where he and others who renounced sorcery discarded their sorcerous paraphernalia. We were advised to keep to the paths at night and avoid the bush.

when he became luluai, Kuluah Kaso appropriated a number of powers that had not hitherto been his.

In the long run, however, colonisation served to decrease the power of *lapan*s rather than to augment it, because it undercut the value of the wealth that *lapan*s could control through their manipulations of kinship and ceremonial exchange. The new colonial economy undercut the indigenous system of control over production, and thereby made Manus a dependent outlier of the larger Papua New Guinea and Australian economy. Villages ceased to rely on each other to acquire the means of survival, but became oriented instead toward Lorengau and the world outside, dependent on government assistance, on the sale of food, copra and other commodities in the provincial capital, on remittances sent back to Manus by migrant workers and on the purchase of imported replacements for what was once produced locally. The old articulated system of locality, production, kinship and circulation was replaced as the location of the significant sources of wealth moved out of the region and out of the control of village societies. As a result, villages shifted their orientation away from each other and toward the outside world, and shifted their economies away from specialist production and exchange and toward remittance and consumption. The most important aspects of colonisation leading in this direction were the imposition of colonial peace, labour recruiting and the establishment of missions, while the establishment of plantations, so important in many parts of the colony, had little impact in Manus (*WT&E*: 241, n. 3).

The imposition of colonial peace meant that force could not be used to preserve the ecological and social division of production. Peace also made it possible for people to follow the Administration's urging to settle on the coastal strip. Inland villages that moved to the coast seem to have taken about a generation to reorient their economies toward the sea, however, and it was not until after World War II that they began to sail or to fish extensively. Colonial peace, thus, began to undercut the pre-colonial division of production that underlay much of the integration of the region.

The ending of local warfare released time for other activities, but labour migration absorbed most of this. Migrant labour expanded quickly, and by the early 1920s many adult males were working outside of Manus.[4] Ponams

---

4 The existing data (described in *WT&E*: 78–79) are somewhat ambiguous on this point. Initially we had interpreted them to mean that about half of adult males were indentured in the early 1920s, the peak period. However, Ton Otto (1990: chap. 6) argues that the data point to a much lower estimate, 20–30 percent. While Otto's figure also is an interpretation of ambiguous and partial data, it seems more secure than ours. The degree and impact of labour recruiting necessarily varied around Manus, and as we and Otto both note, it was ameliorated by colonial control. This released for other purposes the effort previously devoted to

explained that this led to a shift in the sexual division of labour, facilitated by the increased security resulting from colonial peace. Women began to travel further afield, participate more widely and directly in marketing and all forms of exchange, and take on productive activities previously reserved for men. This gave women greater effective control over the distribution of what they produced than had been possible before.

With the drain of active men out of the district the remaining producers had to devote more of their energies to the production of food or goods to be exchanged for food, and less to the manufacture and trade of luxury goods. For example, as World War II approached, Ponams seem to have decreased their trade with more distant parts of Manus but maintained their staples trade with adjacent mainland people, with whom they exchanged fish for starch and raw materials. Also, they made less shell money, in part, they say, because women's labour was needed for subsistence production. Likewise, Mead (1963 [1930]: 231) indicates that by the late 1920s in southeast Manus the labour devoted to carved beds and bowls was dropping. This helped break up the region's integrated production and exchange system, replacing it with a collection of pairs of villages — starch and fish producers trading essential foodstuffs and raw materials with each other, but trading less and less with other villages. Of course, this shift in trade was facilitated by the manufactured goods workers brought back with them, goods that gradually replaced Manus manufactures. Migration also began to break up the control that mature men had over the young by giving them enough money to begin to escape from their debts (Mead 1963 [1930]: 231).

To add to this, the missions opposed *lapan* exchanges and thus weakened one of the institutions helping to integrate the region economically. And for Ponams their attacks on sorcery and magic served to undercut the power of *lapan*s. They also attacked the system of arranged marriages, the source of much of a *lapan*'s influence. More important, however, were the schools they started. Their immediate effect may have been slight, though it seems likely that basic literacy in Pidgin helped people get jobs outside the plantation sector. However, the schools helped establish a taste for education and a belief in the benefits of formal schooling that were to be important later on.

As should be clear, these colonial changes had serious implications for the operation of Ponam *kamal*s and *lapan*s. They altered the value of what was owned, the value of the property from which *kamal*s and *lapan*s gained their significance. The value of fish, shell money and other Manus manufactures was

---

warfare. While the effect of labour recruitment appears to have been less than we assumed in *WT&E*, there is every reason to continue to believe that it was significant, and certainly it loomed large in Ponams' minds.

undercut by colonisation. The decrease in the value of what *kamal*s owned in turn decreased the significance of *kamal*s themselves and their significance relative to domestic households. Also colonisation affected the power of *lapan*s by deceasing the control they had over the young through financing marriages. These changes, which had been gradually developing since 1900, became fully apparent after the traumas of World War II.

THE POST-WAR YEARS: REORIENTATION AND DEPENDENCE

The Japanese captured Manus peacefully in 1942 and held it until the allied American and Australian invasion of Manus occurred in February 1944. After this recapture the district was flooded with soldiers, airfields, ships and supplies, as Manus was used as a base for the bombardment of Rabaul and for assaults on islands closer to Japan, notably the Philippines. Ponam was used as a naval air-base.

Although Ponams who had stayed at home remembered the War as an exciting and luxurious time, the men who were trapped away from Manus when the Japanese arrived had different memories. Some hid with villagers in other parts of the country. Some were soldiers or carriers with the Japanese, Americans or Australians, often changing sides time and again as the fortunes of war dictated. Those who were not quick enough to change sides often spent long periods in prison camps, and a fair number lost their lives. When the War ended the survivors came gratefully home to Ponam, and many hoped they would never have to leave again. Many of these men had been away from home for years, and they returned to a place radically different from the one they had left. The economic changes that had been brewing became apparent under the stresses of the War. Equally important, Manus people, both those at home and those who had been away, were determined that change would continue. They were not willing to accept a return to pre-War colonialism.

When the American military left Manus in 1946 they abandoned a staggering abundance of goods, and because there had been an air base on their island, Ponams acquired more of these than most; all of better quality than anything, local or imported, they had known before the War (or since, for that matter). The supplies abandoned on Ponam, like those in other places, quickly entered the *kawas* trade or were simply sold off for cash. By the time these goods wore out, and by no means all had done so by 1986, no one wanted to return to Manus manufactures. No one who had cooked with surplus from the US Navy mess wanted to go back to clay pots. And no one had to: there was surplus for everyone — at a price. Thus, the War and the trade in war surplus that followed it dealt the final blow to specialist manufacturing in Manus. The last people to manufacture specifically for trade were the Ahus potters, who ceased producing around 1952 (PR 3 of 1952/53). After the mid-1950s Ponams no longer traded or purchased any goods manufactured locally.

Ceremonial exchange continued to take place after the War in most parts of Manus, though not all, as we describe below. However, imported goods, which had appeared in exchanges before the War, began to dominate. Thus, Patrol officers in the early 1950s (PR 3 of 1952/53) reported that brideprice payments contained substantial quantities of cash goods and £A50 or so in cash. Enamel dishes replaced wooden ones, cloth replaced grass skirts and so on. Furthermore, as regional specialisation declined, Ponams began to manufacture for themselves many traditional items that they had once acquired from others. By the 1980s, the only indigenous items other than sago that Ponams used in affinal exchange were those made on Ponam itself. Instead of making shell money to trade for the mainland baskets and mats needed for exchange, Ponam women stayed at home, made their own baskets and made almost no shell money at all.

Utility was not the only reason people adopted imported manufactures to replace local equivalents. In addition, those who had money could acquire imported wares outside of trade and exchange relationships, without having to enter into relationships of debt, obligation and clientship with kin. As the need for specialist manufactures decreased, so too did the incentive to control people with rights of access to them. Those who had money no longer had to construct kin links to get the goods needed for exchange or for daily survival. Those who aspired to be important no longer had to construct their *kamals* by judicious patronage and strengthen them by judicious marriage. Influence no longer came through the control of property and trade, but came instead through the control of money.

During the late 1940s and early 1950s, Ponams were fortunate to be able to earn a living by the sale of war surplus and by working as labourers in building, maintaining and finally tearing down military installations, for this gave them a few years to adjust to the fact that the trade relations of market and *kawas*, on which they had relied before the War, were gone forever. Ironically, however, the fact that they, and others like them, had goods to sell was one of the factors precipitating the collapse of market trade.

The Manus markets had always been somewhat unstable and subject to the vagaries of politics and warfare, but they had survived because of the economic interests they served. After the War these interests were no longer so clear and the markets shut and re-opened frequently. The mainlanders no longer had much need for island fish, since they now lived on the coast and had learned to catch it for themselves. What they wanted was cash to buy foreign goods. In order to get this cash, they began to insist that islanders buy their market produce rather than trade fish for it. Ponams had to have market sago, which they could not produce for themselves, but they wanted to spend their cash on imports, just as the mainlanders did. As a result, they resisted the mainlanders' demands for money, conflicts erupted, and Ponam's markets closed, just as did other markets up and down the coast. Patrol officers were sympathetic to the islanders and tried to keep the markets open, but without success. They closed and opened several times during the 1940s and 1950s, closed altogether during the late 1950s and did not open again until the 1970s, at which time they were dominated by cash. Ponams, and lagoon and island people throughout Manus, had to find some other way to live.

SOCIAL AND ECONOMIC REORIENTATION

The War had more than just an economic impact. The American military rule was completely different from the old Australian administration, and exposure to this, plus the fact that many Manus people had occupied positions of power and authority in wartime, led to overt dissatisfaction, especially among young men, with the reimposed Australian colonial rule. It was this dissatisfaction that motivated two deputations of eminent Manus men to approach the Commander of the United States Naval Base at Lorengau in August 1946, and ask that Americans assume control of Manus, as the Australians had done nothing for them (Dept. of External Territories 1946).

Although this discontent was felt everywhere in Manus, it was expressed most dramatically by those, mostly from the south coast, who accepted the leadership of Paliau Molowat and joined his New Way movement (Schwartz 1962). Paliau planned a social and economic revolution. He planned to overthrow traditional leadership and the economy based on affinal exchange, to break the power of ghosts and ancestors and to break the power of Australian colonial rulers.

Paliau's policy for the revitalisation of the Manus economy was precisely to destroy the old divisions of production that he thought were preventing Manus from joining the modern economic world. He wanted to eliminate the ecological and social divisions that underlay the system of village interdependence, including 'all of the old divisions of rank, clan, ethnic group, and ecological type... . The Manus [lagoon dwellers] were to move ashore, the Usiai [inlanders] to move to the beach; both were to practice mixed fishing and gardening' (Schwartz 1963: 93). Likewise, Paliau and his followers wanted to eliminate the extensive affinal exchanges that motivated much of the intervillage trade, to eliminate the sexual shame and affinal avoidance that made relations between the sexes and between affines so tense, and to hasten integration with the expanding colonial economy through increasing commodity production. Finally, and most prominently, they wanted to overturn colonial rule or, at least in the short term, obtain a voice for Manus people in it. The introduction of Local Government Councils in south coast Manus in 1952 was a direct response to Paliau. (For some of the more recent history of Paliau's movement, see Trompf 1983.)

The New Way and Paliau's leadership were not accepted everywhere in Manus. Especially along the north coast, people feared the movement's expansionist political ambitions and resented its opposition to the Catholic Church and to traditional customs. This became particularly strong when the Administration attempted to expand the Local Government Council to the north coast. The Paliau movement, which had heretofore been merely blasphemous because it rejected the Catholic Church and many traditional customs, became directly threatening. The Council was founded as a result of the demands of Paliau and his followers, and was seen by Ponams to be dominated by them. The Paliau movement had its centre among the south coast Titan-speaking people who had long been Ponams' enemies, and the attempt to expand the Local Government Council was seen as another invasion.

Although Ponams did not join Paliau, Ponam young men also wanted the new prosperity, and entered into many new economic activities. In the early 1950s they ran successful trade stores, made a great deal of money from trochus sales, and several island entrepreneurs were employed as contractors by the Australian administration. But this prosperity did not last. They withdrew money from their trade stores to buy back their old plantation (PR 2-57/58), even though it had few trees and produced little copra. The stores were then bankrupt and the government forced them to close (PR 3-58/59). Trochus prices collapsed. The last of the military jobs disappeared. Ponams had no more war surplus to sell. Their local markets were shut. Their traditional trading partners were fishing for themselves and increasingly were demanding cash and cash goods for sago. Their economic position was thus extremely precarious, and for the next decade many Ponams sought to survive by selling their fish at the government centre, a day's sail to the east, and using the money to buy sago in the sago-producing areas a day's travel to the west.

Confronted with the failure of most internal sources of wealth, many Manus people looked to paid employment. Earlier mission education had helped develop a tradition of literacy and numeracy and a desire for Western education, which now began to bear fruit. In the 1950s the government and missions opened essentially-free English-language schools, and many Manus people took advantage of this in two ways. First, in going to school they increased their ability to get desirable, well-paid jobs; second, many Manus taught in the expanding school system. By the 1960s, Manus commitment to education and educational achievement were striking, and remained so through the period of fieldwork (see appendix 1; *WT&E*: 86).

D

For Ponams, with no opportunity to earn money through cash cropping, education was particularly important because it led, eventually, to a dramatic increase in the amount of money and goods that migrants were able to remit to the island. In the 1950s migration produced relatively little direct benefit, as wages were so low that substantial remittances were not possible. However, through the 1960s and 1970s there was a significant increase in real wages at all levels, combined with expanding opportunities for Papua New Guineans at higher occupational levels, so that migrants were in a position to save and send substantial amounts of money home to their families. In 1979, for example, Ponam's 300 residents spent in excess of K30,000 on imported food and other goods, school fees, and so on, and yet they themselves earned no more than K5,000 of this. The money they did not earn was remitted to them by the approximately 100 employed migrants (*WT&E*: 165–168, 172–177).

KAMALS, LAPANS AND EXCHANGES AFTER THE WAR

In the early years of this century *lapans* were key political and economic figures and *kamals* key institutions on Ponam. *Lapans* were able to control the property and kin links of their *kamal* members and dependents. Through this control they were able to trade and interact with people in outside communities and to acquire the various natural and manufactured products that were essential both for daily survival and for success in exchange. By their wealth *lapans* were able to dominate *kamal*-mates and acquire other dependents (whose property and labour they could control) through financing their marriages and other affinal obligations. Thus, the control of people and the control of property were inextricably intertwined, and both of these took place in the idiom of kinship.

During the long course of colonisation this set of relationships was broken apart: *lapans* lost their power to attract and hold dependents; *kamals* ceased to be political constructions, becoming instead largely genealogical and relatively powerless. The most significant factor in this change was the breaking up of the integrated Manus producing- and trading-economy. The local goods that *lapans* had controlled and traded were replaced by imported substitutes that anyone who had money could buy; and the opportunities for earning that money were open almost exclusively to young men. Thus, no longer could *lapans* acquire dependents through marriage finance. In fact, the situation was nearly the reverse, with the old dependent on the charity of the young.

What, then, happened to the three forms of circulation that we described in the first part of this chapter, and how do these relate to the modern institution of the *kamal*?

Markets remained important in the 1980s, and continued to be owned by *kamals*, though they were largely based on cash. They also remained a source of tension, with Ponam's two markets opening and closing frequently as the state of relations between mainlanders and islanders dictated. The markets remained a significant source for sago and betel nut, but Ponams also bought large amounts of produce elsewhere. Opportunistic salesmen from sago-producing areas turned up on Ponam fairly regularly to sell off a few hundred kina's worth of sago and betel nut. And Ponams were frequent visitors to Lorengau and the markets and stores there (*WT&E*: chap. 4).

Kawas trade was also important, but like market trade, it was almost exclusively for cash. *Kawas* were less like conventional trade partners, having become instead people from whom Ponams might conveniently buy mainland produce. Significantly also, when people created new trade partnerships, they did not do so through patronising Ponam dependents and taking over their partners. Instead, they turned to links created outside of Manus, or at least outside of Ponam, seeking out school- and workmates who had returned to the village, or using links created by siblings and children working in towns.

Ceremonial exchange also changed in a number of ways relevant to the understanding of *kamals* (these are described at length in chapter 4). To begin with, the two types of exchange that were most immediately significant for *kamals* and *lapans*, the *lapan* and the men's-house–raising feasts, had both been abandoned. The last Ponam *lapan* exchange was held in about 1920 by Kuluah Kelepe, then the *lapan* of Kamal Kehin. It was large and important, but ended in disaster. Kuluah Kelepe's only son, who was then a student at the Bundralis Mission school, fell ill in the midst of the celebration and died before it was completed. The priest at Bundralis had spoken out against *lapan* exchanges before, and although he did not rebuke Kuluah Kelepe for holding the *lapan*, God's disapproval was patent to all and no more were held in Bundralis Parish.

Men's-house–raising feasts did not evoke the priest's disapproval, but the last one took place in the early 1950s, held by Kamal Nilo. Even that was truncated, with only ten pigs. After that time men's houses were built with little ceremony, some rice, tinned fish and a few turtles. With typical humour, young men hung empty fish and meat tins on the rafters that had once been decorated with the skulls of pigs. A new men's house thus no longer marked the achievements of a *lapan*, his influence over his agnates and kin, his power to pull pigs. It represented far more the achievements of the *kamal*'s migrants who sent home the money to buy the building materials, rice and tinned fish, and the *kamal*'s young men who did most of the work of construction.

Just as a men's-house–raising was no longer an enormously expensive procedure, so it was no longer an enormously significant one. All *kamals* wanted men's houses, and most had one most of the time: even the poorest groups could afford to put up some kind of shelter. More importantly, failure to do so did not presage a fall into dependence. *Kamals* remained independent for as long as they chose, apparently free of economic or other pressure to submit to the patronage of others. In fact, the tendency was quite the reverse. Since the 1920s, a number of once-dependent *kamal*s had broken away from their patrons, and no *kamal*s had become dependent on others.

Although *lapan* and men's-house–raising exchanges had gone, the exchanges focused on individual marriages and life cycles continued. People continued to be born, marry, have children and die, and to celebrate these events with exchanges between affines and between paternal and maternal kin. These exchanges were, however, no longer the occasion for patronage, the creation of dependence and the consolidation of a *kamal* under the control of a *lapan*. Instead, over the course of the post-War years, marriage became almost entirely an affair of the cognatic *ken si*s, and came to be managed by households, not by *kamal*s.

First, for reasons described in chapter 4, few of these exchanges were truly essential, and couples who insisted could be married with almost no expense. Second, marriages and the exchanges that followed were financed almost entirely by migrants, and not by island *lapan*s. When an island couple wished to marry, they looked to their migrant kin for support, and not to *lapan*s, or even parents and resident siblings. Further, the support they sought was cash, not Ponam fish and shell money. It was spent at stores to buy imported commodities, not traded to *kawa*s for indigenous produce. Thus, in the 1980s these exchanges had a very different economic significance. Under the old system the patron *lapan*s used exchange to create obligations that allowed them to extract wealth from the poor dependents of their *kamal*s; on modern Ponam the relatively poor island residents, who dominated the exchange system, used exchange to create obligations that allowed them to extract wealth from rich migrants.

With the dying out of *lapan* and men's-house–raising exchanges, with the decreasing significance of *lapan*s and *kamal*s and with the increased significance of exchanges focused on individual marriages and life cycles, there also came an increase in the overt significance of women's positions and roles in exchange.[5] This was true particularly because of changes in the distribution of wealth. In the 1980s, male-owned *kamal* property was not the major source of wealth. Instead, islanders derived most of their wealth from remittances made by migrants, remittances sent not to *kamal*s, but to the individuals who were the

---

[5] The change in women's position on Ponam contrasts interestingly with Glenn Petersen's (1982) descriptions of changes on Ponape, in Micronesia. There, colonisation meant that women's manufactured goods were replaced by imports and their place in exchange was devalued relative to that of men, who continued to produce much valued agricultural produce. However, the role of matrilineages on Ponape changed in ways that parallel some of the changes in Ponam *kamal*s.

migrants' parents and siblings. Women had a great, even dominant, say in the use of this money.

Even though marriage no longer served as an arena for the machinations of *lapan*s or as a conduit for the movement of Manus products, it continued to be a significant source of wealth for Ponams, for it was one of the main ways in which islanders maintained ties to migrants and induced them to remit money to the island. Migrants, especially those married to Ponams, still felt bound to go through the series of exchanges that validated their own marriages and insured the health and good future of their children, and to contribute to the exchanges put on by their own close kin. The reasons for this were two-fold. People were concerned for their own reputation on the island and concerned to do things properly in their own eyes and the eyes of others. And they were concerned for the health and welfare of themselves and their families, and thus concerned to put on the correct rituals and to stay on good terms with island kin, lest disputes between them should invoke ancestral anger and lead to ghostly illness (A. Carrier 1989).

Migrants also expected to receive positive benefits from the contributions they made. They received ritual blessings, the good fortune that followed from good relations with kin and ancestors, and the benefits of a community in which to spend holidays, to retreat in times of sickness or other problems, and to return to on retirement or in the event of unemployment. Although formally any Ponam had, simply by virtue of *kamal* membership, an inalienable right to land, reef, sea, and fishing techniques, as well as claims upon kin for their labour, in practice matters were less certain. Land was in short supply and there was always the fear that neighbours would fiddle the boundaries and kin would challenge the genealogies. The generous migrant of good repute was not immune to these dangers, but was threatened by them much less than miserly absentees who stayed away. As urban migrants themselves explicitly stated, through their contributions to Ponam, Ponam provided them with the social welfare services that the state of Papua New Guinea did not provide.

Migrants who were significant parties in an exchange were expected to participate, by proxy or preferably in person. And resident Ponams did everything possible to assure participation: they announced their intentions two or three years in advance, scheduled exchanges to suit the holidays and financial resources of significant migrants and endlessly wrote letters to keep them informed and involved. If a migrant were not a significant party, his or her parents or siblings might ask for money so that they could participate, though this depended on the importance of the exchange and their place in it.

Migrant men and women contributed a substantial amount of money to island exchange. Thus, during the early 1980s residents were consistently able to raise among themselves about K1000 to put into brideprice payments. But, as they themselves said, this did no one any good, for the money just circulated pointlessly from one resident to another. It was contributions from migrants that inflated this sum and brought a profit to the island. During these years, migrants provided additional sums to these payments, ranging from K500 on one occasion to more than K5000 on another. (Additional money came from the bride's family to make return payments, much of it from migrants as well.) Husbands without close migrant kin simply made smaller prestations. There was no resort to financiers. Even though migrants contributed the bulk of the wealth to exchange, they could not profit directly from it. Anything received by absent migrants was redistributed automatically in their names to their kin and affines, so the money and goods stayed on the island. Migrants present for the exchange were expected to distribute most of what they received, and to use the remainder to help their island families. They could not take what they received away from the island.

In other words, the change in the value of Manus produce, and the shift to dependence on imported commodities, changed the significance of Ponam *lapan*s and *kamal*s. The mutual need of a *lapan* for dependents and of the poor for a *lapan* was erased, as both came to need a migrant instead. The economic impact of Western encroachment meant that the practical importance of *kamal* property changed: in the 1980s this property figured largely as an element of the social identity of groups, the members of which increasingly relied for their subsistence on remittances from migrant workers. Property was no longer what it had been, an important prop for sheer survival and a manipulable key to prosperity. As a consequence of this, the property-owning *kamal*s became, perhaps largely by default, far more rigidly agnatic than they had been before. There was no pressure to recruit outsiders and little pressure on outsiders to seek recruitment. The groups that had been largely political units constructed in an idiom of kinship became real kin groups. It is not clear, therefore, that the Ponam *kamal*s that existed in the 1980s were the same as those that existed fifty or sixty years before. On the contrary, the *kamal*s of the 1980s, the *kamal*s whose structure was so like the classic segmentary lineage, were an artifact of the colonial era.

CONCLUSION

This and the preceding chapter serve dual purposes. On the one hand they are ethnographic. They provide a background description of kin groups essential for any understanding of Ponam society in the 1980s and they provide a general sketch of Ponam history. In addition, however, they present the two sides of the tension between a formal analysis of social organisation and a processual description of the non-structural forces that shape people's actions and the organisations they create. Like the processualist writers of the 1960s described in the introduction, we focus mainly on political and economic processes that shaped Ponam kinship, but unlike those writers, we locate these processes in history.

The highly genealogical, largely descent-based elements of Ponam kin structure in the 1980s resemble the kinds of groups found by and predicted by classic structural kinship analyses. However, the fact that these structural units match classic anthropological descriptions does not mean that one can treat them as "primitive terms", basic units that are so fundamental that they require no further explanation. Instead, the history presented in this chapter shows the limitations of a structured, genealogical presentation of kinship. It does so by showing the way that the operation, and thus significance, of this structure can change over time — though saying this does not mean that a structural view is invalid or irrelevant for understanding contemporary Ponam. The highly genealogical construction of kinship and *kamal*s that Ponams favoured in the 1980s, like the highly fluid, openly-political system of the 1920s, was a consequence of a particular set of economic conditions in conjunction with a set of cultural values and expectations. It was not a logical outcome of a set of cultural structures.

A committed structuralist, of course, could argue that while the operation and significance of kinship structures may have changed over time, the structures themselves have not; could argue that all we have presented is the way that a core set of structured cultural elements manifest themselves in different ways in changing circumstances. We do not have the evidence to refute this, for there is little evidence on the structured set of cultural elements that may have motivated Ponams earlier in this century. We can, however, attack this hypothetical structuralist argument by pointing to its own key flaw. That flaw is the difficulty in deciding what it is that is persisting. If we cannot specify the elements of a core Ponam cultural structure, we cannot decide that they have survived.

We can show the nature of this problem by asking a practical historical– ethnographic question about the important Ponam institution of the *kamal*: What is the key of a *kamal* as a cultural construct? Looking at the *kamal*s of the 1920s without the benefit of hindsight it is difficult to identify what their main aspects were. Reasonable candidates include: ownership of real property, high economic significance, kinship flexibility through adoption and patronage, rank, agnation and regulation of marriage. But it is apparent that most of these candidates for core status have changed significantly. While *kamal*s remained property-owning groups, it is not clear that Ponams at the time of fieldwork construed them as having economic significance in anything like the way that seems likely for the 1920s. Similarly, while Ponams continued to conceive of *kamal*s in a way that includes the notion of rank, it is difficult to see how the meaning and understanding of that rank bears more than a passing resemblance to that of the 1920s. Even the notion of agnation seems likely to have undergone important change. Ponams, like Peres, seem to have practiced extensive adoption. If Mead's reports are anything to go by, they appear to have accepted a notion of the flexibility of agnatic descent that seems very much unlike their understanding of the relationships of agnation and *kamal* membership in the 1980s.

Certainly with the benefit of hindsight it is possible to identify some aspects of *kamal*s that have survived for 50 years or so, and if we like we can decide that it was they, after all, that were core structural elements. However, this merely elevates the benefit of hindsight to a theoretical first principle.

CHAPTER THREE

Marriage and ceremonial exchange

Ponam kin groups can be analysed in terms of descent, as we showed in chapter 1, and certainly Ponams themselves conceptualised these groups this way, referring to kin groups as *ken si* ("one origin") and identifying them by the name of their focal ancestors. It is also true however, that the neo-structuralist thesis that Melanesian kinship is organised in terms of principles of exchange applies to Ponam. Island kin relations often derived their content and meaning from exchange and were inexplicable except in terms of it. This was less true of *kamals*, though even here exchange was important, as we show in chapter 5. However, the cognatic *ken sis* and the relations between line-of-the-woman and line-of-the-man that comprised them were inseparable from the realm of ceremonial exchange. These relationships had almost no content other than that of giving and receiving, reciprocity and obligation. We will describe these groups in structural terms in this chapter. However, as our historical description in the next chapter will show, the elegant logic of the sort that neo-structuralists have revealed is rather less compelling and rather less satisfactory as explanation than those neo-structuralists suggest.

We begin by describing marriage, the institution around which almost all significant exchanges revolved. Then we turn to the formal rules governing exchange in the 1980s, and show how the structure of exchange and the structure of kinship described in chapter 1 are inter-related. In the next chapter we show how the system we describe here was affected by the same sort of historical contingencies that shaped Ponam *kamals*.

The most renown systems of ceremonial exchange in Papua New Guinea are the elaborate, enchained systems of competitive exchange of valuables, such as *tee, moka* and *kula*. Ponams too once had something like this, in *lapan* exchanges and competitive men's-house–raising exchanges, but by the 1980s these were no more. Instead, Ponam exchanges were part of the system of marriage and the continuing relations between inter-marrying families, and as such lacked a specifically competitive edge. Rather, their explicit purpose was to create and perpetuate the relations of mutual dependence and obligation that followed from and were an objective of marriage. Marriage, brideprice and prestations made for the benefit of the children of a marriage were the most important of Ponam exchanges. Marriage, then, is the appropriate place to start.

COURTSHIP AND MARRIAGE CHOICES

The older political and economic marriage strategies that we described in chapter 2 had disappeared by the 1980s. Parents wished to guide their children into wise choices, but by and large they agreed that marriage was a matter for young people themselves and felt that parents should submit to their children's desires, so long as these desires fell outside the range of prohibited close kin and affines and were not otherwise manifestly unwise.

Occasionally, however, people could put pressure on others to marry, as an example will illustrate. A man of about fifty who had been working in Rabaul for many years arranged for his family to offer a proposal to an island woman of about thirty, the mother of two illegitimate children. Her eldest brother strongly urged that she accept the proposal, which was in many ways a sensible one. The woman in question was something of a burden on her kin, and her brother assumed that she would be better off in the care of a hard-working, responsible, though by no means wealthy, man. The woman herself resisted the proposal for some time, and had the support of public opinion, which held that the discrepancy in ages was far too great. As one middle-aged matron argued, 'Why should she get married? She has all the lovers she wants right now.' In the end, however, the woman agreed to her brother's demands and the marriage took place.

The matron who said that there was nothing wrong with the single life, provided it had sexual satisfaction in it, was flippant but not unusual. Ponams did not see marriage as essential or inevitable. Single people were not socially disabled in the way that they often are in Papua New Guinea, and most young men and women were in no great hurry to marry. Both men and women tended to marry late, and there was a high rate of non-marriage. Of the 46 women age 20–29 in 1979, only 43 per cent had ever married. By 30–39 this had increased to 76 per cent of 26. For men the figures were similar. For the 59 men age 20–29, 32 per cent had ever married; for the 28 men age 30–39, 82 per cent had ever married.

Although young people were expected to choose their own spouses without too much interference from their elders, they were expected to choose from within a fairly narrow range. As already described, there was a strong preference for island endogamy, and an expectation that those who married outsiders would be lost to the island. Consequently, most residents married within the island and thus married kin. However, they preferred to marry kin related as distantly as possible. It was considered both wrong and impractical to marry into any of the *ken sis*, the cognatic stocks, that were important contributors to one's own family in exchange. People said it was wrong to marry into one's own or one's mother's *kamal*; it was wrong to marry any kind of cognate until four generations after the original marriage that was the basis of the cognatic relationship; and it was wrong to marry any of one's siblings' close affines. Given their small population, Ponams could not possibly obey all of these prohibitions. The one that gave way most readily was that on marrying distantly-related cognates. Islanders did not marry first-generation cousins, and rarely married second-generation cousins, but marriages of third- and fourth-generation cousins were common.

Ideally, girls were expected to remain chaste and closely supervised by their parents until marriage, and girls with any sense of discretion certainly attempted to maintain this public image. But in private most young women, like young men, had active sex lives during their late teens and twenties and enjoyed a number of partners. However, young people's private courtship and sexuality were not unregulated. To be morally acceptable, even to the young themselves, courtship had to be conducted through the intermediary of the young people's *tamatus*. In the past these *asis* and *tamas* both chose marriage partners and financed marriage arrangements. In the 1980s young people chose their partners themselves, but love affairs, courtship and marriage usually were still arranged through *tamatus*. Without these go-betweens and the approval that they, in their position of special ritual authority, had to offer, any sexual relationship was illicit.

When a young man wanted to court a young woman, he began by asking one of her *tamas*, usually one of his own age, to be an intermediary. Because of their close relationship, a *tama* could talk freely to the girl and tell her that the young man in question wanted to meet her. If he disapproved, however, he could refuse, and would be remiss if he did not. This refusal, with its possible cursing sanction, should be heeded, though the persistent could try to seek out another intermediary. Although young women were not expected to initiate affairs, they too could pass messages to boys who were courting them through the intermediary of the young men's *asis*.

These go-betweens passed messages and arranged for the couple to meet, the business of the meeting being to arrange the initiation of their sexual relationship. (As one man put it, 'We have seen a lot of foreign films, and we know that for Europeans sex is the last question. But for us, sex is the first question.') In a properly-conducted affair, the couple would meet in a house loaned to them for the evening by one of the young man's older, married *tamas*. Illicit meetings took place in unused buildings, canoes or even in the bush. If their sexual relationship were satisfactory, the couple could begin to exchange small gifts such as betel nut and jewellery, which could be easily consumed or explained away. As one might expect from this, pregnancies among unmarried young women were common, but they were not regarded very seriously except by the families immediately involved.

Young people were not expected necessarily to pair off into mono-
gamous couples, and both girls and boys sometimes had a number of partners
at the same time. The president of the young women's club, however, advised
her members not to do this because of the problems these simultaneous affairs
could cause. Sometimes these affairs were sad. For example, two sisters discovered that, unbeknownst to each other, they were both sleeping with, and had
hopes of marrying, the same young man. When it all came to light, the young
man solved the problem by announcing that he had absolutely no intention of
marrying either one of them, or anybody else for that matter. And sometimes
these affairs were seen as particularly funny. One popularly-retold story was of
a young woman who brought an appeal for the maintenance of her illegitimate
child to the village court. When the magistrate asked her whom she wanted to
pay the maintenance, she produced a list of five or six names, could not choose
between them, and the case was dismissed.

When a young man finally decided that he wished to make a formal
proposal of marriage, he first approached some of his *asi*s or *tama*s, most
probably those who had been sympathetically involved in his courtship and
whose opinion would carry weight with his parents. The intermediaries then
presented the suggestion to his parents, and arranged a meeting with the boy's
parents, mature siblings, grandparents and parent's siblings. Those at this
meeting considered the reputations of the young woman and her parents as
individuals and prospective exchange partners, and as well they considered the
implications of the marriage for the family's existing exchange networks. If
they disapproved, the young man might submit, or he might try to wear them
down by persistence, a tactic that was likely to be successful, especially if the
woman he wished to marry became pregnant.

When the family had agreed to make the proposal, they sought out a
person who was kin to both bride and groom to act as an intermediary. Preferably the intermediary should be *tama* to both bride and groom, but other
relationships were possible. The go-between presented the proposal informally
to the bride's kin and moved back and forth between the two groups trying to
ensure that everything was arranged privately before the formal proposal was
made. All of these arrangements were made as secretly as possible, out of fear
of the embarrassment of a failed proposal. This was a reasonable fear for,
despite the precautions of prior negotiations, proposals were sometimes
refused, especially if the young woman involved felt that she had not been
properly consulted. Unlike many other places in Papua New Guinea, on Ponam
the size of future marriage payments was not part of the engagement negotiations. The bride's kin simply had to accept what they were given. When the time
came, they might be dissatisfied, but this did not affect the validity or perman-
ence of the marriage.

In order to make a formal proposal, the groom's family collected contributions of tobacco and money (usually with a value of K200 to K400) from a wide range of kin and affines. The groom's close kin went as a group to present this to the bride's family, usually at her parent's house. When they arrived there, her immediate family was called together to hear the proposal. If the bride or her family refused the marriage they would refuse to accept the tobacco offered to them. If they accepted the marriage, they accepted the tobacco, and the engagement was made public immediately, as the bride's family began to distribute the tobacco and money among their cognates and affines. From this point on the arrangement was virtually binding. The couple were referred to as husband and wife; affinal terms were used between their families; all the rules of affinal avoidance came into play; and the two families began to exchange as they would continue to do for the life of the marriage. Usually, however, the couple did not marry and begin to live together for several years.

For Ponams, as for people elsewhere in Papua New Guinea, the engagement gift was merely the first in a long series of major gifts formally presented by one family to the other. Its role as the initiator of a series was indicated by its name, *aribihi sal*, "opening the road". The word "road" (*sal*) had a range of connotations very similar to those of the English word "way". It meant road or path, and also manner of acting, thinking, or doing something. In kinship usage it meant both the genealogical relationship between two people or groups, and a particular individual who linked two or more others as kin. The significance of the name, *aribihi sal*, is that with the gift of tobacco marking the engagement, the couple became a road linking her kin with his kin. Once this road was opened, gifts flowed continuously between the two families for several generations.

This constant flow of gifts was a key objective of marriage. Thus marriage, and the individual exchanges following it, can only be understood when placed in the context of the entire exchange process. As John Comaroff (1980: 30–31) argued in the introduction to his collection, *The meaning of marriage payments*, 'both the symbolic value and the structural implications of marriage (and its associated prestations) are rendered largely meaningless once they are ... excised from the context of which the other elements are equally a part'.

In his contribution to that collection, Andrew Strathern made these points explicitly in his description of Melpa and Wiru exchange. He couched his discussion in terms of a consideration of Meyer Fortes's jural view of marriage payments. Fortes said that for patrilineal societies, these payments 'signalize the transfer to the husband of marital rights over his wife and parental rights over any children that will be born to her' (1962: 9). In accord with this view, he argued that these transfers are of two types. First is the Prime Prestation, which 'is the part of the marriage payments which stands for the nuclear sexual and parental rights and relationships of the spouses. ...

Bargaining cannot enter into this. ... [I]ts significance lies in its binding power as a jural instrument'. Second are Contingent Prestations. These 'are not a jural instrument for the transfer of rights but a means of winning and preserving good will. ... There is an element of barter in them' (1962: 10). Thus, Fortes separated gift exchanges between affines from other types of exchanges, and argues that the most important of the affinal exchanges is the single non-negotiable payment that transfers jural rights in the bride from her father to her husband. Other gifts are incidental to this one.

Strathern argued that, on the contrary, continuing relations of exchange between affines are no more contingent or negotiable than are the major gifts that formally transfer jural rights. For both Wiru and Melpa, prestations are intended to compensate the bride's kin for some of the losses they suffer when she moves, but compensation is not the prime purpose of marriage prestations.

> Since a marriage itself is seen as but one "item" or "event" in a much larger process of exchanges between people, the aspect of marriage as a focus for regenerating exchange relations is centrally important. Hence the prestations which would be regarded as contingent, optional or peripheral in the Fortesian scheme, centred as it is on a jural view of rights established through individual acts of marriage, may in terms of an exchange model be rather regarded as central (A. Strathern 1980: 64–65).

And reciprocally, it is this larger process of exchange, rather than specific prime prestations, that serves to legitimate marriage. Thus, for the Melpa, 'a marriage is fully established when the affines make *moka* with the breeding pigs a young couple have been endowed with'. Likewise, for the Wiru a marriage 'is properly established when the couple have a child and enter into the nexus of payments for pearlshells in return for ribcages of pork' (1980: 65).

For Ponams the continuing prestations and exchanges that took place through and on behalf of married couples were of the greatest importance in creating their relationship. Marriage did transfer rights in women and children from one group to another, but equally important, it created a new relationship between two sets of kin. A man married not only in order to gain a wife and children, but also in order to gain rights of access to her family: the right to contribute gifts to their exchanges and to receive contributions from them, the right to give and receive labour and the right to give and receive political and emotional support and allegiance. It was, after all, just these aspects of marriage that motivated financier-*lapans* to make the adoptions and marriage arrangements that we described in chapter 2.

In spite of Fortes's assertion that the parties concerned in the transfer of these rights can be understood in part as players in a game which 'requires that they be defined as opponents, each aiming at profiting rather than losing by the outcome' (1962: 3), on Ponam, as in many places in Papua New Guinea, these were not zero-sum rights. Quite the reverse: the more these were given away, the more they returned to the giver; the more they were exercised, the more powerful they grew, for both parties. Because affines had the greatest interest in maintaining and promoting this relationship, from which both sides could benefit, they were allies far more than competitors. Thus, for example, the long negotiations that took place between the bride's and groom's relatives before the presentation of any marriage prestation rarely involved competition or disputes between them over the quantities to be paid and rights to be alienated. The negotiations were intended instead to smooth out in advance all possible problems of procedure and protocol, in order to prevent public quarrels or the appearance of disunity between the main parties and allow them each to present a united front to their own relatives.[1] Further, the bride's kin did not stand together as a group, persistently demanding gifts as compensation for the woman taken from them. In fact, demands that the groom's kin make marriage payments usually came either from the bride's distant kin, or from the groom's kin, who wished to use these payments to strengthen the groom's obligations to them and, in a sense, wean him away from his affines.

Thus Ponam marriage did not bridge two competing groups. Instead, it created a kind of alliance, though not one based on the prospect of future exchanges of women of the sort analysed by Godelier (1986). It was based on the opposite supposition, that from this alliance would emerge a single *ken si*, the descendants of a brother and sister, who would act together and derive their strength from continued exchange. Necessarily, then, marriage exchanges were not merely a means to an end; they were an end in themselves. They were not only a jural instrument or an instrument for alliance; they were also an objective for which marriage itself was the instrument.

Although affinal prestations did more than transfer rights, it is true that Ponams said this was one of their purposes. These prestations marked stages in a couple's relationship and in some instances were specifically associated with the transfer of rights. Even so, they were not obligatory in any simple jural sense. Most people made some prestations, some made all, a few made none at all. People could change the order of prestations, combine them with others and invent variations; none of these appeared to influence the legitimacy of the marriage. Furthermore, neither the bride's nor the groom's kin had any formal recourse if prestations were not made. Cases of non-payment never appeared

---

[1] Anthony Forge (1972: 534) suggests that in competitive Melanesian exchange, the main element of competition frequently was between leader and followers, rather than between leaders. The tensions that existed in these relatively non-competitive Ponam affinal exchanges suggest that Forge's point may apply more broadly.

in village court, and could not do so because the ethic underlying affinal prestations was that they were freely given and not debts. The bride's kin were expected simply to accept whatever was offered. Perhaps more significant, payments were not necessary for the legitimation of the marriage or its children. Non-payment of brideprice was not grounds for the bride's kin to reclaim her or her children, for the bride herself to initiate divorce or for the groom's agnates to disinherit his children in later years. In the heat of the moment people could bring up such non-prestation as a taunt or as an attempt to attack the prestige of others, but it could not be more than this, for marriages could not be dissolved.

They were indissoluble, Ponams said, because when islanders became Catholic they accepted the doctrine that human beings could not dissolve a marriage made by God. Following their adherence to this doctrine, not only was non-payment of marriage prestations no grounds for divorce, but neither were infidelity, laziness, physical abuse, barrenness, insanity or any of the other problems that Ponams thought were far more serious than failure to pay brideprice. Further, none was grounds for more than the most temporary of separations. Families would intervene in a troubled marriage with prayers, curses, exhortations, bribes and threats, but they would not take in a run-away spouse for more than a short time. Not only did Ponams accept the indissolubility of marriage, they also accepted a ban on polygamy, a practice that had, in any case, never been common. Further, they did not encourage widow or widower remarriage. They said that women would not remarry because they did not want to leave their children behind, as they would have to do if they joined new husbands. But there was also a more deeply-rooted sentimental reason behind this. Husbands and wives were expected to care very deeply for one another, and the distress of bereavement was thought to be too deep to be solaced by another marriage.

These principles were strict, but generally Ponams kept to them. Among Ponams themselves there appeared to have been no polygamous marriages and only two divorces and two remarriages since the War. The two divorces both involved couples who had not been married in church. In one case a woman married and left, or was abandoned by, a man from elsewhere in Manus. She then moved in with a Ponam man in the provincial capital, Lorengau, and had two children. They later separated. She came back to the island and raised her two children into her natal *kamal*; he remained in town. The children took their mother's brother's name as their surnames and their kin addressed them as though they were the children of that mother's brother's children. This was the conventional manner of dealing with illegitimate children. In the second case a young man and woman lived together in Rabaul and had no children. They then separated, and each married a non-Manus. These second unions lasted about five years, when they separated again and remarried each other. Similarly, there were only two cases of remarriage following the death of a spouse. In one a widower of about 50 remarried a single woman some ten years his junior. In the other a widower of about 70 remarried a widow almost his own age.

While Ponams were very concerned that marriages between Ponams should be permanent, the situation with marriages to non-Ponams, and especially to non-Manus, was different. Islanders had little control over the fate of these marriages and they seemed relatively unconcerned about them. In general, marriages with outsiders were recognised as fragile, and men and women sometimes divorced outsiders even after their marriages had been solemnised in church and sanctioned by marriage payments. There was no objection to these divorced men and women returning home. Those whose marriages had been made outside of church were free to remarry. Those who had been married in church could remarry without objections from other Ponams, but were then denied confession and holy communion. Perhaps for this reason there was only one such remarried couple on Ponam.

Effectively, intra-island marriages were permanent regardless of whether or not they were made in church, while others did not have to be. One reason for this lay in the place of affinal relations in the day-to-day operation of island exchange, in the fact that Ponam couples were so deeply enmeshed in networks of exchange. The major prestations were of some importance here, but more important was the flow of contributory gifts between the couple and their kin.

Although major prestations could be postponed, combined with other gifts or even skipped altogether, these small contributory gifts could not. A man might not pay his own brideprice, but he would not fail to meet his obligation to assist his wife and her kin to pay a brideprice when they chose to do so. Nor would his wife fail to assist him in a like manner. People were not reluctant to admit that they had not made marriage prestations, but no one admitted failing to help his or her affines with the prestations they chose to make. And indeed it would be almost impossible to do so, for two reasons. First, failure to assist one's affines would shut one off from the constant round of prestations on which many depended for economic survival; it would be a kind of economic suicide. Second, in order to shun his or her affines a would-be non-contributor would have to turn away others who wished to give along the road of his marriage. And since this giving was something those others had a right to do and an interest in doing, this could be very difficult. It appeared, for example, that some very tenuous new marriages were held together largely by the fact that the two partners' kin refused to recognise that the marriage might fail. They continued to exchange and interact with each other as though they were oblivious to troubles in the marriage, and made it almost impossible for the couple to separate.

In conclusion, then, Ponam marriage prestations served not merely to legitimate or facilitate the transfer of women, but they served to open the road for the continual exchange of gifts that lay at the heart of all social relationships. Much more was involved in marriage than the movement of people between two independent and unchanging groups. Marriage not only moved women and children around among existing groups, but it also created something new. It created new kinds of groups, the line-of-the-woman and line-of-the-man, and it created a sphere of exchange activities that was conceptually independent of marriage and was valuable in and of itself. The rest of this chapter describes something of the universe of exchange relations that followed marriage, the context that gave marriage payments their meaning.

THE ORGANISATION OF EXCHANGE

With few exceptions, exchange on Ponam consisted of the presentation of a major gift and very shortly thereafter the presentation of a return gift. To keep these processes clear, we use "exchange" to refer to the entire event in which gifts were accumulated, presented and a return gift made and distributed; we use "prestation" or "initial prestation" for the first gift and "return prestation" for the second one. Initial prestations for different occasions had different names; return prestations were all called *kahu*. Both initial and return prestations had three stages: the contribution and accumulation of the prestation; the handing over of the prestation; and the distribution of what had been received. Thus, each complete exchange normally passed through six stages. We will describe each of these briefly.

1. Contribution and accumulation. Once all the preparations for an exchange had been completed, the leaders (*ke-gwok*s) who were to make the major prestation announced the day on which the goods to be given would be accumulated. On this day all of those who wished to help brought contributions to the leaders. These contributions were called *sor*, the process of bringing them together and displaying them in one place was called *njaharun*.

2. Initial prestation. After having accumulated and displayed the gift at their hamlet, the givers, with the help of kin, carried the gift to the hamlet of the intended recipients and put it on display there before presenting it formally.

3. Distribution. The recipients (who were also *ke-gwok*s) accepted the gift and then distributed it among their kin. These secondary recipients would later redistribute their shares among other kin, who could redistribute to their own kin, and so on. This process of distribution and redistribution (*kendi'i*) was the reverse of the process of contribution and accumulation.

4. Contribution and accumulation. Once the distribution was complete, the primary recipients announced the time for the accumulation of the return gift.

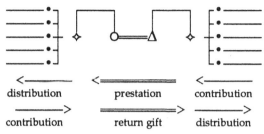

<————	<═══════	<————
distribution	prestation	contribution
————>	═══════>	————>
contribution	return gift	distribution

Figure 5   *The dendritic pattern of exchange*

All those who had received a share of the initial distribution were expected to bring contributions (*sor*) toward the return gift. These were accumulated (*njaharun*) in the recipient's hamlet and displayed.

5. *Return prestation.* Having completed the accumulation, the return prestation was carried to the hamlet of those who had made the initial prestation and displayed there.

6. *Distribution.* After having been displayed, the return prestation was then distributed among all those who had contributed to the initial gift.

Figure 5 shows the dendritic pattern of contribution and distribution in an exchange held for a married couple.

There were many different occasions for exchange on Ponam, all of them following the same basic process we have just described (some are described in *WT&E*: 221–224). At this point, however, we shall discuss only those that bear particularly on the issue of marriage. These occasions fall roughly into two categories, which we call affinal exchange and *tamatu* exchange. We use "affinal exchange", rather than the "bridewealth" or "marriage payments" more common in anthropological writing, because these took place over a long period of time and included gifts made both for the bride and for her children. We use "*tamatu* exchange" because these took place between the child's *tamatus* and the child's other kin. Ponams did not name these different exchanges as separate categories, but our distinction is a reasonable one. Affinal exchanges were explicitly seen as a linked series: each exchange calling forth the next, with obligations being carried forward from exchange to exchange. *Tamatu* exchanges were not so explicitly part of a series, but they all took a similar form, and it is easiest to describe them together.

In addition to exchanging in these major affinal and *tamatu* prestations, inter-marrying families constantly gave smaller and less formal gifts back and forth. Each helped the other with contributions toward their respective major prestations and even helped with contributions to exchanges held by yet others. Even though these contributions were much smaller and less dramatic than major prestations of the sort that have attracted anthropological attention, they were of great importance.

Prestation from groom's kin to bride's kin	Prestation from bride's kin to groom's kin
1. Engagement, *aribihi sal*, "opening the road" [cash, tobacco]	Return prestation, *kahu* [raw food]
2. Marriage, *joso* [beds, cooked & raw food, pig]	Simultaneous prestation [baskets, cooked & raw food, pig]
3.	Bride's marriage prestation,* *nonou*, "decoration" [baskets of lesser valuables]
Return prestation, *kahu* [raw food]	
4. First pregnancy,* *paruhu, marasus,* "nipples" [raw food]	Return prestation, *kahu* [raw food, coconuts]
5. Brideprice,* *njakenjak*, "crawl" [cash, shell money, dog's teeth, pig]	Return prestation, *kahu* [raw food, pig]
6. Late marriage prestation, *rovwel* [cash, shell money, dog's teeth, pig]	Return prestation, *kahu* [raw food]

Figure 6   *Affinal prestations in the 1980s*

* Prestation made by some people only.

AFFINAL EXCHANGE

Affinal exchange consisted of a series of exchanges between the bride's and the groom's siblings, assisted by their respective kin. Ponams explicitly saw these as forming a sequence. Figure 6 lists the affinal exchanges commonly carried out in the 1980s. Not everyone made all of them and they were not always made in this order, but this is roughly what was expected.

Affinal exchange began with the engagement prestation, already described, made by the groom's kin to the bride's. Those who accepted a share of this accepted, at least in principle, a commitment to participate in exchanges through the life of the marriage. The series concluded with a final gift from the groom's kin to the bride's, which was made when either he or she died.

The system by which Ponams accumulated contributory gifts for affinal exchange (or any other exchange for that matter) was very rigidly structured. The leaders in an exchange did not receive contributions from simply anyone — friends, dependents, debtors or distant kin. On the contrary, only specific, limited categories of kin contributed. Some of these are shown in figure 7, and we describe this process in further detail in later chapters. For the moment, however, it is sufficient to say that these contributions came from *kamal*-mates, line-of-the-woman, affines and maternal kin. The bride's kin distributed what they received in the same highly-structured manner among their own *kamal*-mates, line-of-the-woman, affines and maternal kin, who then prepared their contributions for the return prestation. This clear emphasis on genealogy and kinship obligations, rather than relationships created through friendship and obligation, distinguished Ponam from many other areas in Papua New Guinea.

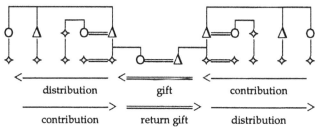

Figure 7   *Some contributors to and recipients of affinal prestations*

Those assisting the bride's and groom's siblings with contributory gifts were paired in partnerships called *parakau*. These partnerships worked this way. Contributions given to help the groom's kin make a prestation were identifiable, so that when they were distributed among the bride's kin each recipient knew who had given the contribution that he or she received. These two people, the original giver and the ultimate recipient, were *parakau* to each other. Return prestations were organised so that each person's contribution went back to his or her *parakau*. Ideally, relations between *parakau* lasted throughout the life of a marriage: those who were *parakau* in a marriage exchange remained *parakau* until the funeral exchange. However, in practice these partnerships rarely lasted beyond an individual exchange.

Items given by the groom's kin included cash, dog's teeth, shell money, pigs, wooden beds, raw food, and cooked food, different ones predominating on different occasions. Return items from the wife's kin were primarily raw food, and by convention of less value than the main prestation. Frequently the groom's kin gave cash and the bride's kin reciprocated with purchased food, and therefore people could and did calculate the relative value of these contributions in monetary terms. Return prestation were usually about one-third to one-half of the value of the initial prestation. However, the bride's kin were also required to provide gifts of cooked food to the groom's kin throughout the days of the prestation, and the cost of this could be substantial. There was considerable debate among Ponams about whether or not the bride's family's gifts ended up equal to the groom's, and a general feeling that they should not.

TAMATU EXCHANGE

In addition to these prestations made to affines, prestations were made throughout a person's life to his or her *tamatu*s. As we said, a person's *tamatu*s (those he or she called *tama*, "father's brother", and *asi*, "father's sister") had ritual powers to bless and to curse that person, and the moral obligation to supervise and look after him or her. Throughout the course of a person's life, that person's maternal kin, siblings and even children would make numerous gifts to those of that person's *tamatu*s who helped in any way, small gifts to

1. Birth,* *palam, kani ara inapwilaf,*
   "food for the child" [cooked food]   Return prestation, *kahu* [raw food]
2. First return to the island from a distant
   place,* *brolofau* [baskets of lesser
   valuables, coconuts]   Return prestation, *kahu* [raw food]
3. Death of close relative,* *kani ara i
   njau* (etc), "food for the widow, etc"
   [cooked food]   Return prestation, *kahu* [raw food]
4. Death, *lutung, susuat* [baskets of
   lesser valuables, pig]   No return prestation

       Prestations from maternal kin,   Prestations from *tamatus*
         siblings and children

Figure 8   Tamatu *prestations in the 1980s*

    * These prestations were made in association with major *kowun* rituals.

individuals for individual assistance and major prestations to all of the person's *tamatus* when they came to make a blessing as a group or to work as a group. Here we discuss only the major public prestations to *tamatus*, for which contributions were received from and distributed to many people. However, these large public exchanges were merely one end of a continuum, the other end of which was the private relationship between an individual and each of his or her individual *tamatus*.

Figure 8 lists the major prestations to *tamatus* that were made commonly in the 1980s. At the child's first return to the island from a distant place and at its funeral, the maternal kin repaid the *tamatus* for their services by the public presentation of gifts of baskets containing valuables to individual *tamatus* for their specific named services. On other, lesser occasions, the maternal kin made prestations of cooked and raw food. *Tamatus* made smaller return prestations of raw food to the child's maternal kin on all of these occasions except the last and most important one. That is, they made no return for the prestation they received following a funeral. Further, *tamatus* never made initial prestations to the child or to his or her kin. In these *tamatu* exchanges, as in affinal ones, return prestations were significantly smaller than initial ones, and thus the overall flow of wealth was from the maternal kin to the paternal kin. This cycle of *tamatu* exchanges began after the child's birth and continued through his or her burial, at which time *tamatus* performed their last services. Ideally, then, this series of *tamatu* prestations lasted much longer than did the series of affinal prestations, which ran only from engagement to the death of a spouse.

The early prestations to a child's *tamatus*, at birth and at first return to the island from a distant place, were led by the child's maternal kin, who were the major contributors. In later prestations, made after the child was grown, his or her siblings, and later own children, began to lead the ceremony. These siblings and children were considered as part of the maternal kin for this purpose.

The maternal kin, siblings and children accumulated contributions for these prestations in the same way as for affinal prestations. However, the prestation and distribution took place somewhat differently. The maternal kin, siblings and children would not present a single joint gift to a single leading *tamatu* (as was done in affinal prestations). Instead, each group would present individual gifts directly to individual *tamatu*s for their specific named services.

Prestations such as these are rather unusual in patrilineal societies in Papua New Guinea, though not in matrilineal ones (e.g. Battaglia 1985). The more common pattern is the inverse of this one: the child's agnates or paternal kin make compensatory payments to the child's maternal kin for their services and for the child that the paternal kin have taken away (e.g. A. Strathern 1980). Why should maternal kin on Ponam have compensated paternal kin for the care of a child who was no longer theirs? For Ponams, the answer to this lay in the institution of *tamatu* itself. The child concerned in these exchanges was *tamatu* to members of his or her maternal kin, and would bless them and care for them if he or she grew strong and sound. The maternal kin compensated the child's *tamatu*s in order that they might later have a good *tamatu* of their own.

Ponams themselves did not explicitly relate the affinal and *tamatu* prestations to each other. However, at least in logical terms, these two systems formed a neat pair, which is interestingly similar to paired cycles of exchange that have been described in Milne Bay (we look at one such description at the end of this chapter). The affinal cycle began with engagement and concluded with the death of either spouse; it involved the movement of people from the wife's side to the husband's and the return of wealth. The *tamatu* cycle was longer. It began with a child's birth and ended with its death; it involved the movement of strength and power from the husband's side (indirectly through the child) to the wife's and the return of wealth.

These implicit cycles affected the relations between members of inter-marrying families over time, relations particularly apparent in the way that they exchanged contributory gifts. Describing how exchange linked inter-marrying families requires detailed descriptions of exchange obligations over a number of generations. This does not make easy reading. But the logic of Ponam exchange and kinship was contained in these very precise kinds of obligations, and not in a series of simple symbolic generalisations.

CONTRIBUTORY GIFTS AND RELATIONS BETWEEN AFFINES AND CROSS-COUSINS

The series of affinal and *tamatu* exchanges constitutes the set of main prestations that flowed between the families of a married couple and provided the major occasions for exchange on Ponam. Such exchanges have been the main concern of those describing exchange in Melanesia (e.g. Forge 1972; M. Strathern 1984*b*; Damon & Wagner 1989). While these exchanges were important on Ponam and certainly merit the attention we have paid to them in this chapter and will pay to them later on, they were only a part of exchange activity, and from some perspectives the less significant part. For each family, they were intermittent, and even the largest and most active families would give one only once every few years. Furthermore, they did not exhaust the universe of gift transactions between inter-marrying families, they merely began it. Smaller gifts were exchanged with great frequency — scores of times every year — for each person was obliged to help his or her affines, maternal and paternal kin with contributory gifts whenever they wished to participate in exchanges made on behalf of other kin, and each person expected to receive similar help in return. These lesser givings and receivings, brought about by yet other people's main exchanges, were central to maintaining the relationships generated by marriage, as well as to the ways those relationships were transformed over the course of time. Such minor transactions have been relatively ignored in Melanesian anthropology (a notable exception is Lederman 1986). However, we cannot understand Ponam marriage and exchange without paying close attention to them.

Though major prestations were rare, contributory gifts were common, and most island residents were eager to participate as minor contributors to major prestations. As we described in chapter 2, much of the wealth that circulated on Ponam came through the contributions that working migrants made to island exchanges, and people planning a major prestation devoted considerable effort to seeking out migrant participants who might make major contributions. But they had little trouble encouraging other islanders to join in with their small contributions. This was because residents were best able to get a share of this migrant wealth by participating in exchange (*WT&E*: 213–217). By contributing to the prestations made by their kin, individuals entitled themselves to a share of prestations received by those kin on other occasions. Therefore, most people wanted to participate in exchanges whenever they could, and actively sought out roads on which they could contribute. All adults knew the kin links through which they were related to every other Ponam, through which they could legitimately contribute to prestations made by others and through which they might expect to receive a share of migrant wealth in return.

We have described how affinal and *tamatu* prestations linked inter-marrying families through the life of the marriage and the children of that marriage. But in another way these prestations served to link inter-marrying families for a much longer time. This was because the process of collecting contributions for prestations meant that families continued to activate their connections with those groups into which they had married before, their line-

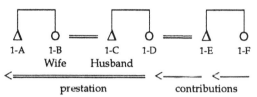

Figure 9   *Contributions through affinal links to a marriage prestation*

of-the-woman and line-of-the-man. It is important, then, to look at the origin and operation of these groups.

When a couple married, they became a road for the exchange of contributory gifts between their families. The bride's kin used her as a road by which they could contribute to prestations arranged by various members of the groom's family and their affines; the groom's kin used him in the same way. We will illustrate this by tracing out the way that contributory gifts are accumulated in order to make marriage prestations for a hypothetical Wife and Husband in figure 9. This discussion will, moreover, show how the structure of exchange gave a place to women as independent actors, rather than as mere links between men.

Our presentation will entail working through a set of exchanges and contributions to exchanges over the course of generations. As our purpose in this is to couch what we observed in structuralist terms, we will describe the logic of the Ponam system of kinship and exchange, a logic that worked itself out in cycles of four generations, beginning with the generation of the Wife and Husband and continuing to the generation of their great-grandchildren. This system is summarised in figure 15 at the end of this chapter. (In the next chapter we will, of course, undercut this structuralist approach by looking at the historical circumstances that have shaped Ponam exchange practices.) We are aware that only the most dedicated enjoy reading about imaginary people with memorable names like 3-E, just as only the most dedicated enjoy referring back and forth from text to figure. To ease this chapter for those less dedicated, we present this discussion in terms of a series of generalisations, each supported by a more detailed argument. These supporting arguments are set off from the main text and may be skipped by the weary.

During the course of their married life, Husband's siblings make a number of affinal prestations to the siblings of Wife. In these prestations, Husband's siblings do not act on their own, but receive contributions from cognates and affines. We will show how Husband's sister receives contributions from her affines through her own husband, for these contributions are not made in quite the simple, direct way one would expect from figure 9.

We said that Ponams conventionally gave contributory gifts to only a very limited range of kin. In fact, the basic principle is that people contributed

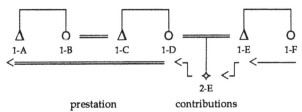

prestation   contributions

Figure 10   *Husband and wife exchange on the road of their child: contributory gifts in the generation of marriage*

only to their own parents, siblings and children. If they wanted a contribution to end up in the hands of a more distant relative, they had to give it to one of these immediate kin, ask that it be passed along a series of parent-child-sibling links to its destination, and trust to the good faith of the people along these roads. (This process was complicated by the fact that people could contribute on the road of dead kin as well as living ones, as we describe in chapters 6 and 7.) This basic principle had implications for the movement of contributory gifts between inter-marrying families, because it meant that affines did not exchange directly: they exchanged only by giving to the married couple themselves. And married couples did not exchange directly, but exchanged only through their mutual cognate, their child.

> Figure 10 shows how the system worked. Husband's (1-C's) brideprice for Wife (1-B) is arranged by his siblings, represented in this instance by his sister 1-D. (Siblings are kept to a minimum in these figures to ease present-ation.) In an actual case the sister would lead the exchange only if she had no mature brothers, though she would always play an important role. We use a sister in this example, however, because we want to illustrate the movement of contributions between the descendants of brothers and the descendants of sisters in later generations.
>
> 1-D does not raise this contribution on her own, but receives help from her husband, 1-E, and his kin (as well as her cognates and maternal kin who are not pertinent to this illustration). Her husband, 1-E, never con-tributes to her directly, however, in the way that she contributes to her brother. Instead he contributes to her "on the road" of their child, 2-E.

In most cases a married couple's children were far too young to be en-trusted with contributions, or were absent from the island at school or work. Instead, they were only nominally involved in these transfers. What usually happened was that the husband or his relatives simply handed their contribut-ions to his wife; in practice the child never entered into the affair at all. But when they talked to us about their participation in exchange, Ponam parents invariably made statements like, 'I received this contribution from my child', while pointing to an infant in a sling; 'I gave that contribution to my child', who happened to be serving in the army in Daru. They never volunteered to us the statement that they contributed directly to or received directly from a spouse, though they were not offended if we happened to phrase it that way. Couples who had no children contributed on the road of the children they expected to have in the future or on the road of the children they should have had in a better world, but still they did not contribute directly to each other.

It was this observation that married Ponams thought of themselves as giving contributions to minor, non-participating children, rather than directly to spouses, that first began to make clear to us the extent to which islanders saw their exchange activities as based on a system of clear-cut genealogical principles that was independent of personal volition. They did not think of themselves as individuals giving to other individuals by choice. Rather, as they described it to us, contributions moved through a series of genealogical steps. In the case of living, resident, adults, this series of steps was explicitly mapped in the physical movement of contributions as they were carried from one house to another before reaching their final destination. In other cases, such as when people contributed on the road of children, absentees and the dead, these steps might be implicit.

Following the principle we have mentioned, an unmarried child could only give to someone within his or her natal family, so that the role of the child as a road for the exchange of contributory gifts between husband and wife was a passive one throughout that child's youth. An unmarried child who received a contributory gift gave it to his or her parents. This meant, in effect, that any contribution from the mother went to the father, and vice versa. An unmarried child did not receive from siblings, because they could always contribute to a parent directly on their own roads. Of course, as the child matured he or she would begin to participate in exchange actively, giving his or her own contributions to either parent for that parent's siblings and thence their children.[2] But even though the child's role relative to his or her parents remained that of a purely passive link, parents never forgot that role. The reason why it loomed so large in their minds becomes obvious when we see what happened to the couple's relationship after their children married.

The second convention structuring exchange was that on marriage, that child's spouse began to replace the child's parents as an exchange road. Thus, married children who received contributory gifts from any parent or sibling gave the contribution to their spouses, and not to a parent or to another sibling.

---

[2] In this way a child could contribute to FBs and their children, the child's *kamal*-mates; MBs and their children, the child's line-of-the-man; FZs and their children, the child's line-of-the-woman; and MZs and their children. (These last were of one *kowun* but this relationship was not invoked in exchange and they exchanged merely as cognates, *lowa-*.)

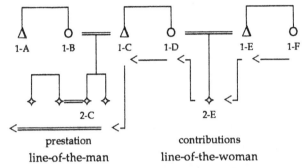

prestation   contributions
line-of-the-man   line-of-the-woman

Figure 11   *Exchange between line-of-the-woman and line-of-the-man: contributory gifts between first-generation cross-cousins, the first stage*

Figure 11 illustrates the effects of this convention, continuing the example from above. When 1-D's children are grown and capable of taking part in exchange on their own, they contribute their own gifts to her for her kin. They gather these contributions through their own labour and through contributions from paternal kin. When 1-D dies they continue to contribute to her name and thence to her brother, 1-C, and his children. At this stage contributions move reciprocally between 2-C and 2-E, the child of the brother and the child of the sister: line-of-the-man contribute to line-of-the-woman, and vice versa. So long as 2-E remains single, he or she can be a road for the transfer of contributions from the father, 1-E, to the mother, 1-D, and on to her siblings. Also 2-E can send contributions in the opposite direction, from mother's kin to father's.

Thus, the married child is no longer a road between its parents (see figure 12). Instead, when the child has obligations to mother and maternal kin, he or she receives help only from a spouse on the road of their child (or from the children themselves if they are married). Reciprocally, any contribution that the child receives from maternal kin is passed on to a spouse, not paternal kin. The same conventions govern the child's relations with paternal kin. Obligations to these kin are met with contributions from the child's own children and spouse; contributions received from the child's paternal kin go to the child's own children and spouse. Thus, as a couple's children grow and marry, the couple exchange less and less. When their children are married, they might continue sending small contributions along this road, from one parent to the other. But if they do so, it is largely out of sentiment: it is not expected. After the parents' deaths, contributions are not usually exchanged along this road. There was no rule forbidding this sort of exchange. People could continue to send contributions along the road of couples whose children were all married. But they were not obliged to. Failing to send such a gift did not cause offence; sending one was a mark of a particular or unusual sentiment.

This decay of the exchange road between husband and wife was the first stage in the demarcation of the cognatic group, *ken si*. The relationship between

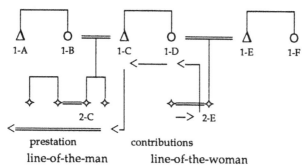

1-A   1-B   1-C   1-D   1-E   1-F

2-C   2-E

prestation   contributions
line-of-the-man   line-of-the-woman

Figure 12   *Exchange between line-of-the-woman and line-of-the-man: contributory gifts*
between first-generation cross-cousins, the second stage

affines, between husband's kin and wife's kin, was gradually transformed into
a relationship between the descendants of a sister (the children of a husband
and wife) and the descendants of a brother (the children of the wife's brother).

> The stages of this transformation are shown in the shifting positions of the
> arrows representing contributions in figures 9 through 12. By the time the
> children (2-C, 2-E) of the initial marriages are themselves mature and
> married, those (such as 1-E and 1-F in figure 12) who are not the descend-
> ants of the brother (1-C) and sister (1-D) at the apex of the pair of line-of-
> the-woman and line-of-the-man lines, are excluded from participation in
> their exchanges.

Understanding how the *ken si* is bounded in this way makes it possible to
understand Ponams' conception of relations between cross-cousins. Logically,
the relationship between the children of cross-sex siblings can be conceived of
in two ways. First, they can be thought of primarily as affines, as the children of
wife-givers and wife-takers. In a patrilineal system, the children of the sister
would be identified with their father (the sister's husband) and his agnates, and
the children of the brother would be identified with their father (the brother)
and his agnates. This produces a pair of counterpoised agnatic groups. Second,
the children of cross-sex siblings can be thought of primarily as the children of
a brother and sister, a cognatic relationship that is independent of their oppos-
ing patrilineal statuses.

Ponams understood the cross-cousin relationship in this second way. Because husband and wife did not exchange on the road of their married children,
the cross-cousin exchange relationship did not act as a relationship between
agnatic lineages. It is true that an unmarried child could be seen as a road
through which contributions could pass from mother's to father's agnates or
the reverse. However, this illusion of exchanges between agnatic groups shat-
tered when the child married. The married child did not contribute gifts from
his father's agnates to his mother and her kin, as would be expected with wife-
givers and wife-takers. Instead, the contributions that married children gave

to their mothers, mothers' brothers, and maternal cross-cousins came from their own children (and ultimately from their spouses). Hence, the relationship that appeared to exist between wife-givers and wife-takers in the generation of marriage disappeared with the marriage of its children. Cross-cousins did exchange, but not as members of mother's and father's agnatic lineages linked through marriage. Instead, the relationship between cross-cousins was defined as a cognatic relationship. They were *ken-si*.

By examining the implications of the convention that a couple did not exchange after their children had married, one can see why it was that men and women were under great pressure to be on good terms with their affines, to cooperate rather than to compete. A person who was obliged to contribute to a prestation made by any of his or her patrilateral and matrilateral kin could expect to receive direct help from only his or her spouse (and through the spouse, his or her affines). But a person who wished to contribute to a spouse could expect to receive help from among a wide range of patrilateral and matrilateral kin on the roads of both father and mother. A person could afford, therefore, to sacrifice or break off relations with one or more cognates (though not, of course, all cognates). But because ego depended on his or her spouse alone for help with contributory gifts to all cognates, ego could never afford to sacrifice the relationship with spouse and affines in favour of any other. This was all the more true because divorce was impossible. One could not get a new set of affines if relations with the first set broke down.

INEQUALITY BETWEEN
LINE-OF-THE-WOMAN AND LINE-OF-THE-MAN

We said in chapter 1 that relations of exchange between line-of-the-man and line-of-the-woman were unequal, because contributions moved from line-of-the-woman to line-of-the-man but did not move back again. This was an over-simplification, for as we have just explained, the children of a brother and the children of a sister contributed to one another equally. The line-of-the-man, 2-C in figure 12, contributed to the line-of-the-woman, 2-E, and in turn received contributions from him or her. In the next generation, however, the relation becomes unequal. In particular, the way that line-of-the-woman and line-of-the-man contribute to one another is influenced by the position of the two families in the series of *tamatu* exchanges. The relationship changes after the funeral of 2-E, the child of the sister, 1-D.

A child's maternal kin, along with his or her siblings and children, make prestations to the child's paternal *tamatus* in order to repay them for blessing and caring for the child. The most significant *tamatus* in this regard are the father's sister (1-F) and her children. The last of these *tamatu* prestations is made

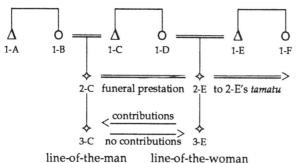

Figure 13 — *The effect of funeral exchange on relations between line-of-the-woman and line-of-the-man: contributory gifts between second-generation cross-cousins*

at the funeral of the last child. After this funeral prestation is complete, the relationship between line-of-the-woman and line-of-the-man becomes a-symmetrical. Once the maternal kin pay the funeral prestation, they have fully compensated the child's *tamatus* for their care of the child. At this point the obligation of the maternal kin to the child is complete. They have given prestations for his or her birth, upbringing and funeral, and rarely give anything more. They rarely contribute to payments made on behalf of this child's children. The maternal kin are line-of-the-man to the child, who is line-of-the-woman to them. And after this funeral, line-of-the-man give much less and much less often to line-of-the-woman. It was not obligatory to abandon the relationship at this point. It was simply no longer obligatory to keep it up. People sometimes gave small amounts along this road on major occasions, but rarely gave on minor ones. However, line-of-the-woman continue to contribute to their line-of-the-man over numerous generations. Ideally, they are expected to do so until a new marriage is made within the group. Figure 13 and the explanation below restates this more specifically.

> Affinal prestations begin to flow from 1-E's siblings to those of his wife, 1-D, when their marriage is first arranged, and continue to flow through the life of the marriage, until either 1-D or 1-E dies. *Tamatu* prestations for 2-E, the child of 1-D and 1-E, flow from 2-E's maternal kin (1-C and his children) to 2-E's *tamatus* (1-F and her children). These end with the funeral prestation made when 2-E dies. This funeral prestation is led by 2-E's child, 3-E. At this point, the relations between 2-C's children and 2-E's children begin to change. Formerly, their parents, 2-C and 2-E, exchanged contributory gifts reciprocally. After 2-E's death, however, this is no longer so. 2-E's child (3-E), who is line-of-the-woman, will continue to make contributory gifts to 2-C's child (3-C) whenever that child has affinal or other obligations. But 3-C will no longer contribute to 3-E. Having paid for 2-E's funeral, 2-C's descendants no longer contribute to 2-E's child.

Thus, relations among the cognates who were the grandchildren of a brother and a sister were restricted, in the sense that these people did not act as

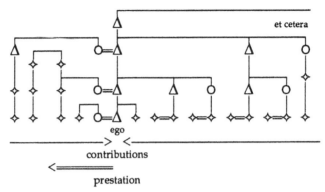

Figure 14   *Contributors to an affinal prestation*

undifferentiated members of a group. Rather, their relationship was asymmetrical. The descendants of a sister continued to contribute to the *kamal* from which they sprang, to their corresponding line-of-the-man. But the descendants of an agnatic line no longer contributed to their off-shoots through women, to their line-of-the-woman.

By extending the conventions we have described it is possible to work out the composition of the set of people who contributed to an affinal prestation made on behalf of any individual. Figure 14 shows this.

The right side of the figure is easiest to understand. The siblings of the groom (ego) receive contributions from their FB's and FZ's descendants, from their FFB's and FFZ's descendants, and so on for as far back as the patriline is remembered. All of these people are *ken si* to the groom and to each other.

The groom's siblings also receive a contribution from their mother. This will include contributions from her father's siblings (and her mother's siblings, though these are not shown in the figure). But it will not include contributions from her FF's siblings, for they are line-of-the-man to her and are unlikely to contribute after her father's death.

If the groom's father is living, the groom's siblings will also receive contributory gifts from their father's mother's siblings and their descendants. The groom's FMF's siblings probably will not contribute, however, for they are line-of-the-man to the groom's FM. Because the groom's FF is almost certainly dead by the time the groom's affinal prestations are made, nothing will be received from the groom's FFM's sibling's descendants.

LOGICAL SYSTEMS

Figure 15 shows the general pattern in which contributions and prestations moved between inter-marrying families over four generations. They moved reciprocally between the two families in the generation of marriage and

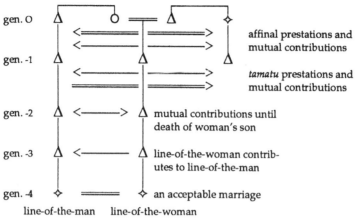

gen. 0

affinal prestations and
mutual contributions

gen. -1

tamatu prestations and
mutual contributions

gen. -2   mutual contributions until
death of woman's son

gen. -3   line-of-the-woman contrib-
utes to line-of-the-man

gen. -4   an acceptable marriage

line-of-the-man   line-of-the-woman

Figure 15   *Ponam exchange over four generations*

through the lives of its children. In the course of the second generation, however, they shifted so that contributions moved almost exclusively from the
descendants of the sister to the descendants of the brother, and continued to do
so through the third generation. In the fourth generation, however, marriage
became once again acceptable, as it was not in preceding generations.

The usefulness of a structural analysis like this one is illustrated by the
fact that it does make sense of this otherwise peculiar marriage rule. Ponams
often said that line-of-the-woman and line-of-the-man could marry again after
four generations, because then they were no longer "too close" to marry. Initially it was difficult to see why they should have picked four generations rather
than three, or six, or some other number, especially given that they did not
follow the rule anyway: in a largely-endogamous population of 500 it really
could not be followed. Figure 15 illustrates that four is a logical number of
generations to select, representing the completion of a series of exchange obligations. It is the obvious point at which to begin to reproduce those relations.

It is interesting to observe that the structure of the exchanges that took
place between inter-marrying families here is much like the various structures
of relationships that have been described in Milne Bay. For example, Frederick
Damon (1983) described a pattern much like that shown in figure 15 when
writing about the inter-generational operation of affinal exchange in Muyuw
(Woodlark) Island. To simplify drastically his careful description, in matrilineal
Muyuw a husband makes gifts to his wife's brother throughout the marriage,
concluding with the gift of a *kula* valuable at her death. The gift of this valuable
signifies the end of the married woman's existence. At the death of each of the
children of the marriage, the grandchildren make gifts in the opposite direction,
gifts to the husband's sister's descendants, gifts that are supposed to compensate for the husband's out-marriage. These prestations finally end the marriage,

E

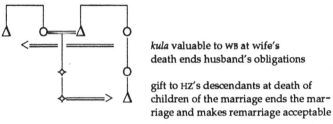

kula valuable to WB at wife's
death ends husband's obligations

gift to HZ's descendants at death of
children of the marriage ends the marriage and makes remarriage acceptable

Figure 16   *Muyuw exchange over three generations*

and remarriage of the two lines is then permitted. This cyclical logic is shown in figure 16. This sort of system is not, moreover, peculiar to Muyuw. In fact, variants of it appear in many parts of Milne Bay (see, e.g., the contributions to Damon & Wagner 1989).

This pattern is obviously similar to that found on Ponam: there is a short cycle of prestations from husband's kin to wife's kin, followed by a long cycle of prestations from wife's kin to husband's kin. The discovery of such cyclical systems is interesting. However, that discovery presents a problem: What are we to make of them? Without giving any of the details of Damon's argument, we simply want to quote from his conclusions. He says,

> Muyuw kinship exchange spheres form a coherent set. The logic of that set can be viewed in Muyuw production notions. ... But it also seems to inform the relationships and rituals central to their kinship terminology. By considering the meaning of the elements in this system, male labour and female labour, the differences between vegetables and tools in the *takon* exchange, I discern a logic to the practices and terminology not revealed by other approaches. This logic, the temporal transformation of gender-defined persons and things, leads to what I call forms of circulation, one of short duration following from a brother separated from his sister, the other, longer, from a sister separated from her brother. The first, departing from female labour, leads into Muyuw's other main productive activity, the Kula. The second, proceeding from male labour, starts the kinship cycle over again (1983: 322).

This is quintessentially a structural analysis, an interpretation of a system in terms of the logic of the meanings that are held to underlie it. It is also an interpretation in terms of structural time. That is, the logic that is investigated and described is the logic of the system as extended hypothetically through a particular sort of time. That is, the sort of time that is defined and given significance by the logic of the system itself. Thus, the temporal extension and consequences of the logic of the system are synthetic and self-supporting. They are not derived from the investigation of the actual history of actual events (we return to this point in the next chapter). This synthetic, structural orientation has a further undesirable, albeit probably unintended, consequence. Because this extension of exchange into a hypothetical, structural time makes the reproductive potential of this system's logic obvious, it tends to imply that it is, in a sense, this reproductive logic itself that generates the system in the first place.

However, it is important to bear in mind that the early Fortesian writers got into dilemmas when trying to derive social organisation from the logical potentials of lineage theory. Put in the simplest way, they found that the system did not actually operate on the ground in the way that their models suggested it should. In the next chapter we want to look at the recent history of Ponam marriage and exchange, and raise questions about the operation of Ponam exchange over time, and thus about the significance of the cycles, and their logic, that appeared to exist in the 1980s.

CHAPTER FOUR

Changes in marriage
and ceremonial exchange

By the 1980s at least, anthropologists writing on kinship and exchange in Melanesia had become concerned with the issue of time. The idea that the meaning and significance of ceremonial exchange is best understood by looking at the temporal cycles of exchange, rather than just at non-temporal relations of reciprocity, was attracting growing attention. This was particularly true of those working in the Milne Bay area of eastern Papua New Guinea. These writers argued that individual exchanges must be understood as part of a temporal sequence based primarily on life cycles. Because they follow life cycles, exchange sequences themselves are cyclical. They begin with marriage, proceed through the life of the marriage and its children and conclude, perhaps several generations later, with the mortuary ceremonies that both complete the cycle and allow it to begin again, as we described for Ponam in the preceding chapter. This is why much recent analysis has featured mortuary ceremonies (e.g. Damon & Wagner 1989; Mosko 1989; see M. Strathern 1984 *b*: 50).

Although anthropologists such as Annette Weiner and Frederick Damon constructed exchange in terms of temporal cycles, this does not mean that they thereby introduced notions of contingency, much less history, into their descriptions. Instead, their use of temporal cycles opened the way for a new form of functionalism and for the structural orientation it entailed. The key concept used here is reproduction.[1] This, as Marshall Sahlins (1981: 67) said at the time, 'has become a fashionable term these days, rather taking the theoretical place of, or specifying, the notion of "function".' From the perspective of these writers, exchanges are linked together in long-running cycles and the logic and meaning of these cycles is seen to give logic and meaning to society generally, and more significantly, to contribute to the continuity, indeed the reproduction, of society itself. Thus, the functional imperative in these theories is not the maintenance of order, as it was in the structural-functionalism of the 1950s, but its reproduction over time. One of the most extreme exponents of

---

[1] It is important to distinguish the way writers like Weiner use the term "reproduction" from the way the same term is used by other writers (e.g. Gregory 1982) in a more Marxist and less purely functional sense. We do not discuss the more Marxist writers here, though some of these criticisms apply to them as well.

this viewpoint has been Annette Weiner, who worked in the Trobriand Islands. We want to review her interpretation of exchange here.

Weiner described her stance in opposition to what she saw as the Maussian analysis of exchange, in which reciprocity is the key element (though her interpretation of Mauss is not itself free from criticism [e.g. Howell 1989]). She argued that reciprocity is an inadequate idea because it is linear and timeless, concerned with discrete acts of giving and getting rather than with the process these acts are intended to promote.[2]

> The traditional priority given to the obligation to give and receive will simply not account for the complexity of the range of transactions within a society when it becomes apparent that although transactions may operate in totally different contexts, they still remain linked to each other... . It also becomes necessary to account for long-range cycles of interaction, which may involve relationships that continue ... beyond the lifetime of any one individual (1980: 73).

The concept that Weiner used in place of reciprocity is reproduction. She argued that the cycles of exchange that endure through and beyond the lives of individuals have an explicit indigenous objective. That objective is to reproduce and regenerate people, objects and social relationships, "objects of value" that are not eternal but necessarily decay through time. She said, 'basic to all such systems ... is a cyclical world view in which the processes of reproduction and regeneration are perceived as essential cultural concerns' (1980: 72). But she did not claim only that reproduction is a central indigenous value. In addition, she claimed that it is an essential element of society objectively perceived and understood. Thus, she said, 'In formulating a model of reproduction, my basic premise ... is that any society must reproduce and regenerate certain elements of value in order for the society to continue' (1980: 71). Put in other words, 'The life cycles of individuals ... in articulation with the life trajectories of objects of exchange ... establish the temporal dimensions around which a particular societal system is structured' (1980: 82–83). This is, in brief, a simple restatement of the basic tautological fallacy of functionalism, the fallacy of assuming that society is organised in such a way as to maintain or reproduce its essential elements, with the corollary that the prime task of anthropology is to

---

[2] Her view thus departs from that of Pierre Bourdieu, who also launched a criticism of synchronic approaches to exchange, in *Outline of a theory of practice* (1977: esp. 4–7). Bourdieu's criticism is close to our own. He used the fact that there is a lapse between gift and counter-gift to point out that gift relations necessarily contain some degree of uncertainty: Will the gift be reciprocated? When? In what way? How are we to act in the meantime? While this clearly introduces the element of contingency that, we argue, usually is lacking in structuralist studies of kinship and exchange in Melanesia, the way Bourdieu treats this contingency is not entirely satisfactory. We discuss this further in the conclusion.

discover the mechanism of that maintenance. (Margaret Jolly [n.d.] makes an analogous criticism of Weiner's work.)

We said in the introduction that the processualist writers of the 1960s separated society and culture — distinguished group from category, processes of group formation from descent constructs — explicitly in order to argue against structural-functionalist lineage theory. Weiner reunited society and culture in her exchange theory, and in doing so produced a new sort of functionalism, though one that might better be called "temporal functionalism". As she understood it, a society continues to exist not so much through the functional integration of its institutions in social space, but through their functional integration in social time. Each exchange in the lifetime of an individual calls forth the next one in the cycle, in an almost inexorable series, all continually serving, as actors intend, to reproduce the essential values of society.

Reproduction theory is appealing. From the perspective of logic and structure, the Fortesian perspective of the total social system, it seems obvious that exchanges are integrated into multi-generational cycles and thus logical that by their endless revolution they serve to reproduce society through time, the conclusion of the cycle bringing social relations back to the point at which the cycle began, ready to begin again. This is just the sort of reproductive logic we discerned in the structure of Ponam exchange at the end of chapter 3.

But reproduction resembles Fortesian structuralist models not only in its appeal, but also in its shortcomings. These spring largely from the way that exchanges have been analysed, together with the fact that the putatively-indigenous ideology of cycles came to dominate the interpretation of exchange just as putatively-indigenous ideologies of descent once dominated interpretations of kinship. Anthropological analyses of exchange cycles are based largely on synchronous data, the observation of a wide variety of transactions made on behalf of a number of people over a fairly short period of time. These transactions are analysed and placed in a logical sequence that is then transformed into a temporal sequence: the marriage of A in January, the funeral of B in June and the birth of C in November are reconstructed as following the life cycle of a hypothetical X through his or her birth, marriage and death over a period of 70 years. In doing this, researchers re-enacted an anthropological ritual much older and more wide-spread than Fortesian lineage theory. This ritual appears in the early (as well as the more recent but less overt) evolutionist work in anthropology; that is to say, when societies, or even culture traits, existing at the same time are placed in a hypothetical evolutionary sequence, without critical consideration of whether the place, or indeed the sequence, is justified (see Thomas 1989: esp. chaps 4 & 5).

However, this kind of exchange cycle is located in an abstract, hypothetical time, not in concrete historical time, as was the case with the sequence of evolutionary development that it resembles. Such a cycle is temporal but not necessarily truly historical. It certainly does not provide evidence that the funeral for B that the ethnographer observed in June of 1985 was really preceded in 1945 by a marriage like that of A or by a birth ceremony in 1915 like that of C. And it does not provide evidence that the birth of C in 1985 will be followed in 2010 by a marriage ceremony like that of A and by a funeral in 2055 like that of B. Yet, real, historical evidence like this is necessary in order to show that exchange cycles do in fact act the way Weiner says they do, operate over the course of history to reproduce cultural values, gender identities, political inequalities or anything else for that matter. In order to show reproduction it is necessary to show that the cycle that one has isolated synchronically in fact also operates historically. It is necessary to show that the logical structure of exchange is the same as its historical process.

Obviously, this argument is the same as that made years ago against lineage theory. Schneider's point can be made to apply equally well here. 'The muddled part of that model is the notion that somehow the segment is not only a conceptual segment, but also in some way a physically distinct and concrete segment' (1965: 63) can easily be updated to read, 'The muddled part of the model is the notion that somehow the cycle is not only a conceptual cycle, but also in some way an historically distinct and concrete cycle'. Our consideration of reproduction theory has to be pursued in the same way that considerations of descent theory were once pursued, by an investigation of whether the theory conforms to the world it purports to explain.

The historical material we presented in chapter 2 allows us an initial answer to that question. If the "elements of value" that Ponam exchange was supposed to reproduce can be discerned in the main outlines of the organisation of Ponam society, then there was not much reproduction going on. One could, of course, argue a more modest position. Even if the Ponam system of exchange did not reproduce the social order, that system itself could be thought of as a distinct segment of society, a distinct way of assigning value to things and relations. If this were the case, it would only be necessary for the system of exchange to reproduce itself.

In this chapter we investigate this more modest claim. We do so by looking again at the years 1920–1980. In chapter 2 we described changes in economy and kinship over those decades. This time we describe the organisation of marriage and ceremonial exchange in the years before World War II and what has happened to them since. This description will show that Ponam exchange did not reproduce itself, much less society as a whole. The very logical, orderly, classically-reproductive picture of exchange presented in the previous chapter has not always existed. Rather, it was created by individual actors out of a variety of contingent circumstances and for a variety of different purposes. To ignore or trivialise this is to ignore or trivialise Ponams themselves as individuals and actors, to portray them as cogs in a mechanistic Melanesian social structure.

MARRIAGE STRATEGIES

We will look now at how people thought about marriage choices in the 1980s and at what we were able to discover about the earlier part of the century. We do so for two reasons. First, we want to investigate the extent to which people saw marriage in terms of the sort of reproduction that concerned Weiner. Second, we want to describe the structure of marriage, which will help us to see whether marriage patterns themselves were reproduced over the course of the century.

In the 1980s, Ponams disapproved of marriage with any *kamal*-mate and with any close cognate or close affine. No one ever expressed any preference for any form of exchange marriage between *kamal*s or other groups, or for any form of cousin marriage. They did say, however, that when adults arranged marriages for the young in the past, they had genealogical considerations in mind as well as the economic ones described in chapter 2.

According to Mead, in the 1920s Peres followed the convention that marriages could only be arranged between the children of cross-cousins. This requirement was one of the incentives for the continual adoption of children by financier-*lapan*s, for they wanted to control children and clients who could legitimately be married to the children and dependents of those other big men with whom they wanted to exchange. Ponams apparently did not have such a strict rule, and cousin marriage did not provide the same kind of incentive for adoption. Nonetheless, they did prefer to arrange exchange marriages, and these were of some significance for political relations.

Ponams said that in the 1920s people could not marry into a father's or mother's *kamal*, and that marriages between the children and grandchildren of siblings were not preferred. Even so, genealogies show that marriages between the grandchildren of sisters or cross-sex siblings did occur. It was also clear that in the past people did not object to marrying a sibling's spouse's sibling, a marriage they most definitely rejected in the 1980s. There are many examples of repeated marriages within two sets of siblings or cousins in the early part of this century. Ponams told us that there were two preferential ideals for marriage arrangements before World War II: one for the continued exchange of women between *kamal*s and one for girls to repeat the marriages made by their *asis* (especially, father's sisters and father's mothers).

Men in particular talked about the first of these preferential ideals, saying that in the old days there was a general feeling that *kamal*s should exchange

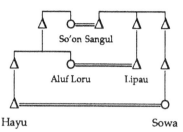

Figure 17   *Exchange marriage*

Note: These marriages took place at about 1880, 1910 and 1930.

women. When a man of Kamal Nilo married a woman of Kamal Kayeh, the men of Kayeh expected, sooner or later, to take back a woman from Nilo, and would feel more than usually slighted if a proposal for such a marriage were refused. They preferred not to take back a child of the out-marrying woman herself, but to take instead one of her husband's relatives, a younger sister or brother's daughter. Thus, when he explained this marriage preference, Mark Kupe gave the story of his mother's marriage as an example. His mother, Aluf Loru of Kamal Kayeh, married Lipau of Kamal Nilo. Some years later Lipau's FBSD, Sowa, was sent back to Aluf Loru's BS, Hayu, to balance out this marriage (see figure 17).

What Mark Kupe did not point out, however, was that the marriage of Aluf Loru, his mother, also illustrates the operation of the second type of marriage preference, in which girls were to repeat the marriage of their *asis*. Aluf Loru had repeated her father's sister's marriage, by marrying her FZHBS.

It is not surprising that Mark Kupe did not mention this, for it was never recognised by the men with whom we discussed marriage. However, older women said that women had preferred to arrange the marriages of their *natue-* (BD, SD) this way. They said that when a woman married, she moved onto her husband's land, where she planted coconuts and worked for him. And when she died she wanted her own cognates to benefit from the fruits of her labour. In order to ensure this, she would try to arrange that a girl whose marriage was in her gift be married to a boy who had claims to the land on which she had worked.[3] For example, Piwayeh Nja Self Kolin and Hikanau Nja Monun, two elderly widows, described their marriages as being of the same type, arranged for the same reason. In about 1935 Nja Self Kolin was married to her father's

---

[3] This echoes the point that Chambri women seek to replicate themselves by arranging the marriages of their juniors (Errington & Gewertz 1987*a*: 52). Certainly there are parallels between the older Ponam marriages and the modern Chambri ones. We want to go no further than noting these parallels, however, for we did not investigate these older marriages with this question in mind.

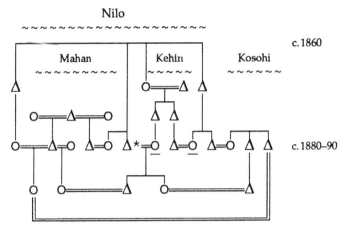

Figure 18   *Examples of inter-marriages among four* kamals

* Kuluah Jaf

Note: Women who repeated the marriage of an *asi* are underlined.

mother's second husband's brother's son. Her father's mother arranged this marriage so that Nja Selef Kolin could move onto the land that that father's mother had cultivated. At about the same time, Nja Monun married her FFBD's own husband. Nja Monun's *asi* (that same FFBD) arranged this marriage when she was dying, to ensure that her own work would not be lost to her family.

Several common sorts of marriage are illustrated in figure 18. It shows a portion of the network of marriages surrounding Kuluah Jaf, *lapan* of Kamal Nilo from the mid-1920s to about 1950. The marriages represented here include those between cross-cousins, those in which girls followed roads made by their *asis*, and those in which brides were exchanged between *kamals*.

Logically the two preferential ideals that Ponams described are contradictory, one being a form of restricted exchange, the other generalised. But they do not seem to have been so in practice. Neither men nor women claimed that their preference was an exclusive one, and it is perfectly possible both for *kamals* to exchange women and for girls to repeat the marriage of their *asis* if *kamals* inter-married often enough, as indeed they seem to have done.

Although these preferences may have tended to reproduce the kinship order, men and women agreed that the overriding factor in marriage arrangements was economic, not genealogical. Inevitably their first response to questions about how marriages were made was, 'We married wealth'. Men sought to marry their wards to the children of *lapans*, people with land, sea and trade partners, and no concerns of genealogy or reciprocity were more pressing, or more legitimate, than this. It was good policy to repeat the advantageous marriages of previous generations, but there was no point to repeating an unprofitable marriage just for the sake of reciprocity. Further, old men and women repeatedly stressed that their fathers arranged marriages without considering the wishes of their children or the personal characteristics of their partners. From the perspective of these men and women, their *tamas* and *asis* had arranged marriages in order to bring the greatest and most immediate economic gain. Their bitterness at this injustice seems to have motivated their feeling that nowadays children should follow their own desires.[4]

What were these economic motives that Ponams said drove adults to arrange marriages? What did *tamas* and *asis* expect to gain by marrying children off to the children of *lapans*? Briefly, they seem to have expected two things: to receive marriage prestations that they could distribute to their *kamal*-mates and line-of-the-woman, and to receive contributions toward other prestations, those to wives' kin, for children's marriages, for men's-house–raisings, for *lapan* exchanges and so on. Therefore they wanted to marry their wards to the children of families that would be valuable partners in exchange, families that could make major prestations and return prestations and families that could make significant contributions to their affines' prestations. To do this, these prospective affines needed to have land and, more importantly, sea and fishing rights, and they needed wealthy trade partners from whom they could get valuables needed for exchange in return for their own sea produce.

Though we do not accept without qualification the assertion of older Ponams that they were merely passive counters in the game of their parents' marriage strategies, we must accept that they felt themselves to be under strong pressure to accept the decisions that their elders made, a pressure they vowed to avoid putting on their own children. Those decisions reflected in a direct way the changing contingencies and circumstances of the elders who made them. One general change affected almost all those elders. That was the decay of the indigenous Manus economy around World War II, which we described in chapter 2. Prior to then, the labour that *asis* invested in their husbands' land and the resources and trade links that *lapans* controlled made a difference, and these marriage strategies made sense. Later, however, significant sources of wealth lay not in Manus but in urban Papua New Guinea, which meant, for resident islanders, that they lay in employed migrants. Once this change had occurred, the older strategies no longer made sense and the older patterns of marriage disappeared. The logic of the system of marriage preference, then, did not reproduce itself. It yielded to changing circumstance.

Just as marriage strategies and patterns changed over the course of the twentieth century, so did the actual sequence of affinal and *tamatu* exchanges,

---

[4] Their statements do not prove, of course, that adults of earlier generations really did arrange marriages primarily for economic motives. But still, this is what seems to have been impressed on their children.

often enough for just the same reason: changing economic circumstance. The balance of this chapter is a discussion of the changes in these exchanges. We begin with a description of the major exchanges that took place between inter-marrying families in the 1920s. This is not, of course, a description of "tradit-ional" exchange, for Ponam exchange was not an unchanging entity before the 1920s any more than it had been since then. Instead, our choice of this decade is pragmatic. It is the earliest period that Ponams living in the 1980s could remember in any detail.

CEREMONIAL EXCHANGE IN THE 1920S

The general outline of exchange in the early part of this century, like the outline of the 1980s that we described in chapter 3, included exchanges between the kin of husband and wife that were concerned specifically with the institution of marriage, and it included exchanges between an individual's maternal kin and *tamatus* that were concerned with individual life crises. It should be remembered, however, that during the 1920s these individual-oriented exchanges were not the only important form of exchange, as they were in the 1980s. Prestations organised by *kamals* — the men's-house–raisings and *lapan* prestations — were equally important, if not more.

AFFINAL EXCHANGE IN THE 1920S

Figure 19 lists the affinal prestations that were commonly made in the 1920s.[5] Of these, only the first two, the engagement and marriage prestation, were made by almost everyone. In order to make an engagement a boy had to have a father or patron wealthy enough to attract the prospective bride's father and father's sisters; in order for the boy to marry, the groom's family had to have built and equipped a house for his bride and clearly be capable of spons-oring the wedding feasts. For the groom's family to be willing to go through with the marriage, the bride's family had to be similarly capable of bearing their share of the wedding feasts. Weddings varied considerably, from the expensive ceremonies of the wealthy to the more minimal ceremonies of the

---

[5] According to Mead (1934: 318) the major prestations made in Pere in the 1920s were the following: (1) Betrothal payment by the bridegroom's kin: *komambut*; (2) Minor exchanges at the first menstruation of a betrothed girl; (3) Large pre-marriage payment by bridegroom's kin: *mamandra*; (4) Payment by bride's kin at the actual marriage: *mwelamwel*; (5) Post-marriage payment by bridegroom's kin: *matiruai*; (6) Exchange at birth of first child; (7) Minor exchanges for birth of each child, ear piercing of each child, and first menstruation of unbetrothed girls, and at the death of any child born to the marriage; (8) Last marriage payment made after children are half grown: *metcha*; (9) Series of mourning exchanges made at the death of either spouse.

Prestation from groom's kin to bride's kin	Prestation from bride's kin to groom's kin
1. Engagement, *aribihi sal*, "opening the road" [tobacco and betel]	Return prestation, *ke tabac*, "after the tobacco" [small gift of raw food]
2. Marriage, *joso* [beds, cooked food]	Simultaneous prestation [baskets, cooked food]
3.	Bride's marriage prestation,* *nonou*, "decoration" [baskets of lesser valuables]
Return prestation, *kahu* [cooked food]	
4. First pregnancy,* *paruhu, marasus*, "nipples" [raw food]	Return prestation, *kahu* [raw food]
5.	First birth,* *palam* [cooked and raw food]
Return prestation, *kahu* [cooked food]	
6. Groom's marriage prestation,* *masaf* [dog's teeth, shell money, pig]	Return prestation, *kahu* [cooked food]
7.	Bride's prestation,* *piru* [coconuts, shell money, dog's teeth]
Return prestation, *kahu* [cooked food]	

Figure 19   *Affinal prestations in the 1920s*

*   Prestation made by some people only.

poor. But it was virtually unknown for couples to marry without any ceremony at all (as did happen with some regularity in the 1980s). After the marriage had taken place, however, prestations were more or less optional. People could not legitimately fight or sue (in the colonial courts) for later gifts. People made prestations when they could afford to do so and skipped them when they could not. Families that did not make prestations were of low repute, and might find it hard to marry off future children without becoming dependents of others, but they did not lose their wives or children through this failure.

There follows a description of the affinal and *tamatu* prestations that were made during the 1920s. After presenting this, we discuss some of the ways that these changed over the course of the next 50 years.

ENGAGEMENT, *aribihi sal*, "opening the road". A marriage could be arranged at any time during childhood, but was usually arranged during a girl's teens and a boy's early twenties. Initial marriage arrangements were secret, usually conducted through go-betweens. In order to settle the affair, however, the groom's close *asi*s and *tama*s and his parents paid a private visit at night to the prospective bride's father's house to ask for her hand. They presented the father, his brothers, sisters and wife with a gift of a basket containing 10–20 sticks of tobacco and a similar number of betel nuts, which were commonly used as a solicitation to exchange. The bride's father discussed the proposal with his brothers and sisters. If they were agreed, they accepted the gift and distributed it to their kin, thereby announcing the engagement. There was no large public return prestation for this gift, but the bride's family were expected to bring a gift of raw food to the groom's shortly afterwards, called *ke tabac*.

If the bride and groom were mature, the two families began to prepare for the marriage, preparations that might easily take several years. The bride's kin cultivated their relatives, especially their mainland trade partners, in order to find food, especially sago, taro and coconut oil. The groom's kin not only had to find food, but also had to build a house for the bride and equip it with beds, pots, dishes, mats, all obtained from elsewhere. At this stage in their lives neither the bride nor the groom had the wealth to engage in *kawas* trade, and they participated in these arrangements only by helping their parents or patrons as they had always done.

MARRIAGE, *joso*. When the new house was completed and both families had accumulated enough obligations to call in food for the wedding feasts, they would agree on a day for bringing the bride to the house. The bride's parents decorated her with shell money and dog's teeth and other valuables, to found what Ponams in the 1980s described as the couple's bank account. This was not distributed, but was held by the young couple to be used later as they saw fit. Once married, the bride would begin to make shell money herself to add to her own and her husband's bank.

After the ceremony of bringing the bride, she went into her new house and remained there for five nights, in all her decorations, sitting on a ceremonial bed (*kayau*) given by her husband's *asis* and attended by her close female kin, while her family continually brought cooked food for her husband's kin, and her husband's kin brought food back to hers. After the fifth night the members of her matrilineal totemic group performed a small ritual for her and took her fishing on the reef. When she returned, the two families held the final exchange. The bride's kin gave baskets and cooked food, the groom's gave beds and more cooked food. The bride would then abandon her decorative clothing and ceremonial bed and begin to cook and work for her husband's family. Gradually her kin would move out of her house, and when they were gone the couple's conjugal relationship began. The wife began to cook for her husband, and they began to have sexual intercourse, hoping to conceive a child as soon as possible. However, the husband did not live with his wife in her house, but merely visited her there. He was expected to spend most of his days and nights in the men's house, where he was to assist, by fishing and trading, his father and the other men who had arranged and financed his marriage.

The marriage prestations and ceremonies changed during the course of the 1920s as Ponams converted to Catholicism. They added Catholic marriage rituals to their own, expanding the time and wealth needed for a marriage ceremony. One or two days of feasting were added so that islanders could sail to the Bundralis mission and sleep the night there while preparing for a wedding mass the next day, before returning to the island to bring the bride to her new house. Probably more important was the fact that the Catholic Fathers disapproved of marriages that were too close, particularly between first and second cousins. One of their first projects was to collect genealogies (unfortunately lost during the War) for members of their parish, and they refused Christian rites to any couple who were too-closely related. While Ponams had not normally married first cousins, second-cousin marriages occurred from time to time. However, none at all occurred from the late 1920s until after the War.

BRIDE'S MARRIAGE PRESTATION, *nonou*, "decoration". After the new couple had settled together, there was a prestation from the bride's kin to the groom's. The bride returned to her father's house, where once again she was decorated as she had been for her marriage. Then, supported by one of her *asis*, she was carried on a ceremonial bed (*kayau*) to her husband's *kamal*. Her family accompanied her, bringing gifts of woven baskets filled with small valuables, mats, skirts and dishes for her husband's kin. The groom's father distributed these, each basket being presented to a genealogically-equivalent member of the groom's family: the bride's father's basket to the groom's father, the bride's mother's basket to the groom's mother, the bride's sister's basket to the groom's sister and so on. This created the *parakau* partnerships described in chapter 3, and partners would give to one another directly in the subsequent marriage exchanges. Within a few days the groom's kin would bring a return prestation of cooked food: sago, fish, taro and so on. While this was presented all at once, it consisted of a number of individual gifts from *parakau* to *parakau*.

The bride's first pregnancy and the birth of her first child provided occasions for further major exchanges between affines. Ponams in the 1980s did not really think of these as really part of affinal exchange. Particularly, the prestation made after the birth of the child, or at least part of it, seems to have been thought of as a prestation to the child's *tamatus*. However, we describe these first pregnancy and birth prestations here (and refer to them again in the discussion of prestations to *tamatus*) because they seem to fit in with affinal prestations in other ways. These prestations are a worthwhile reminder that the division between affinal and *tamatu* prestations is an abstraction from Ponam categories, not a classification they themselves made.

FIRST PREGNANCY, *paruhu* or *marasus*, "nipples". This prestation seems to have formed a link between the series of affinal exchanges and that of life-crisis exchanges. While its procedure was like that of affinal exchanges, it was specifically linked to the first of the life-crisis prestations held for an individual, not to the sequence of affinal prestations.

When it became apparent that a women was pregnant for the first time, her husband's family brought her to her parent's or brother's house to bear her child there. Those families that could afford to do so also made a substantial prestation that included uncooked food and one particular form of cooked food, a large sago cake as much as two metres across. This cake was distributed to the bride's kin by her family, but first the bride's kin measured its circumference with a rope, for they would have to bring back a cake of the same size when they made the first of the life-crisis prestations for the couple's child. The bride's kin brought a return prestation of cooked food and coconuts.

FIRST BIRTH, *polot*. The series of rituals and exchanges held to commemorate individual life crises began with a long period of ritual and seclusion called *polot*. A woman gave birth to her first child in her parent's house. After the birth she and her child were secluded in the house for several months, adhering to a regimen of totemic taboos and being fed by her husband's kin. When sufficient food had been accumulated to bring her back to her husband's family, her totemic matrilineage performed a series of rituals for her and the child, designed to ensure the child's good health and the mother's ability to care for and nurse it, and to bear and nurse future children. Seclusion and these rituals took place only for a first child, but were held to be beneficial for all.

When the rituals were complete, the child's maternal kin made two prestations to its paternal kin. The first was a small prestation called *palam*, in which the mother and her close kin presented dishes of cooked food to her husband's close kin. The child's mother took a dish to the child's father, the child's mother's sister to the child's father's sister and so on. Although formally analogous to *parakau* partnerships, Ponams did not suggest that there was any relationship between the two. Then the mother's family prepared a large gift of food (*kana mahan*, "big food") for the *polot*. This was primarily raw food, but it also included a large sago cake to match that given in the *paruhu*. These were presented to the groom's parents and siblings and distributed to all of their kin, in the same manner as other affinal prestations. The child and its mother then returned to her father's house. The next day the mother's kin decorated the infant with valuables, carried it to its father's house and put it into the arms of its father's sister, who kept the decorations for herself. Later the father's kin made a return prestation of cooked food.

GROOM'S MARRIAGE PRESTATION, *masaf*. Once the *nonou* was completed and *parakau* relationships established, attention turned to the major prestation of shell money and dog's teeth, *masaf*, that was expected to follow when the marriage was well-established and the couple had a number of children. Throughout the long interval between *nonou* and *masaf* the bride's kin were expected to keep their *parakaus* constantly in mind, sending them gifts of food whenever they had a surplus. Although each separate gift was not necessarily large, over the years they could mount up, particularly if the groom's family were wealthy, in which case the bride's family would give generously in hopes of receiving a large *masaf*. When it was announced that *masaf* was being planned, the gifts would become larger and more frequent. If the groom's family were poor, however, and no *masaf* were expected, the *parakau*s would give little or nothing at all.

When the groom's father (or, by this time, probably his father's younger brothers and sisters and his own elder siblings) finally felt that he and his kin had accumulated a sufficient burden of gifts that they were obliged to do something, he would announce that it was time to plan for *masaf*, time to accumulate dog's teeth and shell money. On the appointed day, his kin would bring their contributions and hang them on a long rope before the door of his men's house for all to see. Then the contributions were taken down and loaded onto the *kamal*-members' canoes to be poled around the island to the bride's men's house. The groom's *asi*s and *tama*s decorated themselves, danced as they travelled and finally came ashore to dance before the bride's *kamal*. While they danced, the bride's kin bought from them the decorations with which the dancers had adorned themselves, paying with dog's teeth and shell money. This performance, called *sasaw*, was also part of many other exchanges, particularly funerals and men's-house–raisings.

Once the bride's kin had bought all the dancers' decorations, the groom's kin would hang the rope from the door of the bride's men's house and string their valuables on it once again. The bride's kin would then *sasaw* in their turn. Then the bride's father would take down the valuables given by each member of the groom's family and present them to the appropriate *parakau*. Within a few days the bride's kin would bring a *kahu* of cooked food to their *parakau*s, and the *masaf* was complete. The bride's own father (or whoever had taken his place at his death) kept none of this wealth for himself, but was obliged to distribute all of it, primarily to those who had financed his own marriage prestations. In this way he fulfilled his own obligations to them. However, if the bride's family were being led by a patron or sponsor, rather than by her true father or other close relative, the patron could keep a portion of the *masaf* and divert it into other uses. Thus, men who could afford to finance the marriages of clients gained from this a return that they could use to finance the marriages of other dependents.

BRIDE'S MARRIAGE PRESTATION, *piru*. A final further prestation could be made from bride's kin to groom's, though this seems to have been abandoned entirely during the 1920s. In *piru*, the bride's father built two great towers outside the groom's men's house. The bride's family then brought hundreds of coconuts and heaped them around the towers to form two tall cones. Coconuts were valuable at this time, and had to be imported from the mainland, for most of Ponam's land was given over to the plantation, whose coconuts Ponams could not use. The bride's kin then decorated her with valuables and brought her, along with a small gift of valuables, back to the men's house. The two

1. First birth, *palam* [valuables, cooked
   food]   Return prestation, *kahu* [cooked food]
2. Ear-piercing,* *kaaput* [raw and cooked
   food]   Return prestation, *kahu* [cooked food]
3. First return to the island from a distant
   place, *brolofau* [coconuts, baskets of
   lesser valuables]   Return prestation, *kahu* [cooked food]
4. Death of a close relative, *kani ara i
   njau*, etc. "food for the widow, etc."
   [cooked food]   Return prestation, *kahu* [cooked food]
5. Death, *lutung, susuat* [baskets of lesser
   valuables, pig]   Return prestation, *kahu* [cooked food]

          Prestation from   Prestation from
       maternal kin to paternal kin   paternal kin to maternal kin

Figure 20   Tamatu *prestations in the 1920s*

* Prestation made by some people only.

families then indulged in a mock battle, throwing coconuts at each other, all intended to be humorous or even ridiculous.

This was the last of the marriage prestations. Neither family made a prestation at the funeral of either bride or groom.

This series of affinal prestations was different from that of the 1980s, described in chapter 3. Notably, these prestations were complementary rather than asymmetrical (Comaroff 1980: 10). Initial prestations were made alternately by bride's and groom's kin, rather than all being made by the groom's kin as was the case in the 1980s. This complementarity facilitated or even fostered the competition for prestige among the big men who sponsored most of these prestations, in a way that the later asymmetrical prestations did not.

TAMATU EXCHANGE

In the 1920s, as in the 1980s, Ponams also made prestations throughout an individual's life to his or her *tamatus*. Though generally these were similar to those of the 1980s, more prestations were made in the 1920s, and people said they were made more elaborately. These prestations are shown in figure 20.

FIRST BIRTH, *polot*. The first prestation made explicitly to a child's *tamatus* was the final part of the prestation called *polot*, made after a child's birth, which we already described. The bride's matrilineal kin held totemic rituals for her and the child while she was in seclusion, and then brought large gifts of food to her husband's kin. The next day the child was decorated with valuables and brought back to its father's sister.

EAR PIERCING, *kaaput*. The next major prestation to *tamatus* was likely to be made when the child was ten to fifteen years old. Every five years or so, villagers would arrange to have the ear-piercing ceremonies for their teenage children. Although several children had their ears pierced at the same time, this was not a communal ceremony. Each family made arrangements and cared for its own children, and families who could not afford it, or chose not to, did not have their children's ears pierced. On the appointed day the participating boys and girls would be brought together to have their ears pierced by an island specialist (Maiye of Kamal Puyu or Halasai of Kamal Lamai, at that time). Then each girl was taken back to her parents' house and each boy to his men's house. They remained secluded there until their ears were healed, were cared for by their *tamatus* and members of their *kowuns*, and followed totemic taboos like those of *polot*. When all of the children's ears had healed, they were brought out of seclusion to parade through the village. Villagers then held a community-wide celebratory feast, and later each child's maternal kin made a prestation to the child's *tamatus*, receiving a return prestation of cooked food. Boys and girls were eligible then for marriage.

RETURN TO PONAM, *brolofau*. Another ritual and exchange was held for men or women each time they returned to Ponam from a new, distant, and possibly dangerous place. Because children did not travel very often, we place this prestation after the *kaaput*, when it was most likely to be held. However, in fact it could be held at any appropriate time and as often as necessary, or as often as the subject's family could afford it.

When a person returned to the island after visiting a distant place, his or her *tamatus* would come to the shore, dance, shout blessings, and wash his or her face with leaves and salt water. These blessings were intended to drive out any malevolent spirits or influences that the returning person had picked up in his or her travels, as well as to give that person new strength for life on Ponam. A few days later, the returning person's maternal kin would make a prestation of baskets containing lesser valuables to these individual *tamatus*, and would receive a return prestation of cooked food. Apparently at this time there was no totemic ritual held in association with this blessing and prestation, though they were held in conjunction with other prestations to *tamatus*. As we describe below, a totemic ritual was introduced into these ceremonies after the War.

BEREAVEMENT, *kana ara njau, pe njau*, etc, "food for the widow, widower, etc". When any person died, his or her closest kin, particularly parents, spouse and senior siblings, entered seclusion and mourning, most strictly observed by widows, that was concluded by a ritual washing in the sea held by the bereaved's *kowuns*. Following this there was a prestation of cooked food from the bereaved's maternal kin to his or her spouse's kin in the case of widows and widowers, or from the bereaved's maternal kin to *tamatus* in other cases.

Generally this mourning was undertaken only by the deceased's spouse and by those close kin who would normally have been expected to die first: the dead person's parents and elder siblings. However, younger siblings who felt greatly grieved could mourn this way as well. People other than parents and siblings had other recognised ways of expressing their grief. Parents and siblings of the deceased were given special mourning names, by which they were addressed until that death was superseded by another one.[6]

BURIAL, *lutung* or *susuat*.[7] The last prestation to a person's *tamatus* was made after his or her burial. When a person died, his or her *tamatus* assumed responsibility for the management of the burial: washing the body and caring for it, digging the grave, building the coffin, carrying it to the graveyard, making sure the deceased's spirit went to the graveyard instead of remaining in the village and so forth. After the burial was complete, the deceased's maternal kin repaid them with gifts of baskets and valuables, which were presented directly to individual *tamatus*, as in *brolofau*. The mourning period, *kaapet*, continued for a considerable time after the burial, and was concluded with a major prestation from the dead person's kin to all the chief mourners (*toweni heping*, "waiting for morning", referring to the all-night vigils of the chief mourners), to all of the deceased's kin (*lo pahis*, "on the mat"), and to all Ponams (*sahai*). (We describe the modern versions of these in chapters 5 and 6.)

CHANGE AND INNOVATION

Was this system of exchange an instrument for continuing social reproduction? Using the historical sketch in chapter 2, we have argued already that it did not succeed in reproducing the social order as a whole. What we want to demonstrate here is that the system of the 1920s that we have just described did not even reproduce itself in any obvious sense. We do so by describing the more substantial and durable changes in the system of affinal and *tamatu* exchanges. We organise this description by decades, beginning with the 1930s, because it has been impossible to date changes any more closely than this.

These changes have many specific causes that we describe, but there is one recurrent attitudinal cause we need to mention here. At least by the 1980s, Ponams did not take the reverential attitude toward their exchanges (or much else in their social order; J. Carrier 1987a: 124–128) that seems implied by the notion of reproduction (see, e.g., the discussion of Weiner in the introduction). Instead, Ponams seemed to think of their exchanges and those held elsewhere

---

[6] The mourning names in common use in the 1980s were: Njampe: man whose young child has died; Njandon: woman whose young child has died; Kuluah: man whose mature child has died; Nja Kuluah: woman whose mature child has died; Njaron: woman whose sister has died; Nja Piso'on: woman whose brother has died; Sanei: man whose brother has died; Pe-nja: man whose wife has died; Nja: woman whose husband has died.

[7] The former term was commonly used by younger people in the 1980s. The latter, apparently older, term was known and used only by the elderly.

in Manus as forming a pool of available options for innovation and change. Similarly, their descriptions of the past show that they continually borrowed exchanges, ceremonies and rituals from other communities, though they always did so through kin connections. (This borrowing may account for the fact that so many Ponam exchanges had untranslatable or ungrammatical names.) At the same time, islanders continually abandoned customs that came to be seen as redundant or too difficult, or perhaps simply too old-fashioned. And likewise, people from other villages borrowed, and presumably abandoned, customs from Ponam. The reasons people gave for these changes were always highly pragmatic: they adopted new prestations because of the prestige and wealth they were thought likely to generate, and adopted new rituals because of their hoped-for efficacy, or because of the prestige of sponsoring them.

1930s

The most important change in this decade was the importation from the island of Ahus of a new affinal prestation called *njakenjak*. According to Sowakiki, daughter of the Lapan of Kamal Nilo, *njakenjak* was brought to Ponam by her father, Kuluah Jaf, and father-in-law, Sanuen of Kamal Kosohi. Kuluah Jaf, whom we have mentioned several times before, was an important and ambitious man, the island's war leader before pacification and the man who began Ponams' conversion to Christianity. He was also wealthy and sought more wealth. As part of this plan he engaged his daughter to Kakaw, the son of the Kosohi *lapan*, Sanuen, despite her protests. Kuluah Jaf wanted dog's teeth and shell money from Sanuen, and he got them. Legitimated by his Ahus connections, Sanuen sponsored the first Ponam enactment of the Ahus prestation *njakenjak*, a major affinal prestation made before marriage took place, instead of after it, as *masaf* had been before. *Njakenjak* became instantly popular, and was the standard for the next twenty years or so. Within a few years of the introduction of *njakenjak*, the payment of *masaf* was abandoned.

One consequence of this was to place young men even more firmly in the debt of their seniors, by requiring a major prestation before young men had the time to develop exchange links of their own or set up their own households. This change was particularly expedient in view of the spread of migrant labour, for the engagement could be contracted and the *njakenjak* paid before the young worker returned to Ponam, thus establishing an even greater lien on whatever he was fortunate enough to bring home with him. Certainly Pere elders sought to appropriate the wealth of their returning migrants in just this way (Mead 1963 [1930]: 234).

During this decade Ponams also adopted a *tamatu* prestation from Sori Island, their neighbour to the west. Women of a *kowun* with Sori antecedents held a ceremony and prestation for their sons and daughters in which the child's hair was allowed to grow long, and was then cut by the child's *asis* in return for a gift of dog's teeth and shell money. As we describe later, however, this prestation never caught on generally for it was not practiced by those without Sori kin, and was abandoned in the 1960s.

Although *njakenjak* represented an increase in elders' power over the young, other changes began that eventually undercut the power of men like Kuluah Jaf. Both the Church and the Administration disapproved of imposing arranged marriages on unwilling boys and girls. Bearing this in mind, and perhaps with the further motive of taking additional authority on himself, the village luluai (Kuluah Kelepe, *lapan* of Kamal Kehin, Kuluah Jaf's WFBS and main rival) tried to make marriage arrangements the business of the luluai, not just of the prospective couple's *asis* and *tamas*. In completely revolutionary fashion, he began to arrange marriages by asking the marriageable girls which boys they fancied, which boys flirted with them by throwing sticks and leaves at them as they walked about the village. When he had his answer he then went to the boy's family to try to open negotiations. Thus, while he did not override parental authority, he did begin to introduce the idea, totally accepted by the 1980s, that marriage should be based on the mutual attraction of a man and a woman. This was a legitimate procedure in the eyes of the Church because it made marriage begin with a statement of preference by the young women concerned. Also, it placed the luluai on the side of the bride and hence entitled him to a share of her marriage gifts.

Luluais and tultuls continued this practice through the War, and when the patrol officers returned in 1946 they reenforced it by attempting to arrange marriages themselves (PR 2 of 1944/45). The last Ponam to arrange marriages this way was Joseph Karin, tultul (luluai's assistant) in the 1950s, who was particularly concerned with those girls who seemed likely to be left single and with the increasing number of unwed mothers. In the 1980s he was still receiving gifts from, and standing as a kind of patron father to, women whose marriages he had arranged thirty years before.

1940s

The War exaggerated many of changes that had been emerging gradually. Young men had been working, earning and developing ambitions for independence from their seniors, and the War concretised their ambitions. It gave many the experience of leadership and authority, and provided them with a clear model on which to base their ambitions, the Allied (and especially the American) army. The young men who came back to Ponam after the War were simply unwilling to accept the kind of dependence that had been expected ten years earlier. Mark Kupe, for example, returned to Ponam at age 30 with six years of experience in the police and four years as a sergeant major in the army.

Joseph Karin returned at age 45 after 30 years of work, including fifteen years as a policeman and a prominent role in the Rabaul Strike of 1929,[8] two years as an executioner for the Japanese and almost two years in an Allied prison camp. When they looked for wives, such men did not consider for a moment submitting to the domination of what they saw as the ignorant old men at home. And because the end of the War meant the wholesale return of angry, not-so-young men to all parts of Manus in 1946, the old tactics of coercion and shame no longer worked to bring them to heel. Further, it is not clear that the elder generation really wanted to maintain the old system. They too had been infected with enthusiasm for the new kind of life they had experienced during the American occupation and they too thought it might be worth abandoning at least some of the old ways for new ones. Thus, as the returning soldiers began to settle into island life and to work and to earn money, they began to be more and more independent of their elders.

Women had far fewer opportunities for employment than men did, but they too had new freedoms. Colonial peace had made it safer for women and children to travel, and the draining away of male labour made it necessary for them to take on some of the traditionally male work of fishing and marketing. War and the Paliau movement led to further changes. The Paliau movement brought to its followers a great sense of sexual freedom and release, as Mead (1968 [1956]) has described. Men and women were no longer expected to avoid one another, but to live and work openly together, and this erupted, at least periodically among some of Paliau's followers, into sexual license. Ponams even claimed in the 1980s that, 'In Paliau's church, they worshipped sex.' Ponams never worshipped sex (despite a brief abortive attempt to introduce Paliau's custom of mixed bathing), but a sense of sexual freedom swept Ponam after the War as it swept all Manus. Affinal avoidances were lessened, girls were no longer so closely watched at home, Government and Church were enthusiastic about sending young girls to school and women began to feel that they too could achieve things outside the island and their families in a way that men had begun to do before the War. Young couples began to associate more freely, and extra-marital pregnancy became more common.

1950s

As we described earlier, this decade saw the disappearance of indigenous manufacturing in Manus, as tin dishes and imported clothes replaced wooden dishes and grass skirts and as cash began to replace both shell money

---

[8] Karin is the Joseph Selep mentioned in Gammage's (1975) account of the Rabaul Strike. Gammage shows the high level of involvement in the strike by Manus people, especially those in the constabulary.

and dog's teeth, though it would not really displace them in exchange until the next decade. It also saw the breakdown of the system of village specialist manufacture of exchange valuables, as Ponam women began to make for themselves the baskets and mats they had once imported from the mainland, and stopped the large-scale production of shell money.

The decline of customary exchange valuables was foreshadowed during the 1940s by a controversy about whether cash should be a substitute for valuables in brideprice payments. Old men said it should not. Young men, supported by the administration, said it should. The young men won. Old men could not resist because they, and more importantly those to whom they would distribute the prestations they received, had far more use for cash then for shell money. As cash became more and more important in affinal prestations, so the old men, who had no means to earn it, lost ground to the young men, who did.

There were two major changes in prestations made during this decade. First, Ponams abandoned the ear-piercing ceremony, *kaaput*, because, they said, it was too wasteful. People lost too much blood and were made weak. It also seems to have been a matter of regional fashion, for people throughout the district gave up piercing ears at about this time.

Second, there was another change in brideprice. The *njakenjak* prestation had been adopted in the 1930s as a pre-marriage payment. During the 1950s it was gradually moved, becoming a post-marriage prestation. This was the position occupied by the *masaf* prestation in the 1920s, and one could argue that this move was really the re-emergence of the traditional order, a return to the pre-War structure of marriage prestations and their significance. In Ponams eyes, however, this change represented something quite different. For islanders, it was not the re-emergence of an old pattern, but the confirmation of something new, the elder generation's loss of control over marriage arrangements and marriage prestations.

After the War, the wealthy men of a *kamal* ceased to dominate and finance the marriages of their younger *kamal*-mates or dependents from other *kamal*s as they had previously. Instead, they participated in exchanges only as kin, closely if closely related, but peripherally if the relationship was a distant one; they did not dominate financially, and so could not use marriage to set up competitive partnerships with other wealthy people. The place of elders and wealthy men was taken by siblings. Older *tama*s and *asi*s gave way to younger siblings, who had greater access to necessary resources and who began to bear the major financial responsibility for affinal prestations. If siblings could not raise large sums then prestations were small, but they were not taken over and financed by outsiders; they received assistance from kin, but the amount that kin gave reflected their relationship to the married couple more than it reflected their personal wealth.

When wealthy elders could no longer finance marriages, they lost the power to arrange them. As the old men lost control of valued wealth, so the young men gained it. And they used it to attract the women of their choice. One old men in the 1980s explained it this way. 'Women liked money and they liked men who had money to buy them things. They would flirt with them and sleep with them and what could the fathers do? They let the children marry right away without *njakenjak*. Later, if they wanted to, the sons made *njakenjak* on their own.' This speaker exaggerated the problem of premarital pregnancy in the 1950s, but he correctly brought out the independence that money gave to young men and to the women who hoped to be their wives. Young men had money, and they felt that they had knowledge and power and were the inheritors of a new earth. And they had the support of the administration in their ambitions. They began to choose their own brides and to finance marriages with the help of their siblings rather than with the patronage of their elders.

As arranged marriage came to an end, so too did the old preferences for continued inter-marriage between *kamal*s and repeating the marriages of *asi*s. Instead, the only genealogical consideration of importance in contracting marriages was that the two parties be as distantly related as possible, which meant in practice that one should not marry anyone who contributed significantly to one's family in exchange. As we noted earlier in this chapter, Ponams very explicitly attempted to diversify marriages as much as possible, within the limits of their preference for island endogamy, so that they could take advantage of the new source of wealth, migrants and their remittances. Because migrant wealth circulated primarily through the system of ceremonial exchange, it became important to have rights to participate in more exchanges and with a broader network of kin. The marriages between close kin and affines of the 1920s were no longer practical because they turned perfectly good would-be contributors into would-be recipients.

This description of changing marriage preferences raises an important question: What was the system of contributory gifts like before the War? In the 1980s Ponams rejected marriages with close kin and close affines on the grounds that they blocked the road for the exchange of contributory gifts. This suggests very strongly that the rules for exchanging contributory gifts were different in the past and did not present obstacles to these sorts of marriages. By the 1980s, contributions to ceremonial exchanges were governed by a comprehensive array of genealogical rules and calculations that generally overrode considerations of friendship or obligation. In the past, however, exchange, like the rest of Ponam life, seems to have been dominated not by kinship, but by patronage. Thus, prestations were dominated by big men and contributions to these prestations came primarily from their dependents. If this tentative reconstruction is correct, then the marriages to avoid would not have been those within the *ken si* or those with groups with whom marriages had previously been made, but would have been those within the patron's set of dependents, a set defined more by economics and politics than by genealogy.

1960s

A number of different changes took place during the 1960s in both affinal and *tamatu* prestations. Ponams introduced a new affinal prestation from the mainland, *rovwel*. This was a final marriage prestation from the groom's kin to the bride's made after the funeral of the first of the couple to die. Before this there had been no major exchange of gifts between affines after a death.

They also began to abandon the prestation called *nonou*, which had been made by the bride's kin to the groom's shortly after marriage. This was made by only two of the ten couples married with ceremony between 1979 and 1986, and it caused controversy. Particularly, people felt that the real value of the brideprice payment was decreased by the amount the bride's kin spent to put on the *nonou*, and this devaluation was an insult to the woman and her family. However, what also seemed to have happened during this decade and the 1970s was that the *nonou* prestation was absorbed into the wedding ceremonies. Before, the bride went to her husband's house with a gift of two or three baskets from her closest kin. As the *nonou* prestation began to die out, more and more of the bride's kin began to contribute baskets to her wedding. Some people said that the separate *nonou* was no longer necessary because it was made during the wedding.

A number of changes were also made in the *tamatu* prestations in this decade. First, the ceremony of cutting a child's hair, which had been made for those children whose mothers' came from Sori Island, gradually disappeared, never having managed to become popular with those who were not from Sori.

However, and at about the same time, another Sori ritual was imported and added to the *brolofau*, the prestation made when a person first returned to Ponam from a foreign place. This one, called *senget niu*, quickly caught on, even among those without Sori connections. The ritual was performed by members of a person's *kowun* and his or her *tamatus* just before the maternal kin made the prestation of baskets to the *tamatus* that was part of *brolofau*. The maternal kin brought a great heap of coconuts to the subject's father's house. The subject sat on them, shaded by cloths and a pandanus mat, while *tamatus* danced and shouted blessings and a senior *kowun* male struck an unshelled coconut with an adze and at each stroke invoked the names of *kowun* ancestors. The mat, coconuts, and cloths were then distributed to the *tamatus*, along with the other gifts distributed to them as part of the *brolofau* prestation.

A change also took place in the prestations made for a first child. We described how the prestation made by the husband's kin to the wife's on her first pregnancy included a large sago cake that was matched by a return of an identical cake in the prestation made by the bride's kin after the birth of the child. In the 1960s, however, this was dropped, and the link between the two prestations was broken. Further, the prestations made by the bride's kin were abbreviated. Instead of giving three separate gifts of different kinds, they simply gave one gift of cooked food to the child's *tamatus*, making this prestation virtually identical to other *tamatu* prestations.

During this decade people also changed the *lutung* prestation to *tamatus* made after a person's burial. Previously the *tamatus* receiving this prestation made a return prestation, as they did for other prestations. However, in the 1960s they stopped making a return. Before, Ponams said, *lutung* consisted of a prestation of a small number of baskets, five or six, to the dead person's closest and most important *tamatus*, each of whom distributed the contents of the basket and organised a return prestation. However, when Ponam women began to make baskets of their own instead of importing them from the mainland, they began to give more and more in *lutung* to more and more *tamatus*. Consequently there were no longer any obvious leaders to organise the *kahu*, and people simply stopped paying it. Unfortunately, this perfectly plausible Ponam explanation is belied by the fact that people continued to make return prestations for *brolofau*, despite the increased number of baskets given there.

Finally, a third change began to take place in the 1960s which affected all prestations and, by the 1980s at least, was seen as one of the more significant changes to have taken place since the War.

For as far back as people could remember, most island food prestations involved cooked food, and the return prestations (*kahu*) that followed almost every major prestation included only cooked food. During the late 1960s, however, people began instead to give raw food in *kahu* and other prestations. People who were prepared to hazard a guess about why the change occurred, came up with a very pragmatic explanation. Gifts of cooked food were wasteful because people gave more than the recipients could eat. With sago this was only a mild problem, because cooked sago could be stored and reheated, though it would never again be appetising. But rice, which began to be used regularly during this decade, presented a problem. Cooked rice could not be saved for more than about a day, and people ended up throwing the left-overs to the pigs and chickens. People said they began giving raw food in order to prevent this waste.

Although people were not sure about why the change took place, they were sure about its consequences: larger return prestations and a shift in the balance of relations between the giver and receiver. The reason people gave was a simple, almost aesthetic one. Raw food is less bulky and therefore less impressive than cooked food. One bundle of sago produces three large dishes when it is cooked, a much more impressive contribution to a return prestation than one raw sago. So, the person who used to give three dishes of sago felt unsatisfied with only one sago bundle, and gave two or three instead. The same is true of rice: what would fill a big dish when cooked was only a small puddle in the bottom of the dish when raw. No one wanted to look like a miser, so everyone gave more. There was some feeling that this had fuelled a general inflation in exchange, with larger initial prestations given in expectation of larger return prestations leading to even larger return prestations, all in the effort to make and maintain reputations for lavish giving.

1970s

The major change during the 1970s was the growth of the initial engagement prestation. Early in this century, this involved just a few sticks of tobacco and some betel nut, collected from the groom's close kin, brought secretly and at night and having a minimal *kahu*. In the 1970s, however, it expanded, as more kin began to contribute. Also, money was added, and grew until it overwhelmed the tobacco, and betel nut was dropped out. As the size of the prestation and the number of contributors grew, it became a major public affair, though more tension-ridden than most, for there remained the real chance that the proposal might be rejected despite all the careful negotiations carried out beforehand. As the engagement prestation grew, so did the return prestation, its *kahu*. In 1985 people said that receivers were expected to return one bundle of sago for each stick of tobacco received, despite the fact that a stick of tobacco cost 30 toea while a bundle of sago cost K 1.50.

CHANGING PATTERNS AND CHANGING LOGICS

From the 1920s to the 1980s, there were a number of changes in *tamatu* prestations. One major one was dropped and another added; rituals were added and dropped; the kinds of objects given changed. However, the general outline of the form of prestations remained essentially the same. Gifts moved from an individual's maternal kin to paternal *tamatu*s in recompense for the *tamatus'* blessings and care. Figure 21 compares the series of prestations in these two decades.

While the general pattern of *tamatu* prestations remained the same, the pattern of affinal prestations changed. In the 1920s, the system had been one of complementary exchange in which the groom's and bride's kin made major prestations and return prestations to one another alternately. By the 1980s, it was a system of asymmetrical exchange in which the major prestations were made by the groom's kin, while the bride's kin responded with return prestations but no major prestations of their own. Almost as if to compensate for this,

1. First birth, *palam*
    [valuables, cooked food]
    　　　Return prestation, *kahu*
    　　　　　[cooked food]

2. Ear-piercing,* *kaaput*
    [raw and cooked food]
    　　　Return prestation, *kahu*
    　　　　　[cooked food]

3. First return to the island from a
    distant place, *brolofau* [coconuts,
    baskets of lesser valuables]
    　　　Return prestation, *kahu*
    　　　　　[cooked food]

4. Death of a close relative,
    kani ara i njau, etc.
    [cooked food]
    　　　Return prestation, *kahu*
    　　　　　[cooked food]

5. Death, *lutung, susuat* [baskets
    of lesser valuables, pig]
    　　　Return prestation, *kahu*
    　　　　　[cooked food]

Prestations in the 1920s

1. First birth, *kani ara inapwilaf*
    [cooked food]
    　　　Return prestation, *kahu* [raw food]

2. First return to the island from a
    distant place,* *brolofau* [coconuts,
    baskets of lesser valuables]
    　　　Return prestation, *kahu* [raw food]

3. Death of a close relative,
    kani ara i njau, etc.
    [cooked food]
    　　　Return prestation, *kahu* [raw food]

4. Death, *lutung, susuat*
    [baskets of lesser valuables]
    　　　　　No return prestation

Prestations in the 1980s

Figure 21   Tamatu *prestations in the 1920s and the 1980s*

* Prestation made by some people only.

however, the size of the return prestations given after each initial prestation increased, so it may well be that the balance of wealth exchanged between the two parties did not change significantly. Figure 22 compares the affinal prestation sequence of the 1920s with that of the 1980s.

This and the preceding chapter extend the points made in chapter 1, with its structural approach, and chapter 2, with its historical approach. They do so by adding information on exchange to the earlier discussions of Ponam kinship. Chapter 3 showed how exchange is an inextricable element of the kin relations described in chapter 1. Although descent and group structures are important, Ponam kinship cannot be understood in terms of these alone, but must be understood as created as well out of the reciprocal obligations of exchange. The present chapter extends the argument in chapter 2. While that chapter showed how the history of colonisation affected the structure of *kamals*, the present chapter shows how that history affected the structure of exchange.

These changes that we have described here and in chapter 2 were profound and involved many aspects of life: the old relations of inequality between *lapans* and ordinary men and women disappeared; the domination by parents of their children was wiped out, or may even have been inverted; the sexual division of labour was changed, with an important consequence that women's participation in many areas of life increased; the arranging of

1. Engagement, *aribihi sal*
   [tobacco, betel]
         Return prestation, *ke tabac*
             [cooked food]

2. Marriage, *joso*
   [beds, valuables, cooked food]
         Simultaneous prestation
         [baskets of lesser valuables,
             cooked food]

3.   Bride's prestation, *nonou*
             [baskets]
   Return prestation, *kahu*
   [cooked food]

4. Groom's prestation,* *masaf*
   [dog's teeth, shell money]
         Return prestation, *kahu*
             [cooked food]

5.   Bride's prestation,* *piru*
         [coconuts, valuables]

Prestations in the 1920s

Groom's   Bride's

---

1. Engagement, *aribihi sal*
   [cash, tobacco]
         Return prestation, *kahu*
             [raw food]

2. Marriage, *joso*
   [beds, valuables, raw food]
         Simultaneous prestation
         [baskets of lesser valuables,
             cooked food]

3. Groom's prestation,* *njakenjak*
   [cash, dog's teeth]
         Return prestation, *kahu*
             [raw food]

4. Last prestation, *rovwel*
   [cash, dog's teeth, shell money]
         Return prestation, *kahu*
             [raw food]

Prestations in the 1980s

Groom's   Bride's

Figure 22   *Affinal prestations in the 1920s and the 1980s*

    * Prestation made by some people only.

marriages by elders ceased; the preferences for repeating marriages made by father's sisters and for the exchange of women between *kamal*s and between *lapan*s, disappeared; the pattern of affinal prestations changed from one of reciprocating prestations to one in which the husband's family initiated almost all prestations; the cycle of affinal and *tamatu* prestations changed as new prestations were introduced, old ones were dropped and existing ones were moved about within the sequence.

Further, we need to repeat a point apparent in our discussion of the changing nature of *kamal*s in chapter 2. That is, even those elements of Ponam life that appeared to have remained stable, did so in a changing setting, so that the part these elements played and the practices associated with them also underwent substantial change. For example, ceremonial exchange continued to involve the transfer of gifts between bride's kin and groom's, and between a person's matrilateral and patrilateral kin. However, success and failure in these exchanges no longer turned on men's and women's ability to produce fish and valuables and to trade and control trade with *kawas*. It depended instead on their ability to produce, control and maintain relations with successful migrants.

Thus we have demonstrated that this system of exchange not only failed to bring about the reproduction of the Ponam social order as a whole, it failed to bring about its own reproduction. The logic of the system of exchange that we observed during fieldwork and described in chapter 3 may be compelling to ethnographers, and it may even have been compelling to Ponams themselves. But compelling or not, this logic was impotent in fact. The changes that we have described amounted to a transformation of both social structure (the logic of Ponam social order) and social process (the circumstances and constraints within which individuals had to operate). But it should be quite clear that the failure of this system to reproduce itself was not the consequence of the disintegration or even weakening of society or culture. The exchange system continued to flourish and the process of exchange was still highly rule-bound and culturally important. Ponam remained Ponam, it did not turn into the poorer quarters of Sydney or Melbourne, but it changed as circumstances and people changed.

The historical view of Ponam kinship and exchange presented in this chapter contrasts with the structural and synchronic view presented in chapter 3, which described the structural logic of the systems of affinal and *tamatu* exchange as they existed in the 1980s. This logic was genuinely present in exchange as it took place in the 1980s. However, one cannot choose between these two perspectives, between history and logic or structure. A purely historical analysis, one that traces a series of changes, misses the logic that, in this case at least, is genuinely contained in the system seen synchronically. Yet this synchronic perspective misses the fact that this logic may not in fact be causal or reproductive. The logic of the moment is undoubtedly influential, for it is in terms of their interpretation of circumstances that people act and thereby create history. But, as Marshall Sahlins has written,

> the worldly circumstances of human action are under no inevitable obligation to conform to the categories by which certain people perceive them. In the event they do not, the received categories are potentially revalued in practice, functionally redefined.... At the extreme, what began as reproduction ends as transformation (1981: 67).

CHAPTER FIVE

The representation
of *kamal*s in exchange

In the preceding chapters we showed the strengths and limitations of structural and processual approaches for the analysis of Ponam kinship and exchange as a system or institution. We looked at the logic and order of that system and at how it was shaped by history. The three remaining ethnographic chapters continue to contrast structural and processual views of kinship and exchange, but at another level.

Here we are concerned not with systems, but with individuals and individual practices: what people did and were supposed to do as they participated in exchange. We are, then, concerned less with the logic of a system of practices than with the way people carried out those practices. Our viewpoint is less the logic of the total social system or cultural system or exchange system, and more the viewpoint of the individual actor in exchange. The structures and processes at work here are far more modest than those of the Ponam social order writ large or the historical sweep of colonisation, but they are no less real and important for making sense of what we saw on Ponam Island. At this more individual level there was a structure that defined and gave meaning to people's situations, but it was by no means determinant, for it also provided the framework through which people commented on and tried to alter their situations. Illustrating this requires greater attention to individual people and events than was the case with the earlier chapters of this book, and greater than is the case with much ethnography, which, as Nicholas Thomas (1989) notes, often uses individual people and events to illustrate not complexity and contingency, but structure and uniformity.

The logic of a social system or a body of social practices may, as Fortesians claimed, be immanent, but frequently its elicitation and expression appear to depend to a large degree on the analyst, typically the anthropologist alone or assisted by an informant of remarkable insight. The case is different with the structures of Ponam exchange. What we present here is a structure that was presented routinely by Ponams in the course of their frequent exchanges, though it is embarrassing how long it took us to understand what they were doing. Like many anthropologists, Ponams conceived of their society as involving orderly and logical relations among groups and categories of people that existed, in some sense, independently of the behaviour of individuals or the processes of social life. This structure, Ponams' collective self-represent-ations, if you will, is what concerns us now.

Self-representation attracted a growing interest among Melanesianists during the 1970s and 1980s, but usually it seems to have been pursued through talk, through what people had to say about their social organisation (J. Carrier & A. Carrier 1990). Here, however, we look at another way that people objectify and represent social order to themselves. During the course of contribution and distribution in Ponam ceremonial exchange, gifts were arranged in displays that diagramed the relations among the contributors or recipients. These dis-plays represented Ponams' own conceptions of the structural relations among individuals and kin groups; these were the routine Ponam representations of their own society that it took us so long to understand.

Perhaps one reason these displays did not attract our attention is that they seemed so utilitarian and routine. They were not, seemingly, the focus of oratory and debate. Neither were they associated especially with significant prestations or with the most intense moments of exchange. They seemed, in other words, to have nothing in particular to do with the political and symbolic significance of the main moments of main exchanges, which have been the focus of anthropological attention in Melanesia. Instead, they seemed just as much at home in what we had at first assumed to be the petty housekeeping chores of exchange: filling in the time while waiting for things to happen, or the tasks of subsidiary accumulation and distribution that were the prelude and epilogue to the main event, the ceremonial prestation. What made us begin to understand the importance of these displays was something we saw after we had been on Ponam for six months.

In May of 1979 Damien Self Njohang was in his late fifties, short, heavy and hale. He was at the culmination of the ceremonies commemorating the death of his younger brother, Camilius Pari, six months earlier. The death was sudden, and rumours had it that the ancestors had killed Pari because of unresolved bitterness among Pari, Self Njohang and their close agnates. Self Njohang was renowned for his ability to perform ceremony, and because he was indirectly implicated in Pari's death, this was a crucial ceremony.

Over a hundred adults, just about everyone on the island over 16 and not senile, formed a large semi-circle, as they sat in what shade they could find at the edge of the large clearing in front of Self Njohang's low, thatched house. Self Njohang himself sat on a bench under the eaves of his house. Next to him was a bony old woman who was his adviser on the fine points of kinship for this display. His wife stood in shadow just inside the doorway of his house, looking out.

Watching villagers chatted amongst themselves until Self Njohang began the hardest work of the funeral ceremonies, arranging the display that was the core of the distribution of cooked food to the dead man's

F

relatives. He directed a young nephew to get three dishes from the mass of over eighty that were at Selef Njohang's left at the edge of the clearing. At the man's direction, his nephew laid the first dish about ten feet away from the door of Selef Njohang's house. The second dish was placed about six feet beyond the first, the third a like distance beyond the second. The nephew got three more dishes and laid them beyond the first three, making a line of six. By this time the only noise from the watching villagers was mothers murmuring to their infant children to quiet them.

Selef Njohang sat looking at the line. He leaned to talk quietly to the old woman and to listen to her when she, after some deliberation, answered him. Then he stood up and walked to the third dish. Hesitating and still considering, he picked it up. He then walked to the fourth dish. He picked it up as well, and looked quickly back at the old woman. Then he placed the third dish on the ground where the fourth had been, and the fourth on the ground where the third had been. He walked back to the bench and sat down.

For over an hour, Selef Njohang continued. The nephew brought out two or three dishes and placed them singly on the ground where he indicated. At times he would direct him to move one to a new spot. At times he would heave himself up from the bench to move a dish or switch two. The watching semi-circle of Ponams remained silent.

VISUAL REPRESENTATION OF SOCIAL RELATIONS

Anthropologists have long attended to the way that people's models of social order are contained in the arrangements they make of social space. Lévi-Strauss's discussion of village plans (1968) and Bourdieu's description of the Kabyle house (1973) are classic examples. Likewise, in his paper on the Dorai market, Alfred Gell showed that the spatial arrangement of sellers and their various products in the market maps the geographic origins of the sellers, their status in the local social hierarchy and the status of the goods they sell. The market thus provides 'an indigenous model of social relations' that 'gives tangible expression to principles of social structure' (Gell 1982: 471).

These kinds of social models appear to be largely unconscious. The representations of social order that Ponams made in gift display, however, were conscious and intentional. In their intentionality, these Ponam displays were perhaps more like the representation of social relations made in rituals than like those encoded in enduring physical structures (though we would not call these prestations rituals). Despite differences in media and context, these Ponam representations resemble those that Robert Thornton described for Iraqw in Tanzania, in which a sacrificial animal and the rites conducted with it provide the media for 'the objectification of spatial and social relationships', objectifications that, furthermore, could 'be manipulated to produce changes in such relationships once they have been diagrammatically represented'

(Thornton 1982: 544). Ponams were different from Iraqws, however, in that their representations were purely intellectual. They had no power of their own to alter social relationships, though it is undeniable that they, like all models, had significant potential power to persuade people that they were an accurate and proper representation of social relations. And the social constraint that repetitive display generated could oblige even the un-persuaded to accept convention, however unpalatable it might have been.

Ceremonial exchanges in Melanesia often appear to contain a potential for representation of this sort, in the way that the prestations, or indeed those making the prestations, are arranged and displayed. Several writers have discussed this representative aspect of prestation. For instance, Michael O'Hanlon (1983) has described how dance and self-decoration, important parts of exchange and other occasions in Wahgi, serve as ways of representing the dancing group and its relations with others. Displays are intended to illustrate group size and strength, and more subtly its solidarity and the state of its relations with ancestors. 'The displays are both assertions of power in a turbulent social landscape, and at the same time are regarded as revelations of the moral relationships prevailing within the displaying group' (O'Hanlon 1983: 331). A significant element of Wahgi display, apparent in the dancers' preoccupation with the idea of betrayal, is that those who display do not fully control the image they put across. Weakness may be revealed instead of strength, confusion instead of unity.[1]

Expressive and representational potential is inherent in the arrangement of gifts as well as in the arrangement of people. Robert Foster looked at the representational nature of gift display in his discussion of the Enga *tee*. He described the iconography of *tee* prestations and said that the way that the presenters of *tee* display their pigs on the ceremonial ground embodies many of their conceptions of relations among men. *Tee* pigs are presented staked out in a set of long parallel lines, one line for each man presenting pigs to his partners, all the lines together pointing to the direction in which the pigs will go.

---

[1] O'Hanlon subsequently elaborated and extended his arguments in *Reading the skin* (1989: esp. chap. 7), and although his book is about Wahgi dancers rather than Ponam exchangers, it parallels our concern with the difference between the structure and logic that underlies events and the contingency that shapes their execution. O'Hanlon shows that there is a set of rules or principles for assessing the appearance of a set of dancers. At the same time, however, contingent events strongly influence the way that these principles are invoked and manipulated in any real assessment. As he puts it, 'there may be a considerable discrepancy between the general ideological perception that a particular process does generate information, and the extent to which, in practice, consistent, agreed-upon information, is actually produced' (1989: 236).

[T]he longest line of pigs in a *tee* ceremony unambiguously expresses the pre-eminent productive capacity of the individual with whom the line is associated... . [A]n obsessive concern with straightening the lines reveals the attention given to creating a unity out of diversity — that is, a single line metonymically related to a single man out of the pigs (the productive capacity) of others... . *Tee* lines ... crystallize the productive capacity of others into a physical icon — the line of stakes — which is then directly identified with the personage of an individual man. The internal segmentation of the line with bark fibres ... fulfills a dual symbolic function. On the one hand, the number of discrete segments expresses the extension of a man's influence to the places where the pigs will be received; on the other, the creation of a straight line out of pigs from various sources, encoded by a segmented straight line, reflects the influence of a man in the groups from which pigs have been "pulled" (Foster 1985: 192).

The way Ponam gift displays illustrated social relations was even more explicit than the line of *tee* pigs or the appearance of dancing men. This is because Ponams arranged their gift displays intentionally to represent relations among and within groups of kin. In this way, these displays resemble what Michael Young (1971: 200) has described of *abutu* competitive food exchanges on Goodenough Island, in Milne Bay. He says villagers there displayed their gift in the presenter's village by the type of good and by the category of giver before they formally presented it to the recipient. Such an arrangement allowed people to see at a glance the proportionate contributions of the various categories of people contributing. But although they resembled these Goodenough Island displays, Ponam Island displays were even more clearly intended as kinship diagrams.

Like other types of kinship diagrams, these displays illustrated what Pierre Bourdieu called "official kinship" or "representational kinship", 'the group's self-representation and the almost theatrical presentation it gives of itself when acting in accordance with that self-image' (Bourdieu 1977: 35). Such formal, public, collective, and ideal models of social structure are 'produced by the application of the structuring principle that is dominant ... in certain situations and with a view to certain functions' (1977: 34, emphasis omitted). In Bourdieu's view, they are always ideologically-purposeful misrepresentations that serve to slight or devalue certain relations in favour of others. Especially, they obscure what he called practical kinship, obscure the practical uses people make of kin relations, of their connections to others. Practical groups exist not as logical structures, but 'only through and for the particular functions in pursuance of which they have been effectively mobilised' (1977: 35). Thus, practical kinship refers to the process of organising relations among people and groups, and while the constitution of these practical groups might, at certain points, accord with official kinship, more likely it does not.

Bourdieu was, of course, describing a system in which official kinship was enshrined in texts and backed by the state in a far more thorough-going way than was the case on Ponam (though it would be wrong to underestimate the rapidly-increasing role of the state, especially the land courts, in this matter; e.g., *WT&E*: 48–54). Nevertheless, the notion of official kinship, or perhaps semi-official kinship, is useful in suggesting how the practice of externalising kinship in this formal way served to regulate it and subject it to the explicit constraint and political scrutiny of others.

In part, Ponam displays reflected official kinship. But also they were inevitably modified by the processes of practical kinship. This was because they were not abstract representations of neutral genealogies, but were assemblages of gifts put together by particular groups of people who had chosen to act together. Thus, while, in some sense, they served to perpetuate the dominant model of idealised kin relations, they also served to realise and make public the tensions inherent in this model, and the ways that the processes of social life deviated from it. Ponam gift displays are interesting, therefore, because in the process of the display and distribution of gifts, Ponams themselves wrestled with problems of the relation between their own official and practical kinship.

While Ponam display was representational, something islanders used to represent to themselves and to others the social relations they saw around them (or wished others to think they saw), it would be wrong to see display as only representational. Because exchange, and the displays it necessarily involved, took place so frequently, there was also another, more generative dimension to them. These displays could be said to *create or constitute* that world of social relationships. The universe of kinship that was the subject of exchange and provided its rules, was created and defined by the gift displays and the possibilities contained in them as much as it was represented by them.

GIFT DISPLAY IN CEREMONIAL PRESTATIONS

We said that prestations on Ponam involved three stages: contribution and accumulation, prestation and distribution. Major prestations were usually reciprocated by return prestations of *kahu*, which followed these same three stages. We have already given a general description of the genealogical relationships through which gifts moved in these various stages; here we want to look at the practical management of these transactions. What did people actually do?

Preparations for a gift prestation formally began when the individual or siblings who planned to make it announced the day for contributions. On a major occasion such as brideprice, this announcement might be made a number of days in advance and in public, perhaps at church or in a village meeting. For

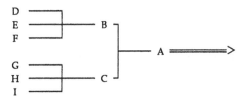

Figure 23   *Contributors to a prestation*

lesser occasions, the news was simply spread by word of mouth. On the appointed day, the various peripheral contributors would begin to send gifts, in the dendritic manner described in chapter 3, to the individuals or siblings who were to make the final public prestation. We describe this process thoroughly in chapter 6, but want to illustrate it schematically here.

Figure 23 shows the contributors to a prestation given by A. B and C are A's close kin: parents, spouse, siblings or children; D, E and F are kin to B; and G, H and I are kin to C. The people D through I may receive contributory gifts from others, but for simplicity's sake we ignore this. We will describe D's gift, but the same observations apply to the other contributors. In the morning of the day on which the prestation was to be made, D would begin, in consultation with his or her spouse, to prepare a gift for B. This would include both deciding on and making up D's own contribution, and waiting to see if any subsidiary contributions came to D from others. Having prepared the gift, D would bring it to B's house, where B, or perhaps B's child or spouse, was waiting to receive it.

If the occasion were an important one, D would be welcomed with tea, biscuits, betel nut or tobacco. If not, D would merely place the gift on the ground by B's house and settle down to wait for other contributors to B to arrive. As they trickled in, they would place their contributions on the ground near D's in such a way that they gradually built up a pattern or diagram representing the relations of the various contributors to each other and to B. There might be considerable discussion among the various contributors about the quantity and quality of the gifts to be given and the manner of their arrangement. On important occasions speeches might also be made. When all of the contributions had arrived, or it was too late to wait for more, people would set off as a group to carry their contributions to A's house.

Those waiting at A's house would greet B and B's kin with shouts of 'Welcome, welcome! Come in, come in!' as B's contingent placed their gifts all together in a single pile outside of A's house and settled down to wait for other groups of contributors to arrive. As these other groups came they would place their gifts on the ground near B's in such a way as to represent the relations of all the various contributing groups to each other and to A. When all of A's contributors had arrived, then the *sor ne njaharun*, "contribution and accumulation", was complete and it was time to make the major prestation.

This procedure for the accumulation of contributions was followed for all types of prestation. The procedure was more complex and it involved more people in important prestations than in minor ones. But the basic steps did not vary. Once the accumulation of contributions was complete, however, a variety of different steps were possible, depending on the type of prestation.

On most occasions the person who accumulated the prestation would immediately take it somewhere else and present it to others to be distributed. Affinal and *tamatu* prestations, for example, were always made in this way.[2] In affinal prestations the person who accumulated the prestation carried it (with the help of other kin) to his or her affines' men's house and presented it to the affines, who would then distribute it to their own kin as they chose. In *tamatu* prestations the subject's maternal kin carried the gifts they accumulated to the subject's own house, and there made the prestation to the subject's *tamatu*.

There were also a number of occasions on which a person would accumulate gifts of cooked food to distribute in order to compensate others for something they had done. One important set of funeral prestations, called *kaapet*, was made this way: the deceased's siblings gave to kin and other Ponams who had come to share the mourning. Similarly, a person distributed this way in order to compensate those who had helped with work such as building a house. These kinds of distributions could be made in two different ways. The food could be divided up among the giver's kin, in much the same way that it had been accumulated, or it could be distributed to the community, to the island's moieties and *kamal*s.

We will describe prestations to moieties and *kamal*s in this chapter, and reserve prestations to kin for chapter 6. This allows us to introduce the principles of these displays in a fairly straightforward way, before addressing the more complex features that existed in displays of gifts to kin.

DISTRIBUTIONS TO MOIETIES AND *KAMALS*

Distributions to the community took the form of distributions to moieties or *kamal*s, and these were made whenever an individual or a group wanted to give to others on grounds other than those of kinship. For example, this form of distribution was often used in the type of prestation called *hamisie-gwok*, which a Ponam would give to repay others who had helped with some enterprise like house- or canoe-building. They were also made during the course of funeral celebrations, for it was expected that all Ponams would come to mourn,

---

[2] These were the only occasions on which Ponams gave valuables (*langou*) such as cash, dog's teeth, shell money, baskets and so on. Thus, these were the most important and prestigious types of prestations made on Ponam.

regardless of their relationship to the deceased. On these types of occasions, the decision about whether to distribute to moieties or to *kamals* was determined largely by the amount of food available. If there were enough to produce fourteen sizable shares (one for each *kamal*) then probably the food would be distributed to *kamals*, a form of distribution called a *sahai*.[3] If there were too little for this, then the food would be distributed to moieties, a kind of distribution that had no proper name, but was described simply as *kendi'i kelif Kum ne Tolau*, "distribute to Kum [the south moiety] and Tolau [the north moiety]." Here we call them Kum–Tolau distributions.

Most *sahai* and Kum–Tolau distributions took place in a clear space in front of a dwelling or men's house belonging to the person or people making the distribution. The kin of the person leading the distribution amassed their contributions at one side of the clearing and then joined those who expected to receive, gathered around the edges of the open ground. Watched by this audience, the leader and a few chosen kin would have a last strategic conference, while they arranged single dishes on the ground, each representing one of the categories of people to whom they intended to give, in the way that Self Njohang did in one of the mortuary prestations for Camilius Pari, described earlier in this chapter. Once they were satisfied with the array, they would then distribute the remaining dishes among the categories they had just marked out.

The door of the building in front of which the arrangement was being made gave the arrangement an orientation. The gifts were arranged in parallel lines leading away from the door. The end of each line nearest the door was called *ken*, the "origin" or "base" of the line, the most prominent position. The end farthest away was *pehen*, the "crown" of the line, and least prominent. The image evoked was that of a tree, for *ken* referred to the base of a tree and *pehen* to its crown.

Once the dishes of food were arranged, a public speaker (*sohou*) would address the crowd and announce which category of people was to receive each set of dishes. A male leader could act as his own speaker or appoint someone with a better style of public address to speak for him. A woman could not

---

[3] In one circumstance a *sahai* was not simply a complex way of distributing food, but was obligatory. That was when a group built a new men's house. Then the group members affirmed their status as an independent *kamal* by giving food to each of the other *kamals* and by having the food be accepted. (Later in this chapter we deal with the importance of exchange for *kamal* identity.) This act, central for defining *kamal* identity and *kamal* membership, was the only remaining element of the larger men's-house–raising prestations described in chapter 2. Unfortunately, we have seen only one of these distributions for a new men's house, held two weeks after our arrival, and the information we have does not justify an analysis of this use of *sahai* distribution.

normally act as a speaker, though if an occasion were very informal or attended exclusively by women (itself a mark of informality), a woman might be her own speaker. In the vast majority of cases, however, a woman would ask a kinsman or known speaker to speak for her. Even so, she still directed the work of the distribution and would usually stand beside the speaker, telling him exactly what to say and correcting him openly if he made a mistake.

The speaker would stand near the base of the display and speak briefly, thanking people for attending and perhaps making some humorous or pointed remarks, but the overall tone of his speech was always sober. Then he would walk through the arrangement pointing to each set of dishes and calling the name of the category of people who should come to collect it. He then retired to the edge of the display. In a very small, informal or hurried distribution the speaker did not always bother to walk among the dishes. Thus, a speaker at a small distribution threatened by rain might simply shout out the names of the recipients, and leave people to sort out for themselves which category was to get which dishes, which they could do by matching the pattern of dishes and the sets of recipients. As will become clear, with some forms of prestation this was not difficult.

When the speaker stepped away from the display of food, a few members of each of the recipient categories would come forward to collect their shares and move them away from the centre of the clearing for redistribution. The small quantities of food given in Kum–Tolau distributions were usually redistributed immediately and eaten on the spot. When there was more food than the recipients could finish in one sitting, as should be the case in *sahai*, it was taken away to be redistributed later.

KUM–TOLAU DISTRIBUTION

How were these distributions arranged? The system of display is easiest to understand in the simplest distributions, those made to moieties. And the simplest of these Kum–Tolau prestations consisted of just that: two equal shares, two equal sets of dishes of food, one for each moiety. These were arranged on the ground in a very simple representation of the division of the island into northern and southern halves and the division of islanders into Northerners and Southerners, with the Tolau (North) share being placed to the north of the Kum share. These two shares formed the core of all Kum–Tolau distributions. However, it was possible to expand the number of gifts and thus the complexity of the arrangement as the amount of food to be distributed increased, something that was usually a function of the importance of the occasion. If there were more than enough food to provide five or six dishes for each moiety, then the portions for each were subdivided into shares for men and women, producing the four equal gifts illustrated in figure 24. In dividing

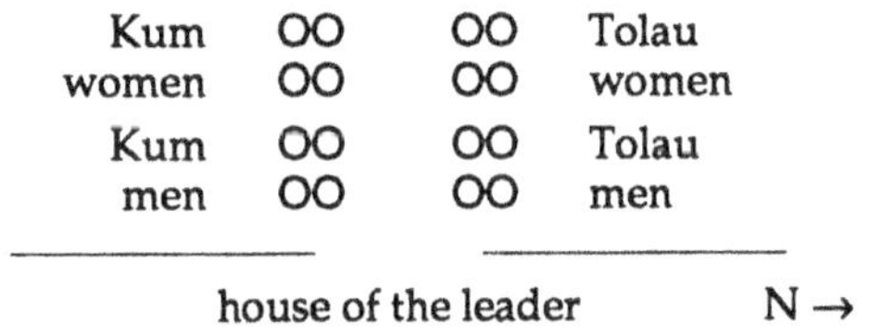

```
         Kum    OO     OO    Tolau
       women    OO     OO    women
         Kum    OO     OO    Tolau
         men    OO     OO    men
```

house of the leader   N →

Figure 24   *An arrangement of gifts distributed to the men and women of the Kum and Tolau moieties*

Note: Here, as in all figures, sets of circles roughly represent the relative sizes of piles of gift items.

the moiety shares this way, the leader of a distribution recognised what always happened in any case, for the etiquette of affinal avoidance made it very difficult for groups of men and women to eat together in public.

Categories other than the two moieties and the two genders could also receive shares. Often special shares were set aside for off-island visitors,[4] by definition not moiety members, as well as for the island's foreign school teachers. Sometimes shares were added for school children, serving both to expand and elaborate the distribution, and to keep the children out of their parents' hair. Gifts for these categories were always placed at the head of the display. Any category of people that was not kinship-based and that had contributed in some special way to the work the distribution celebrated could also receive a special share. This was placed at the base of the display to indicate its importance. Figure 25 shows a distribution in which a number of shares were given to non-moiety groups: teachers, children and the young men's and young women's clubs, Posus and Nai.

The pattern of Kum–Tolau arrangements was simple and thus easy to dismiss as petty housekeeping, merely a convenient way to manage the technical problems of exchange and reciprocity. However, Ponams were articulate about the principles of arrangement and their significance. These same principles, and others, also underlay the more complex distributions to *kamal*s and kindreds. They provided what one can think of as a kind of grid on which Ponams were able to diagram social structure.

The physical space in which Kum–Tolau and *sahai* distributions were made contained three significant dimensions: north–south, base–crown, and size of gift. Positions in social space were mapped onto this three-dimensional physical space. Ponams used the paired oppositions of physical space (north–south, base–crown, large–small) as vehicles that defined the social space in

---

[4] This category included us — foreign anthropologists. However, we refer to our own shares as "anthropologists" in the figures illustrating displays. We reserve "foreigners" for non-Ponams other than the teachers at the island's primary school. We were all outsiders.

```
            O      O    school
teachers   OO     OO    children
Kum        OO     OO    Tolau
women      OO     OO    women
Kum        OO     OO    Tolau
men        OO     OO    men
Posus       O      O    Nai
Club       OO     OO    Club
```

house of the leader   N →

Figure 25   *An arrangement of gifts distributed to the men and women of the Kum and Tolau moieties and to other categories*

which relationships between groups receiving goods in a distribution could be represented. Thus, ceremonial exchange was important not simply because of the relations of reciprocity that it created, but because the very process of prestation and distribution provided a model in terms of which Ponams understood society in the abstract.

The significance of these three dimensions of display varied with the type of distribution, but were always well-known. In Kum–Tolau and *sahai* the north–south dimension distinguished the two moieties, while the base–crown dimension distinguished central from peripheral participants. Thus, as we noted, in Kum–Tolau distributions, gifts for the Kum moiety were placed on the south side of the arrangement and gifts for Tolau on the north. Gifts for the men of each moiety were placed at the base of the display, gifts for women followed these, gifts for outsiders and children went at the crown. Especially-honoured participants could have their gifts placed in front of those for men. The four gifts for the men and women of each moiety were normally of equal size, larger than any of the others. Gifts for honoured participants were usually slightly smaller, and gifts for outsiders slightly smaller again. (However, as these categories had fewer members than the more important ones, usually the amount of food each member received was, in fact, much greater.)

Kum–Tolau distributions were arranged to represent relations among the official categories of Ponam society. However, this idealised structure was not the only factor affecting social processes or relations among individuals, and consequently food distributed to a particular category was rarely redistributed to all category members or only to them. As Ponams were aware, what an individual actually received was determined as much by the contingencies of his or her relationships with other category members as by his or her formal category membership. This was particularly true in the redistributions of Kum–Tolau, which were very informal. After the speaker announced the distribution, people began the task of mobilising the individual members of the categories invoked in the display into groups of recipients. Usually that happened after a few people from each category collected their category's share and moved it to one side of the clearing. Those wanting a portion gathered nearby and the dishes were passed around, usually one dish to be shared among five or six adults. Thus, although shares were distributed to specific social categories, they were redistributed to individuals who came forward to take them.

Normally, a person was supposed to receive a portion of his or her own category's food. However, this did not always happen, nor did Ponams expect it to. No Ponam was in a position to dictate what any adult could do, and the informality of these redistributions allowed people to do more or less what they chose. People could go purposefully to the spot where the share for their own category was being distributed. They were unlikely to stride so purposefully to take from another category, but if they wanted to eat with members of another category or to avoid eating with their own, it was easy enough to do so. They could follow the people they had been sitting with and share what they received, whether or not they belonged to the same recipient category. They could sit and wait for someone to bring something. And if something was being redistributed nearby, they could simply reach out a hand and take some, regardless of the category to which it had been given. No one was likely to interfere, and Ponams recognised a number of reasons why people might want to receive a share from a category other than their own: the desire to do what-ever was simplest, to eat with a particular group of people or to avoid others.

Because of the options available to individuals and the different reasons they could have for exercising them, it would be hard for anyone unfamiliar with the state of play of village relations to see anything meaningful in people's choices. But it was not hard for islanders to do this, and for Ponams the moment of redistribution was a marked time, in which people noticed what others were doing and wondered why, a moment in which ordinarily-insignificant actions took on significance. A person who was out of place was likely to explain why, with statements such as, 'I'm too tired to get up and walk all the way over there', or 'I really want to hear what happened when you went to town yesterday', though such statements were not necessarily taken at face value. And regardless of what a person said, those who were interested would file this action away for consideration.

The categories represented in these distributions were real to Ponams, not merely artifacts created for the purpose of facilitating distribution. They were part of the way Ponams interpreted their society. And yet islanders were perfectly aware that individuals did not always act as members of the categories to which they belonged, that the structural factor of membership did not always determine behaviour. Other factors were important, such as the state of relations among individuals. In other words, Ponams had both a model of the island's social structure and an understanding of its social processes.

SAHAI DISTRIBUTIONS

Kum–Tolau distributions varied little: Ponams saw these distributions as fairly simple and agreed about the attributes of social organisation represented in them. But this was not the case with *sahai*. This was seen as difficult, it normally took half an hour to arrange and it was entrusted only to mature adults. At first blush this is puzzling, for a *sahai* was simple: shares for each *kamal* were laid out in two lines almost exactly in the manner in which their men's houses were arranged in the village, and a few extra shares for others were laid out at the crown of the display. Like Kum–Tolau, however, the simplicity is deceptive. The arrangement did produce a map of the village, but this was constructed over the grid defined by the dimensions described previously, so that each position on the map had social as well as geographical significance.

In the following pages we describe three funeral *sahai*s held in 1979 for two men and one woman who had been born into different *kamal*s and married into yet others. We discuss the way these *sahai*s differed and the way Ponams explained these differences, in order to show how they were used to define and describe the social order.

Like Kum–Tolau, the arrangement of gifts in a *sahai* provided a representation of both the geographic and the social relationships among categories. Also like Kum–Tolau, in principle *sahai* arrangements were invariant, reflecting Ponam as a whole and not the personal ties and obligations of the leader of the distribution. However, *kamal*s were both more complex and more sensitive politically than moieties, and therefore were more difficult to represent. Consequently there were differences of opinion about how *sahai*s should be arranged and variations in their actual arrangement.

There were two sorts of variations, each with a different cause. The first can be thought of as primarily a technical problem. Ponam convention did not determine exactly how the complex geographic reality of *kamal*s was to be simplified and accommodated to the diagrammatic conventions of distribution. Although initially confusing to us, Ponams saw these technical variations as essentially irrelevant, when indeed they noticed them at all. The second sort of variation was more social than technical. It occurred when there was a lack of agreement about how the social groups that existed "on the ground", to use the anthropological phrase, were to be fitted into the representational model of *kamal*s. Which groups really were *kamal*s? Which *kamal*s really belonged at the base of the line and which at the crown? Where were men's houses really located? Who belonged to which *kamal*? These were the important issues. Had Ponams seen the rules of these displays as determinant, they would have accounted for variations in displays in terms of the ignorance of exchange leaders, as indeed they did at times. However, they did not see the rules as determinant of action. Instead, they saw them as providing a vehicle by means

				O	school children
				OO	(10)
Buhai	OO OO		O	O	teachers
(8)	OO OO		OO	OO	(11)
Nilo	OO OO		anthropologists		
(7)	OO OO		(9)		
Kehin	OO OO	OO OO	Puyu		
(6)	OO OO	OO OO	(12)		
Kosohi	OO OO	OO OO	Kahu		
(5)	OO OO	OO OO	(13)		
Toloso'on	OO OO	OO OO	Lopaalek		
(4)	OO OO	OO OO	(14)		
Lifekau	OO OO	OO OO	Mahan		
(3)	OO OO	OO OO	(15)		
Sako	OO OO	OO OO	Lehesu		
(2)	OO OO	OO OO	(16)		
Lamai	OO OO	OO OO	Kayeh		
(1)	OO OO	OO OO	(17)		

Kosohi men's house   S →

Figure 26   Sahai *held for Pe-nja Kapen, a Kamal Kehin man, October 1979 (including separate shares for men and women)*

of which leaders in exchange could comment independently on the state of Ponam social identities and relations. Thus, islanders often explained differences between *sahai*s in terms of leaders' different attempts to make contentious statements about aspects of Ponam society.

All three of the *sahai*s discussed here showed the technical problems of representing social groups in physical display. All contained gifts for the *kamal*s associated with each of the 14 Ponam men's houses then standing (shown in map 3, of Ponam village, p. 39). These were arranged in two lines: one for the *kamal*s of the northern, Tolau moiety, and the other for those of the southern, Kum moiety, with the shares for each *kamal* arranged to replicate the order in which their men's houses stood along the island's northern and southern beaches. (Shares for the *kamal*s were sometimes subdivided into male and female portions, as was possible in the Kum–Tolau distributions.) These *kamal* shares were the core gifts without which *sahai* would not be *sahai*. But *sahai*s could also include gifts for those other categories that attended the prestation or helped with the work of the mourning period that these *sahai*s commemorated. We never saw gifts for groups other than *kamal*s placed at the base of the *sahai*, no matter how important their contribution had been, and people asserted that it would be incorrect to do so. Instead, they were placed clearly apart from the *kamal* shares, usually at the crown of the lines.

Figure 26 shows these points. (The sets of dishes of food shown in each figure are numbered in the order in which they were announced by the speaker, a sequence that introduces time as a meaningful fourth dimension.)

```
                    anthropologists   O
                         (17)        OO
              teachers        O
                (16)         OO
           foreigners    O
             (15)       OO
                                OO    Buhai
                                OO     (8)

                                OO    Lamai
                                OO     (7)
                                           O     net fishermen
        Kahu    OO      OO    Sako  OO          (21)
        (14)    OO      OO     (6)
                                       O       anglers
        Puyu    OO      OO    Lifekau  OO      (20)
        (13)    OO      OO     (5)
                                       O      schoolgirls
     Lopaalek   OO      OO    Toloso'on OO     (19)
       (12)     OO      OO     (4)
                                     O      schoolboys
       Mahan    OO      OO    Kosohi  OO     (18)
       (11)     OO      OO     (3)

       Kayeh    OO      OO    Kehin
       (10)     OO      OO     (2)

       Lehesu   OO      OO    Nilo
        (9)     OO      OO     (1)
     ─────────────────      ──────────────────
            Nilo men's house                 N →
```

Figure 27   Sahai *held for Camilius Pari, a Kamal Nilo man, May 1979*

The dead man's wife's brother arranged this *sahai* at the instruction of the leader, the dead man's sister. He laid out one row of eight sets of dishes and another of six, one for each *kamal* and each set sub-divided into men's and women's dishes. Above these he placed sets for outsiders. Then he announced the distribution. He pointed to the set at the base of the Tolau line (number 1) and called out, 'For Lamai', the western-most Tolau *kamal*. Walking toward the crown of the line, he designated shares for the Tolau *kamals* in the order in which their men's houses appeared along the north shore of the island. Then he called the few special shares at the head of the arrangement (school children, teachers and anthropologists) before crossing to the crown of the southern line and announcing the *kamals* of the southern moiety, beginning with Puyu in the east (number 12) and proceeding to Kayeh in the west. Comparing this with map 3 shows that the speaker announced the *kamals* in the order in which he would have encountered their men's houses had he made a circuit of the village, starting with Lamai in the northwest and finishing with Kayeh in the southwest. By arranging and announcing the *kamals* in this way the leader produced an accurate representation of village geography.

The different convention of arrangement used in figure 27, however, illustrates that a *sahai* was more than a literal representation of island geography. Here the northern, Tolau *kamals* were arranged in an order that was the

```
foreigners    O
      (18)    OO

  teachers    O
      (17)    OO

anthropolo-   O
gists (15)    OO

           Buhai    OO
             (8)    OO

           Lamai    OO
             (7)    OO

            Sako    OO    OO    Puyu
             (6)    OO    OO    (14)

         Lifekau    OO    OO    Kahu
             (5)    OO    OO    (13)

        Toloso'on   OO    OO    Lopaalek
             (4)    OO    OO    (12)

          Kosohi    OO    OO    Mahan
             (3)    OO    OO    (11)

           Kehin    OO    OO    Lehesu
             (2)    OO    OO    (10)

            Nilo    OO    OO    Kayeh
             (1)    OO    OO    (9)
  _____        _____

           house of the leader              S →
```

Figure 28   Sahai *held for Nja Polon, a woman born in Kamal Kayeh and married into Kamal Sako, July 1979*

reverse of that shown in figure 26. The reason for this becomes apparent when the order in which the *kamals* were announced is taken into account. The speaker began with Nilo, the eastern-most men's house in the northern moiety, walked westward to the end of that line, returned to the base of the Kum line and proceeded to announce that line from base to crown, calling the *kamals* as their men's houses appeared from west to east. In doing this he was following the convention, inviolate in distributions to kin, that the lines of gifts should be announced from base to crown, and not the other way around. In order to match this convention to the apparently equally inviolable convention that *kamal* shares in *sahais* be announced in the order in which they would be encountered if the speaker made a circuit of the village, the shares in the Kum line were reversed. The conflicts between these two conventions were the cause of idiosyncratic variations in the arrangements.

Figure 28, which shows a *sahai* for an elderly widow, gives yet a third example of the way *sahais* were organised. Also, it shows how the *sahai* display presented difficulties other than just those caused by the technical limitations of the medium in which social groups were represented. This display is very much like the *sahai* in figure 27, but differs in the placement of two pairs of *kamals*, Puyu and Kahu, and Lehesu and Kayeh. These differences appeared because the arrangers of these displays had different opinions about the social position of these pairs of *kamal*s in Ponam society (we explore this later in this chapter). Many aspects of *sahai* distributions were subject to this sort of variation because *sahai* did more than represent spatial organisation: it also represented social organisation. Thus, the distribution leader's knowledge of *kamal*s (their history, the relations between them and the possible consequences of recognising or not recognising these things) also influenced the way that *sahai* was arranged. The influence of the leader's understanding of social relations and social structure on the arrangement of *sahai* can be seen if we compare explanations of some of the variations in these *sahai*s: variations in the *kamal*s included in the distribution, variations in the particular order in which the *kamal* shares were arranged, variations in the site chosen for a *sahai*.

VARIATIONS IN *SAHAI* DISPLAYS

During the time of fieldwork the *kamal*s recognised in *sahai* did not change, but Ponams did not think that they were unchangeable. This suggests, and the following discussion shows, that Ponams fell between the poles of a distinction that Simon Harrison draws, between a nominalist view of clans, common in the New Guinea Highlands, and a realist view, common in the Lowlands. Ponams would not have agreed with Harrison's synoptic statement of the Highlands view that 'a clan exists at all only by virtue of the individuals who constitute it'; equally they would be leery of the realist view that 'a clan is considered to have a reality quite independent of the existence of its members' (1989: 5). These views are, of course, expressions of the processual and structural views that underlie our discussion of Ponam Island.

As we have described, island history records that new *kamal*s emerged by breaking away from existing ones; existing *kamal*s weakened, were absorbed as dependents and ceased to build men's houses or hold *sahai*s; and sometimes these dependent groups regained strength and reappeared again. At the turn of the century, for example, Buhai, Kahu, Lamai, Lifekau and Puyu were all dependents of other *kamal*s. When a group of agnates had the land and strength to build a men's house and commemorate it with a *sahai*, they could claim recognition in the *sahai*s of others. Even though, in principle, a *kamal* was a conjunction of agnation and real property, in practice that conjunction had to be recognised in exchange. A *kamal* never given a place in *sahai*, like one that never gave a *sahai*, simply did not exist. Exchange, as well as descent, made *kamal*s on Ponam. A group that ceased to be able to give *sahai* could no longer claim recognition in the *sahai*s of others.

When groups stood at the point of transition, there was room for dispute.

When the brothers of the company Molou attempted to declare themselves independent of Kamal Nilo in 1985, as we described in chapter 1, they announced that one of the buildings in their hamlet was henceforth to be a *kamal*. They did not, however, raise a new men's house or distribute *sahai*, and, as a small impoverished group,[5] they could not have afforded to do so. Ponams reported that in the *sahai*s distributed during 1985, no shares were designated for Molou. Molous, however, did not accept part of the *sahai*s given to Nilo as they had done in the past.

Just as Molou was poised to emerge as a newly-independent *kamal*, so Toloso'on stood on the brink of extinction. The last man of Kamal Toloso'on died in the 1950s and only women remained, yet the *kamal* remained in existence. The two surviving Toloso'on women maintained control over their *kamal*'s property and recruited the descendants of previous generations of Toloso'on women to maintain the men's house and sponsor prestations. As a consequence, Toloso'on continued to be represented in *sahai*. However, Ponams were not sure about Toloso'on's prospects, and they knew that ultimately some decision would have to be made about its future. By 1985 their men's house had been allowed to fall down and the fate of the *kamal* appeared to hinge on the last unmarried son of one of the Toloso'on woman — on whether he would choose to marry, settle on Toloso'on land and raise his children as Toloso'ons, or to remain with his father's *kamal*. Because this young man was still defiantly a bachelor (despite continuous pressure to marry one or another of his lovers), the fate of the *kamal* was unsettled and it kept its place in *sahai*.

Thus, the fact that the *kamal*s included in *sahai* did not vary during our stay does not mean that producing a *sahai* was no more than a mechanical repetition of the names of men's houses. In every case someone had to decide how to handle the potentially tendentious *kamal*s, whether or not to be the first one to put Molou in or leave Toloso'on out and so on. One had to know not only which *kamal*s had men's houses, but who was entitled to have one and what the possible consequences of recognising or failing to recognise one might be.

Once the leader of a distribution had identified the *kamal*s to be included in a *sahai*, it was still necessary to determine how to arrange them on the ground and the order in which to announce them. Some held that the *kamal*s should be arranged in a purely geographical order, that the arrangement had no base and no crown, but simply eastern and western ends. Others argued that although the arrangement was largely geographical, certain *kamal*s had the right to claim geographically-irregular positions of prominence at the base of the arrangement.

Kamal Kehin was generally acknowledged to have been the leading *kamal* in pre-colonial times, and its *lapan* was luluai throughout the colonial period. Kehins and their supporters claimed that in the past the Kehin share in *sahai*

---

[5] This is illustrated by the relatively small amount of brideprice that families in Molou could generate (the smaller of the two payments discussed in *WT&E*: 214).

was put at the base of the Tolau line, and that this should continue. After the introduction of council government, however, the leader of Ponam's largest *kamal*, Nilo, was elected councillor, a position he held through 1984 (when a new form of local government was created). The share for Kamal Nilo fell naturally at the base of the Tolau line because Nilo had the eastern-most men's house. In conversations with us the Nilo leader took a strong geographical position. While this meant putting Nilo at the base of the Tolau line, it need not have been only self-serving, for Nilo's leader argued that if, as seemed possible, a *kamal* built a new men's house east of Nilo, then that *kamal* would be at the base and Nilo's position in the arrangement of *sahai* would be changed.

The *kamals* Lehesu, Kayeh and Mahan had common roots on a property called Sapakol, and were thus known as Sapakol I, Sapakol II and Sapakol III. Mahan forewent any claim to be the senior of these three *kamals*, and accepted its status as an off-shoot of Kayeh. However, the relative status of and historical relations between the other two *kamals* were the subject of dispute, each claiming the right to be Sapakol I. Therefore, when arranging *sahai*, most people simply designated three adjacent shares as being for Sapakol I, Sapakol II and Sapakol III, and avoided any attempt to link these three names to specific men's houses or *kamal* groups. They left it to the individual members of Kayeh and Lehesu to work out who should get which share. Sometimes Lehesu got there first and claimed the Sapakol I share and sometimes Kayeh did so.

Even if one accepted, as Ponams generally did, that the position of *kamals* should reflect their location on the island, positioning shares was not automatic, for it was not always clear where a men's house was really located. There were ambiguous cases, in which men's houses were seen to be on the wrong place on the island: they really should have been elsewhere. In these situations, the person laying out the *sahai* had to decide where to place the share of the *kamal* in question: should it be placed according to where the men's house was, or where it ought to have been? The occasion of the display forced the arranger to make a public statement, and so come down on one side or the other of what was, usually, a contentious issue. This conflict between geographic and social positions appears in the displays we describe here.

In one case the position of a *kamal*'s share was based on the position of its ancestral men's house rather than its current one. At the time of fieldwork the Buhai men's house stood in Kum. However, its ancestral land was in Tolau, it was treated as a Tolau *kamal* and in *sahai* its share was normally put in the Tolau line. But people were not sure where in the line it really belonged, because its position was not clearly marked by a men's house. Normally it was placed at the crown of the Tolau line, though some sought to commemorate (or re-assert) an old connection with Nilo by placing the Buhai share next to Nilo (that is, between the Nilo and Kehin shares).

In another case the position of a *kamal*'s share was based on the site of the hamlet in which most *kamal* members lived rather than the site on which they built their men's house or the site on which their ancestors built their first men's house. The share for Kamal Kahu was sometimes placed to the east of that for Kamal Puyu and sometimes to the west of it (compare figures 26 and 27). This shifting reflected people's ambivalence about the proper location of the Kahu men's house. In the mid-1970s Kahu's leader decided to move his men's house and hamlet back to their pre-colonial site on the eastern end of the island. His *kamal*-mates formally supported him, but tended to remain in their old village houses except when the leader came home on his holidays from work. Most Ponams followed their lead: when the leader was absent, *sahais* gave Kahu its old village site rather than the new one, where its men's house stood, a manoeuvre that amused the arrangers of these *sahais*.

It is obvious from comparing *sahai* arrangements with map 3 (p. 39), of Ponam village, that the order in which the shares were arranged was based on the location of men's houses. But it is also obvious from an investigation of the *kamals* whose placement in *sahai* was at odds with the location of their men's houses in the map, that *sahai* represented more than geography alone. And when the geography that *was*, was at odds with the geography that *should have been*, the arranger could opt for the latter instead.

We have described the implications for *sahai* of two points: all existing *kamals* were to be included; their position in the display should follow their location on the island. There was disagreement about what position was pertinent — social, political or geographical — just as there could be disagreement about what groups were *kamals*. Even so, each Ponam felt that the principles that motivated the arrangement of *sahai* ought to be uniform, ought to apply equally to all Ponam *sahais*, without regard for the personal situation of the individual making the prestation. There was, however, one element of these displays that *was* expected to reflect the personal situation of the individual laying out the display. That was the selection of the site on which it took place.

Site was important, because in choosing a site, the leader was claiming a relationship with its current owners, and perhaps its original owners as well. The funeral distributions for a man should be held outside his men's house as a mark of his relationship with that *kamal*. A married woman's funeral distributions should be held at her husband's dwelling house, as a mark of her relationship to him. Those we saw for single women (all elderly spinsters) were held at their own dwelling house, but people said that the distributions for a woman of marriageable age, in her twenties, would be held at the men's house, as a mark of her importance and the group's loss.

Although these were the appropriate sites for funeral distributions, distributions did not always take place at them. Disputes about the death often led to disputes over the control of the body, management of the funeral and the proper site for the ceremonies. The history of the *sahai* in figure 26 illustrates this. It should have been held at the door of the dead man's *kamal*'s men's house. In fact it took place at the door of his mother's natal men's house. The dead man's sister, who led the work, did this because she believed that her brother had been killed by his *kamal* ancestors, who were angry that he and some of his agnates had quarrelled about providing his mother's agnates' with a gift of land on which to build their new men's house. Ponams often held that ancestors would kill an injured party rather than a guilty one (in an attempt to force islanders to police their own morals; see A. Carrier 1989), and the leader felt that her brother's death vindicated him and proved that his agnates were wrong. By choosing to hold the funeral at their mother's agnates men's house, the sister showed that she supported her brother and her mother's agnates against those of her own agnates with whom her brother had quarrelled.

One might infer from this example that a leader who refused to hold a funeral at the deceased's own men's house could deny the connection between the dead person and his or her *kamal*-mates. However, Ponams did not see kinship as mutable in this way, so this denial could only be partial. As Ponam idiom explained it, two people joined by kinship had a road, *sal*, between them along which they could travel in order to interact. When they were separated by dispute, there was a breach, *hakeo*, in the road that prevented interaction. This had economic as well as symbolic consequences, for a breach meant no exchanges or other transactions could take place between the two parties or their kin, for there was no road by which they could reach one another, until they made a formal settlement for which ancestral blessings were invoked.

This breach is illustrated in the case just described, of the man whose funeral *sahai* took place at the door of his mother's natal men's house. One part of the mortuary ceremony was *lo pahis*, a distribution of gifts to the deceased's kindred that followed the *sahai*. In this case, the mortuary leader refused to give anything to the deceased's agnates. Instead, she gave what would have been the agnates' share to her mother's agnates. Further, she placed the share for these maternal kin at the base of the display (where shares for ego's agnates normally belonged) instead of at the crown (the normal position for maternal shares). Following this step neither the leader nor her siblings would be able to exchange directly with the now-cut-off agnates, nor would anyone else who was related to these agnates through the leader or her siblings. Thus, the choice of a site for the *sahai* was not only a symbolic gesture, but was part of a complex of symbolic, economic and political actions.

We must point out, however, that even though refusing to hold a *sahai* at the deceased's men's house constituted an effective breach of relations between the two groups of kin, it did not give the leader grounds for eliminating the deceased's *kamal* from the *sahai*. The leader who arranged the *sahai* in figure 26 had legitimate grounds for breaking off her own family's personal connection with their agnates, but she had no grounds for denying the legitimacy of their status as a *kamal*, for refusing to recognise what was commonly recognised as the Ponam social order. She had to recognise them in *sahai* and allow their leader, her principal opponent, to redistribute their share. Thus, as we pointed out in the discussion of the redistribution of Kum–Tolau, Ponams distinguished between the objective social order and the behaviour of individuals.

This distinction was also important in the redistributions that followed *sahai*. In principle a *kamal*'s share of the *sahai* distribution was received by the *kamal*'s leader, who redistributed portions to all adult sons and adult unmarried daughters of men of the *kamal*. To receive a portion of a *kamal*'s share of a *sahai* was a primary recognition that one belonged to that *kamal*. Thus, when describing how a married woman moved from her father's *kamal* to her husband's, people said she no longer received a portion of her father's *kamal*'s share of *sahai*, but instead partook jointly in her husband's portion of his *kamal*'s share of *sahai*. People usually qualified this explanation, however, saying that if the *kamal*'s share in the *sahai* were large enough, then married daughters could receive some of it as well. This was perfectly possible, as nothing prevented anyone from accepting from more than one source.

In spite of this principle that the *kamal*'s share in a *sahai* went to its members, it did not always go to all *kamal* members, and often it went to outsiders. Because receiving a portion affirmed a link and created an obligation to the *kamal*, leaders could use the redistribution to shape relations between leaders and followers within the *kamal*, snubbing those with whom they were in dispute and recruiting support from others. Also, leaders could use the distribution of a *kamal*'s share to influence relations between *kamal*s. This was particularly important for those small *kamal*s, such as Toloso'on, that needed the support of others in order to avoid extinction or fusion into another *kamal*.

◆ ◆ ◆ ◆

Here we have described the way that Ponams represented two types of groups, moieties and *kamal*s, in the course of the distribution of gifts in their ceremonial exchange. This has allowed us to introduce these displays as a feature of exchange, to demonstrate some of the principles that governed their organisation and to show how display was a form of self-representation. Although relatively simple, these displays clearly represented notions of structure of the sort that Meyer Fortes would recognise, an abstract genealogical and geographical social order that existed independently of the political and other social processes that went on in the context of that structure.

The kinds of social representations that people make in exchange need not take this structural form. An alternative form appears in Frederick Errington's description of a mortuary prestation in the Duke of York Islands:

> the sponsors, each followed by his supporters, seek out other big men with whom they wish to initiate an exchange. The sponsor begins the prestation by dropping a large piece of divara [shell wealth] in front of the recipient, and his followers contribute smaller pieces. Later lesser men lead smaller processions to recipients of their choice (Errington 1974: 230).

This type of prestation illustrates not genealogical structures, but the power of big men to form coalitions of followers for the purpose of prestation, and this form of representation is appropriate to the processual view of society that Errington said was held there (1974: 25).

Although the form of self-representation that Ponams used was clearly a structural one, embodying an abstract version of official kinship, we need to repeat that Ponams were also well aware of other kinds of social processes that influenced action and that were often at odds with the structures represented in these displays. Thus, Ponams recognised a discrepancy between the *kamals* as conceptual categories that were represented in *sahai* displays and the sets of people who actually received a share of which *kamal's* food. Their recognition of this discrepancy between the imperatives of their collective structure and the contingencies of their individual situations is, perhaps, best illustrated in the description of the funeral exchange in which the leader included her agnates in one form of distribution, the *sahai* that represented Ponam social order as a whole, but omitted those agnates from the display that represented her own relations with her kin.

Having introduced the nature and operation of these displays, we will look in more detail at the relation between structured representations of social order and the processes that led to their creation. We will do so by describing how Ponams represented kindreds in displays, our task in the next chapter.

CHAPTER SIX

The representation
of kindreds in exchange

We have described how distributions to Ponam as a community were arranged in displays that mapped *kamals* and moieties, the two elements of their kinship structure most clearly contained in village geography. Ponams also arranged the displays of contributions to, and distributions made by, individuals, and these displays represented other key elements in the social order. These individual-focused displays used genealogy instead of geography as their organising theme. In these prestations, piles of gifts represented not *kamals* and moieties, but *ken sis*, stocks of people descended from a common male or female ancestor, and the arrangement of the piles represented the genealogical relations among *ken sis* as the stocks of an individual's kindred. Ponams could read these displays just as anthropologists can read genealogical diagrams, seeing in them relationships of ascent, descent and siblingship. In this chapter we will describe these displays and the ways that they reflected both structural principles and individual contingency. First we will describe the general nature of these displays and some of their structural properties, looking especially at the effect of the succession of generations on the stocks represented in display. After this, we will look at the ways that individual contingency shaped the displays that people made.

The assertion that relations among Ponam kin were represented as genealogical relations sounds trivial and almost tautological, but as we noted in the introduction, the point of much of the analysis of kinship in Melanesia is that it is not tautological. People do not inevitably think of kinship as a genealogical structure. On the contrary, it is quite possible to organise relations among people who happen to be biological kin in ways that are not genealogical in the sense that we mean, and to make relations other than genealogical ones the most important for organising exchange. The ceremonial exchange systems that have been described in Papua New Guinea do not often seem to use genealogy in the very thorough-going way that Ponams did, and do not make genealogical representations a central feature of gift prestations and distributions. Thus, the focus on genealogical relations that was so pronounced in Ponam exchange is neither inevitable nor commonplace, but instead constitutes a marked attention on the part of islanders to a particular form of understanding social relations that is in no way universal. The fact that this genealogical approach resembles the way that Western anthropologists were trained to envision kinship (though it is not identical to it) does not make the Ponam vision a trivial one.

Indeed, it was Ponams' preoccupation with genealogy, with this formal, abstract principle of social structure, that inspired our focus on the relation between structure and process. While Ponams were certainly aware of the processual side of life, this was, in a sense, the epiphenomenal side of life. To them, real life and the real facts about Ponam society were contained in these fixed genealogical structures and rules, and not in the negotiations and social processes that were an inevitable part of life in the mortal world.[1]

This was brought home to us once when we were watching the arrangement of a display of gifts for a major affinal prestation. One of the men involved suddenly lost his temper and began shouting and hacking apart one of the gifts, a wooden bed, with his axe. The old man who had been explaining events to us turned and said of this most unusual and impressive display of temper, 'Don't write this down; it's not true.' We do not think his choice of words was accidental. He could have said, 'It's not good; it's not moral; it is disgraceful', which was true. He also could have said, 'Look at him. See how he is showing off and trying to impress his elder brother', which was also true. But what he said was that this event was not *true*. It did not represent what Ponam society was really like. And in a sense, he was quite correct.

We argued in previous chapters that a purely structural approach to kinship and exchange is insufficient because it cannot account for the significance of structures, the way they operate in daily life and the way they change over time. These things need to be explained in terms of processes, and thus far we have looked in particular at historical processes. Nevertheless, the models of social structure that we have described in previous chapters, and that Ponams assumed to be real, did have a tremendous influence on people, and especially on the ceremonial exchanges that dominated their lives in so many ways. They were not simply epiphenomenal, reified abstractions from experience; nor were they an isolated realm of culture independent of behaviour. They were, in important ways, "true". They should not, in other words, be separated from social practices in the way that some processualist anthropologists argued and in the way that some structuralist anthropologists presumed.

---

[1] Ponams were not unique in their structural orientation. For example, researchers who have attempted to elicit women's life-histories in Melanesia frequently find that these women present themselves in terms of what we would call structural principles. That is, they present themselves in terms of the cultural principles of woman-hood, rather than in terms of a biography of personal choice and contingency (e.g. Keesing 1985, 1987*b*; Young 1983; this issue is addressed more generally in Errington & Gewertz 1987*b*).

$$
\begin{array}{ll}
\text{B} & \text{FM}^{11} \\
\text{A} & \text{M}^{10} \\
9 & \text{FFFZ}^{9} \\
8 & \text{FFFB}^{8} \\
7 & \text{FFZ}^{7} \\
6 & \text{FFB}^{6} \\
5 & \text{FZ}^{5} \\
4 & \text{FB}^{4} \\
3 & \text{Z}^{3} \\
2 & \text{B}^{2} \\
1 & \text{Ego}^{1}
\end{array}
$$

house

Figure 29   *Hypothetical display of contributions from a person's kindred*

Note: In this and following illustrations of gift displays, superscript characters indicate the order in which gifts were announced.

INDIVIDUAL-FOCUSED DISPLAYS

Ponams put genealogy at the centre of exchanges between individuals. They expected that gifts would be accumulated and distributed only through pre-defined genealogical networks, and the central event of every prestation and distribution was the display of gifts in a manner representing these genealogies. These prestations were displayed and presented in a way that stressed the giver's and recipient's positions within and dependence on a genealogical network, a kindred. As one would expect, however, this genealogical network was not structured in the same way as that normally used by English speakers. Ponam genealogies were structured using the relationships described in chapter 1. In that chapter our ancestor-focused description showed how *ken sis* (sets of people with a common ancestor) were created and linked together through the three relationships of *kamal*, line-of-the-woman and line-of-the-man. However, in the process of accumulating and distributing gifts (or labour or other forms of assistance) individuals inverted this perspective, and re-presented kin relations from the ego-focus instead, as a kindred whose various stocks were related to ego as *kamal*-mates, line-of-the-woman or line-of-the-man. This representation appeared in the displays of contributions from or distributions to an individual's kin. There, the gifts were arranged on the ground in a pattern that represented the genealogical relations within the individual's kindred in just the same way that distributions to the community were arranged in patterns that represented the spatial relations of *kamal*s and moieties in the village. We want to show this first with an idealised illustration.

There were a variety of ways that Ponams arranged these displays. However, they all had a common structure. Figure 29 shows in hypothetical form one common pattern for the arrangement of the display of gifts being contributed by or distributed to an individual's kindred. We shall describe this as a display of contributions to an imaginary man, but exactly the same type of display could be used in distribution as well, and in prestations led by a woman. The gifts in this display are arranged in a single line before the main door of the leader's house. The line includes a number of piles of gifts, each contributed by a separate stock, or *ken si*, within the leader's kindred. The display of gifts for kindreds such as this one was thus completely different from those described in the last chapter. *Kamal*s were not represented in these prestations, except perhaps as maximal *ken si*s; moieties did not appear at all; no distinction was made between male and female recipients.

The line begins with gifts from the *ken si*s that are most closely related to the leader through his own patriline. At the base of the line is the gift accumulated by the leader himself (if the leader were married, as was typical, the bulk of this gift would be contributions by his affines). As one proceeds up the line toward the crown there are gifts from ever more distantly-related stocks: first, the leader's siblings (usually arranged in birth order); then, father's siblings (usually arranged by birth order within genders). Often these father's siblings were long dead, but the gifts were still presented in their names. They were collected from the father's siblings' children (and possibly affines if any children happened to remain unmarried). Following the gifts from father's siblings come gifts from father's father's siblings, and so on, for as many generations as necessary to reach the founder of ego's own *kamal*, and to reach beyond, to include other *kamal*s affiliated with his own, usually through ancient ties of patronage or common origin. After all of the gifts from patrilateral kin come those from people who are related to the leader as line-of-the-man, that is, his maternal kin, father's maternal kin, and occasionally, father's father's maternal kin.

This pattern, gifts arranged in a single line, was used only when a small number of gifts was given or during brideprice prestations, for then gifts were hung up on a single, long rope. On other occasions the display was usually broken up into a number of different lines. However, the gifts were still announced by the speaker in the order described here, proceeding through the leader's patrilateral kin from closest to most distantly related, and then to his matrilateral kin.

These lines of gifts represent a kind of genealogical tree. This image was explicit. As was the case with the displays we discussed in chapter 5, the end of the ego-focused display that was nearest the house was called *ken*, the base of a tree, and the end farthest away was called *pehen*, the crown or canopy of a tree. As one moves from the base to the crown one moves progressively farther away from the leader, whose gift is at the base. The relationship between those at the base and crown was described by the same metaphor used in English,

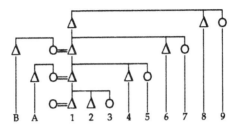

Figure 30   *Genealogy of* ken sis *in figure 29*

that of distance. The kin whose gifts are adjacent to ego's are his close kin, *lowa maraferin*, while others are progressively more distant, *lowa mafun*.

The genealogical relations among these hypothetical groups are illustrated in figure 30, the numbers and letters on the genealogy corresponding to the numbered and lettered gifts in figure 29. The manner in which the genealogy is illustrated here is different from the bilateral branching tree genealogy appropriate for representing English kinship, for it is derived from the representations that Ponams made in their gift displays. We use this form for presenting genealogies in this chapter and the next.

KAHUWE TABAC:
THE RETURN PRESTATION FOR AN ENGAGEMENT

Having described the representation of kindreds in the abstract, we now want to illustrate the display and prestation of gifts in an affinal prestation in a more concrete way, by investigating the accumulation and distribution of a single prestation, a *kahuwe tabac*. This was the return prestation for a gift of tobacco and money that opened the road (*aribihi sal*) for an engagement. This prestation was not a complex one, nor was it trivial. On the contrary it was ordinary, illustrating what most prestations were like most of the time.

Our description will show that the arrangement of gifts in genealogical diagrams was the central activity of the prestation. This was true of almost all Ponam prestations. On a few occasions of particular importance, such as brideprice, marriage and occasionally funerals, people decorated and danced and did things that were not merely instrumental to the process of gift accumulation and distribution. But for most prestations the accumulation and distribution of gifts was the focal event, as they were in this case.

Further, our description will help clarify and qualify the structural picture of the nature of Ponam kin relations that we have presented in previous chapters and that informed our hypothetical sketch of the structured way that these relations were represented in display. Although our concrete illustration will modify this structural picture, it will become clear that these structures were real for Ponams, as the old man indicated. However, they were not over-whelming forces that determined what Ponams did in exchange. Instead, they provided a framework of expectation and meaning. While this framework certainly influenced people's actions, it also provided them with the means by which they could comment on their relations with their various relatives. These relations were not just an expression of that formal structure. They also were the result of contingency, of who had squabbled with whom, of who wanted to express special concern for whom and the like. To make this point, we will describe prestations in detail in this chapter, rather than presenting them in a synoptic way. Synoptic presentation may be useful for illustrating general principles or recurrent patterns, but greater detail is necessary in order to show the nature and force of contingency.

As we will present them, these contingencies are largely personal. How-ever, it is important to bear in mind that squabbles, concerns and the like take their shape in a broader historical setting, as new values and opportunities appear and old ones disappear. Thus, in the first prestation we describe, the early pregnancy of the woman that precipitated the marriage of which the prestation was a part was more likely as a result of changes in gender relations and sexual practices of the sort we described in chapter 2. Likewise, the elimin-ation of this woman's half-brother from the prestation was made easier by the fact that, while *her* mother was a Ponam, *his* mother was a Tolai. The marriage between their father and the Tolai was made possible by the labour migration that occurred in the twentieth century.

In the first week of January 1986, Philip Kemou's family brought a gift of tobacco and money to open the road for his engagement to 18-year-old Sowa-hanu Tapo, who had given birth to his son just three weeks before. Sowahanu's parents were delighted to accept, for this was the best possible outcome for their daughter's injudicious pregnancy. This opening gift included ten one-pound blocks of twist tobacco, worth K178, and K200 in cash.

Sowahanu's parents discussed the distribution of this gift privately that evening. Initially, her father, Michael Tapo, divided it in half, keeping five blocks and K100 for himself and his family, and giving 5 blocks and K100 to his wife, Julie Pipohok. However, she kept only three blocks of tobacco and K80 for her family, and returned the rest.

Julie Pipohok described this manoeuvre with a great sense of pride and originality, as though this were their own idea and not a culturally-prescribed formula. But in fact this was a very common solution to a persistently-felt ambiguity. Convention held that the bulk of the goods in any prestation went to the patrilateral kin of the person concerned, and not to the matrilateral kin. However, couples often told us that this was unfair, especially in the case of a daughter's marriage payments. When we discussed distributions of marriage

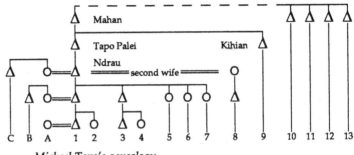

Figure 31   *Michael Tapo's genealogy*

Note: A line of dashes represents a connection other than one of true
siblingship.

prestations with parents of the bride, they said things like 'I don't feel that this
is right. The mother should get more. She looks after the daughter all her life,
and yet she doesn't get much. But that is our custom.' The strategy by which
the loving and generous husband offered half of the gift to his wife, and the
dutiful wife, mindful of custom and appreciative of the brideprice paid to her
family, returned all but about a third of the total, seems to have been a
satisfying way of resolving this recurring conflict.

Having arranged this between themselves, they proceeded the next day
to divide the money and tobacco among their kin. Because of a dispute with his
son, Michael Tapo gave him none of the money and tobacco. The son and
daughter had different mothers (the daughter's from Ponam, the son's from
near Rabaul), which made it possible to exclude the son from his sister's affairs.
But this exclusion led several of Michael Tapo's closest agnates to refuse to
accept the tobacco offered to them. Despite admonitions from the rest of his
kin, Tapo stuck to his original decision and announced that he would go ahead
and make the return prestation without their help. This took place about three
weeks after the initial prestation.

At about mid-morning on the appointed day, the kin who had accepted a
share of the money and tobacco that opened the engagement began to come in
groups bringing the gifts that they had put together earlier in the morning,
while Michael Tapo stood in front of the door of his house, watching, waiting
and helping. As with all other return prestations (*kahu*), this one included only
raw food, primarily rice, with some sago. The bride and her mother did not
welcome the contributors, for the bride was still in seclusion following the birth
of her first child and her mother stayed with her. The contributions were not
in a haphazard arrangement, but were deliberately set out in three lines of
discrete piles.

Once all the expected contributions had arrived, the display was complete. Then the bride's father announced (*polangai*) to the assembled company

C	Kuluah Pakou (FMB)[7]		
7	Sowapulo (FZ)[6]	13	Aluf Ndrakolok[13]
6	Asaf Ndrau (FZ)[5]	12	Mwaka[12]
5	Aluf Ndrau (FZ)[4]	11	Sapakol II[11]
4	Sakati (FBD)[3,a]	10	Sapakol I[10]
2	Sowahanu (Z)[2]	9	Kihian (FFFB)[9]
1	Michael Tapo (ego)[1,b]	8	Ndrau Salin (FFB)[8]

B   Pisa'oh (M)[14]

Michael Tapo's house

Figure 32   *Accumulation of* kahu *for engagement prestation*

a Michael Tapo's FBS's descendants refused to accept tobacco. His FBD's descendants took their place.

b The bride's brother should have led this prestation and his gift should have gone at the base of the display. The bride's mother's gift was included with Michael Tapo's instead of being placed separately as it would have been if her son had led the work.

(most of whom were sitting in the shade around the clearing in front of his house) the name of the *ken sis*, or stocks, that had contributed to him. He did so by walking deliberately through the display, pausing briefly beside each pile as he called out the name of its contributor. He began with his own gift and concluded with his mother's.

Figure 31 gives a genealogy of the groups involved. Michael Tapo's *kamal*, Mahan, included three companies. One company was descended from Mahan's second son, Kihian. The other two were descended from each of the two wives of Ndrau, who was Mahan's grandson through his first-born son, Tapo Palei (who was Michael Tapo's great-grandfather). Therefore, the ancestral Tapo's descendants were divided into two companies: Ndrau Salin (Right Ndrau), the descendants of Ndrau and his first wife, and Ndrau Kamau (Left Ndrau), the descendants of Ndrau and his second wife.

Figure 32 represents the display, which included in the left line the gifts from Michael Tapo's own company, Ndrau Salin, and from Ndrau's first wife. The centre included the gifts of Ndrau Kamau and Kihian, the other two companies of Kamal Mahan. At the end of that line were gifts of other groups associated with Kamal Mahan: Kamals Sapakol I and Sapakol II, which shared origins with Mahan, and two other groups that were once Mahan's dependents. The third line included only a gift from Michael Tapo's maternal kin.

Once Michael Tapo finished his announcements his kin began to take apart the display and put the gifts in a single heap bearing Michael Tapo's name, to be carried to the groom's house. As they did this, two of his kinsmen stood up to speak. Both his FZS and his MZS spoke briefly, quietly and even-temperedly about his dispute with his son, reminding him of the importance of good family relations and getting the marriage off to a good start. Their restraint was typical of Ponam rhetoric, the mildest speeches being reserved for

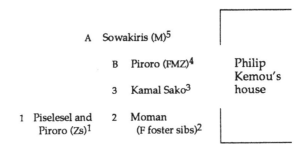

A   Sowakiris (M)[5]

    B   Piroro (FMZ)[4]

    3   Kamal Sako[3]

1   Piselesel and   2   Moman
   Piroro (Zs)[1]   (F foster sibs)[2]

Philip
Kemou's
house

Figure 33   *Distribution of* kahuwe tabac

Note: The base of this display was not parallel to the house door, but at right angles to it.

the most serious occasions. They gave no hint that they had worked through the night to prevent disaster. They had worked to calm the groom's kin, Michael Tapo's would-be affines, some of whom were so angry with what they saw as Michael Tapo's pig-headedness that they threatened to demand their engagement gift back, or at least refuse the *kahu*. But Michael Tapo took no notice of these speeches, his other kin went on piling up the gift, and after the two men had had their say they all carried the gift to Philip Kemou's house.

Once they had put the food down outside Philip Kemou's house, Michael Tapo's relatives retired into the shade, and the groom's father, Chris Pelekai, came out of his house to speak. He thanked Michael Tapo and his kin for the *kahu*, then announced that he had some extra gifts to give. The first was a conventional present to the man who had been go-between in the marriage negotiations. This man was Sowahanu's FZS and Philip Kemou's FMFBDSS (his *nato-*, brother). The second gift, he announced with pride, was an extra K170 and two blocks of tobacco for Michael Tapo. It was not customary to do this, he said, but it was a mark of his pleasure. Then he motioned to his family to bring out a gift of cooked food, called *njomis*, and handed Tapo the gift of twist tobacco that went with it. Tapo said thank you, but did not make a speech. Neither of them mentioned the dispute in Tapo's family, despite the fact that it had been the most compelling topic of conversation in the village all morning.

The *njomis*, the gift of cooked food that Chris Pelekai presented to Michael Tapo and his kin, included 63 dishes of cooked food, a number of kettles and flasks of tea, and twenty sticks of tobacco, with a value of approximately K100. Recipients of a large prestation always gave this, as a kind of compensation for the hard work that had gone into accumulating it. Often *njomis* was redistributed on the spot, to be eaten while watching the recipients worry over the problem of how to redistribute their gift. But this time rain was threatening and everyone wanted to get home. So the bride's family snatched up the dishes of cooked food, rushed back to her father's house thirty metres

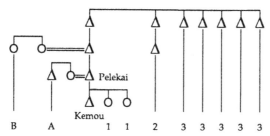

Figure 34   *Philip Kemou's genealogy*

away and quickly distributed it to the major groups of contributors, managing to announce the distribution just as the squall broke.

When the rain ended, Philip Kemou's family began the distribution. This was normally more difficult than the accumulation, when the responsibility for remembering the links that bound the kindred with the prestation's leader was diffused among the various would-be contributors. However, in a distribution this responsibility rested only on the leader and his or her advisers, who had to remember all the appropriate kin and had to consider the state of relations with each of them. Thus, while the job of the person accumulating contributions was not easy, it was much less fraught with risk than the job of arranging a distribution, for here all the responsibility for difficult decisions, with possibly long-lasting consequences, bore down on a small group of people.

Philip Kemou's father and mother looked at the pile of food they had been given and talked over what they would do. Philip Kemou's two married sisters and his FZD began to arrange the bags of rice into piles as his parents directed, marking each group to which they would give. Once they had decided on an arrangement of piles, they began to distribute the remaining food among them. As they did so they frequently stopped to check their distribution against the record book they had made of the original prestation of engagement tobacco, for ideally the return gift should be a just reciprocation for the gift received (which made this much easier than the distribution of an initial prestation). When the arrangement of the display was completed, Chris Pelekai announced the distribution and the recipients quickly removed their gifts.

Figure 33 shows the arrangement of the distribution, and figure 34 the genealogy of the recipients. Philip Kemou's sisters led this distribution, though as women they did not speak. The left line included their gift only, for Chris Pelekai and his children were the only remaining members of their company within Kamal Sako. The right line included gifts for other groups of Philip Kemou's kindred: first, a gift for the company that had fostered his father when he was orphaned as a child; second, a gift for the remaining companies of the *kamal*; third, a gift for his FMZ, his FM's only sibling. Philip Kemou's mother's gift was placed rather indeterminately between these two lines.

G

The bride's and the groom's displays were led by and focused on individuals rather than groups, as was true of all the accumulations of gifts, and of all distributions in affinal exchange. In many parts of Papua New Guinea affinal prestations are managed by clans, so that the clan, under the leadership of its senior members, corporately accumulates a gift and presents it to another corporate clan, a situation that stresses the subsumption of individuals by larger groups and hence betokens the power of those groups (Lederman 1986; O'Hanlon 1989). This was not the case on Ponam, as *kamal*s did not manage exchanges made on behalf of their members. Instead, prestations were led by the individual or set of siblings most immediately concerned. In the two cases we have just described, the prestations were led by, and displays focused on, the bride's father (in default of her brother) and the groom's sisters.

The individual at the focus of an accumulation or distribution received from and gave to a largely pre-determined structure of stocks within his or her kindred. The contributors and recipients were related to the leader as members of particular kin groups, rather than as friends or clients or even as members of terminological categories such as *asis* or *tamas*. As we described in chapter 2, this is different from the pre-War exchange pattern. Because, at that earlier time, *lapan*s both led *kamal*s and dominated the affinal exchanges made on behalf of *kamal* members, exchanges then were much more nearly the business of corporate *kamal*s. This was so much so that the idea that *kamal*s would exchange women made sense, as it did not in the 1980s.

We now turn to another aspect of the organisation and representation of kindreds, by comparing the displays arranged for two closely-related individuals, a man and his brother's son. Because these two individuals were a generation apart, this comparison will show how the composition of kindreds and the *ken sis* belonging to them shifted over the course of generations, even when the people actually participating were largely the same in both cases.

CHANGES IN DISPLAYS OVER GENERATIONS

Here we describe two similar affinal prestations. The first was an unusual prestation made in 1982 on behalf of Sepat Kaso of Kamal Kosohi to his affines. The second was a brideprice, *njakenjak*, given in 1981 on behalf of Sepat Kaso's brother's son, Tony Kakaw. (As will become apparent shortly, the fact that Tony Kakaw was Sepat Kaso's brother's son, rather than son, does not prevent using these two prestations for analysing changes in displays over generations.) For these prestations we will describe the display of accumulated gifts from each man's kindreds and the display of the *njomis* distributed to them. As we have done previously in this chapter, our representations of these displays are keyed to a genealogy. However, in this case the genealogy includes both Sepat Kaso and Tony Kakaw. This genealogy was provided by Michael Nakaw, Sepat Kaso's elder brother, the *lapan* of Kamal Kosohi. Michael Nakaw did not arrange these displays on his own, and there was disagreement and uncertainty about the exact connections among *ken sis* in the distant past, which accounts for some of the variations among the different displays. However, they are similar in their handling of the shift of focus from one generation to another. This genealogy centres on Tony Kakaw, and it is present in figure 35, on page 174, which is rotated on the page so that senior generations are to the left of juniors, rather than above them. In it, Tony Kakaw is shown as "Tony" in line 1 and Sepat Kaso is line 6.

We said that the first prestation was unusual, and we want to describe its background before analysing the display involved. This prestation seems to have been devised specifically to deal with a dispute within the family. In January 1981, Pimeses, Sepat Kaso's daughter, fell ill and died suddenly in Rabaul. Her Papuan husband and her kin in Rabaul chartered a plane to bring her body home for burial. Like any sudden death of a young person, this caused great distress, particularly to her parents, and there was much debate about its cause. One early suggestion, for example, was that she had been killed by the notoriously quick-tempered and vengeful Tolai sorcerers after an argument about a game of cards. But her parents believed that the cause of death lay nearer home. Whatever the truth of the matter, this cause was ultimately most important for the village, because her parents stuck to it and refused to allow her body to be placed in the Kosohi men's house for mourning. (In normal circumstances, as we said previously, this is where her body should have lain before burial.) The dispute raged on, delaying the funeral prestations, and her father threatened to dissociate himself from his own *kamal* and affiliate with his wife's kin instead.

In order to forestall this, Sepat Kaso's brother, Michael Nakaw, made a large prestation to Sepat Kaso's affines, primarily at the urging of the two men's children, who were trying to heal the breach. Sepat Kaso was not involved in his *kamal's* part in the proceedings, as he would have been in more ordinary circumstances. Instead, throughout he remained firmly with his wife's kin, the recipients of the prestation. This prestation was considered a just and amicable way to try to smooth over this dispute, but it was not conventional and normally would never have been made. Pimeses's husband should have given *rovwel* to her kin, and Pimeses's maternal kin should have given *lutung* to her *tamatus* (as they did), but her paternal kin had no conventional obligation to give to anyone. They made a prestation simply because it was politically, and perhaps morally, appropriate to do so. People had different opinions about what name we should record for this prestation (we were the only ones who were obliged to call it anything). Some said that it was a *rovwel*, but it was being

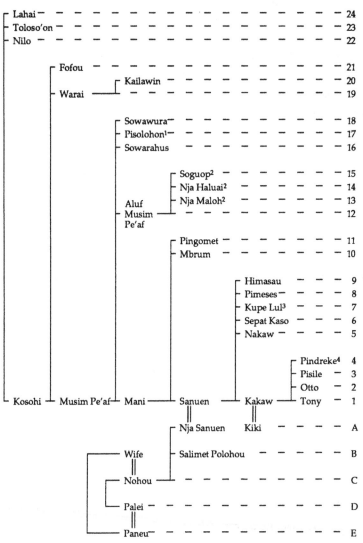

Figure 35   *Genealogy of Sepat Kaso and Tony Kakaw*

1 Pisolohon's only living descendant was more closely related to Kosohi through other roads and did not participate in her name.

2 Soguop, Nja Maloh and Nja Haluai married to Ponam from Sori Island. They were *kawas* to Aluf Musim Pe'af and other Kosohis, who had Sori relatives. This connection was still remembered.

3 Kupe Lul was away from Ponam during Pimeses's funeral.

4 Because of a dispute, Pindreke did not participate in Tony Kakaw's brideprice.

made by Pimeses's father's kin because her Papuan husband could not make it. Other said that it couldn't be a *rovwel*, it had to be something more like the long-abandoned *masaf* instead. Still others said that it didn't have a name, and that it didn't matter that it didn't have a name.

13,	Soguop and				
15	Nja Maloh[7]	21	Fofou[14]		
12,	Aluf Musim				
14	Pe'af and	22,	Nilo and		
	Nja Haluai[6]	23	Toloso'on[13]		
11	Pingomet (FZ)[5]	18	Sowawura[12]		
10	Mbrum (FB)[4]	16	Sowarahus (FFZ)[11]	E	Paneu (MB)[18]
9	Himasau (Z)[3]	20	Kailawin (FFBS)[10]	C	Nohou (MB)[17]
8	Pimeses (Z)[2]	19	Warai (FFB)[9]	D	Palei (MFB)[16]
1	Kakaw (B)[1]	5	Nakaw (B)[8]	B	Salimet Polohou (MZ)[15]

men's house

Figure 36   *Accumulation for Sepat Kaso's prestation*

The contributions to Sepat Kaso from his kindred are shown in figure 36. These contributions were arranged in three lines. On the left were contributions from the various *ken sis* of Sepat Kaso's own company within Kamal Kosohi. Because Sepat Kaso sided with his wife and contributed none of his own wealth, the display began not as it should have, with his own contribution, but with the contributions from his siblings. It then proceeded through the contributions from his father's siblings, his father's father's sisters and other women linked to his family. In the central line were contributions from the other companies of Kamal Kosohi and other *kamals* affiliated with it. The most unusual feature of this is that Michael Nakaw's gift was placed in this central line, rather than in the left line. The third line, on the right side of the display, included gifts from Sepat Kaso's maternal kin, broken down into different stocks, a procedure that was reasonably common in large prestations.

As part of this prestation, contributors received *njomis*, cooked food. This was arranged in a display by Michael Nakaw, Sepat Kaso's brother. This is presented in figure 37. At first glance this display looks very different from the display of contributions in figure 36, but it is not so very different in detail. It was inverted right to left: the gifts for Sepat Kaso's own company were on the right instead of the left, the gifts for the other companies of the *kamal* stayed in the centre, the gift for his maternal kin were on the left instead of the right. The gifts for Fofou (21 in figure 35) and the Sori Island *kawas* of Aluf Musim Pe'af (12–15 in figure 35), two of the oddly-affiliated groups, had been moved out of the line for other companies and into the line for Nakaw's own company. Toloso'on was forgotten, causing a minor row, and Sepat Kaso's mother's kin were given a single share instead of several.

For our purpose here, the important fact about both these displays is that they began with Sepat Kaso's own generation. That is to say, although he and his siblings had numerous adult children, none of them gave or received in their own names. Instead, the members of this junior generation were linked to

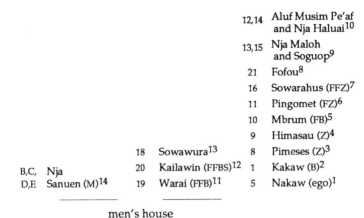

men's house

Figure 37   *Distribution of* njomis *to Sepat Kaso's kindred*

Sepat Kaso only on the roads of their fathers and mothers, and participated only as members of the stocks linked to Sepat Kaso through those men and women. It is this fact that makes it possible for us to compare displays for this prestation with displays for Tony Kakaw (Sepat Kaso's brother's son) as a way of investigating changes between generations: though these two presentations took place only about a year apart, they were a full generation apart in their orientation.

Sepat Kaso and all of his siblings had identical kindreds, and consequently the display of distributions by or contributions to any of these siblings would, all things being equal, be essentially the same. However, the children of these men and women did not have identical kindreds, and their displays would be different from one another's and from their parents'. The following examples of the display of gifts from Tony Kakaw's kindred for his brideprice, and the distribution of *njomis* to them, show this.

In January 1980, Tony Kakaw, a public servant in the national capitol, came home to pay brideprice for his wife Teresia Pindramolat. There were no unusual quarrels to mar this, though Tony Kakaw had a long-standing quarrel with his mother and his sister that led to their exclusion from the celebrations. The gifts given in Tony Kakaw's mother's name in fact came from her brother.

Figure 38 shows the arrangement of contributions of cash given by Tony Kakaw's kin. (Refer to figure 35, page 174, for Tony Kakaw's genealogy.) The money that each stock gave to a brideprice was always sealed in an envelope on which was written the donor's name and the amount of the gift enclosed. The envelopes were then pegged onto a long rope hung up before the men's house door for all to see, before being taken down and re-hung at the door of the wife's father's men's house. This form of display involved only one line instead of three, and as a result the principles of arranging stocks in terms

A	Kiki (M)[21]
B-E	Kupe Lul and Nja
	Sanuen (F unmarried B and FM)[20]
24	Lahai[19]
18	Sowawura[18]
22	Nilo[17]
23	Toloso'on[16]
19	Warai (FFFB)[15]
20	Kailawin (FFFBS)[14]
21	Fofou[13]
14	Nja Haluai[12]
12	Aluf Musim Pe'af (FFFZ)
13	& Nja Maloh
16	Sowarahus[11]
15	Soguop[10]
11	Pingomet (FFZ)[9]
10	Mbrum (FFB)[8]
6	Sepat Kaso (FB)[7]
9	Himasau (FZ)[6]
8	Pimeses (FZ)[5]
5	Nakaw (FB)[4]
3	Pisile (Z)[3]
2	Otto (B)[2]
1	Tony (ego)[1]

men's house

Figure 38   *Tony Kakaw's brideprice display*

of their genealogical distance from ego is more clearly apparent here than in displays where gifts were laid out in several lines. At the base of the line were gifts from the groom's own company, followed by those from the other companies of his *kamal* and from distantly related *kamal*s, and then by gifts from maternal kin.

The distribution of *njomis* to Tony Kakaw's kin (figure 39) was dishes of food arranged into four lines, instead of envelopes of money arranged in one. On the far right was a single gift for his mother's kin, announced last as the superscript number indicates. Next to that was a line of gifts for his own siblings and father's siblings, announced first. In the third line were gifts for the other companies of Kamal Kosohi, and for the various distantly-related groups. And in the line on the far left were gifts for the stocks peripherally attached to Tony Kakaw's own company.

				7	Kupe Lul (FB)[8]			
		21	Fofou[15]	9	Himasau (FZ)[7]			
14	Nja Haluai[19]	18	Sowawura[14]	8	Pimeses (FZ)[6]			
12,	Aluf Musim	16	Sowarahus[13]	6	Sepat Kaso[5]			
13	Pe'af and	11	Pingomet (FFZ)[12]	5	Nakaw (FB)[4]			
	Nja Maloh[18]	19	Warai (FFFB)[11]	2	Otto (B)[3]			
24	Lahai[17]	20	Kailawin (FFFBS)[10]	1	Tony (ego)[2]			
15	Soguop[16]	10	Mbrum (FFB)[9]	3	Pisile (Z)[1]	A	Kiki (M)[20]

men's house

Figure 39   *Tony Kakaw's njomis*

In these prestations the gifts at the base, the first gifts to be announced, were those from Tony Kakaw and his siblings. None of these people were involved directly, in their own names, in Sepat Kaso's displays. Instead, they had shared a single gift given in the name of their father, Kakaw. Kakaw, however, had no name in this display, focused on his son Tony, nor did any of his lineal ascendents. He had been superseded by his children in the process that we referred to in our discussion of the logical structure of Ponam affinal exchange in chapter 3.

The introduction of three new names into the base of this display, Tony, Otto and Pisile Kakaw, was not matched by the exclusion of three old names from the crown. Rather, the number of gifts given and received had increased. Ponams did not perceive, however, that this number would continue to increase forever. They said that all of those who were linked to ego through men should be remembered indefinitely. However, they said that those linked through women would not endure. As we described in chapter 1, those linked as line-of-the-man (which is to say, maternal kin) usually remained for only about two generations. Sepat Kaso's maternal kin participated in his prestation, but not his FM's kin. Tony Kakaw's mother's kin and his father's mother's kin participated, but not his FFM's. Those related as line-of-the-woman endured for somewhat longer, but only until the connection was superseded by a new marriage linking the woman's descendants to ego and his or her siblings (see our discussion of this at the end of chapter 3). Thus, neither Tony Kakaw nor Sepat Kaso received gifts from the descendants of Pisolohon (line 17 in figure 35), for those descendants were more closely related by another route and no longer gave in her name. In Ponams' view the same fate would befall all line-of-the-woman eventually.

DISPLAY AS SOCIAL COMMENTARY

Our discussion of the prestation for Sepat Kaso and for Tony Kakaw illustrates the genealogical principles involved in the arrangement of contributions and distributions. As we said, however, these principles were not a mechanistic constraint that determined the shape of display. Instead, they were a form of communication. While the rules of that form inevitably constrained Ponams, also they allowed (and even obliged) people to express themselves. We now want to consider this aspect of display, by looking at how these arrangements could be used to comment on or represent the way that actual relations deviated from the ideal. It is obvious that genealogy provided the framework for the relations between participants in exchange, as in so much else of life. It is equally obvious, however, that people did not inevitably cooperate with their kin in the prescribed manner. Disputes between kin, particularly between siblings and *kamal*-mates, were endemic. As we have already described, when a dispute occurred between two people or groups, they did not exchange with one another, and this failure to exchange was apparent in the arrangement of prestations.[2]

Because people involved in exchange were obliged to make displays, they were obliged by the genealogical conventions of display to make public those conflicts that they might have preferred to keep private, though not actually secret — secrecy being virtually impossible in this small open village. O'Hanlon's (1983, 1989) description of Wahgi dance displays, discussed in chapter 5, stresses the importance of this revelatory aspect of display, an importance manifest in the dancers' compulsive concern with the revelation of "betrayal" in the appearance of the dancing men. Ponams were not frightened that weakness would be revealed through betrayal. This was because the units involved in Ponam exchange were not fixed, competitive groups vulnerable to betrayal to like groups, but individuals trying to balance and manipulate a network of kindred. Islanders worried not about being betrayed, but about being forgotten or ignored (*pale esumi*).

They worried that their kin would forget to come with contributions, a reasonable fear since the complexity of islanders' involvement in exchange was such that people really did forget others from time to time. And they worried that they would be intentionally ignored or slighted, and the dissensions within their families thus made an object of ridicule. Of course, the tactical response to the negative fact of being ignored in this way was to make a positive claim for power with the assertion, or at least the implication, that one would not have accepted the other party's gift in any case. To a certain extent, then, the manipulations that people made with gift displays were intended to put this best front on the weaknesses in a person's kin network that were publicly revealed in display.

To illustrate this expressive use of display, we describe several prestations, beginning with two different examples of a single type of prestation called *lo pahis* ("on the palm-leaf mat"). This was one of a number of prestations usually made during the course of funeral celebrations, often immediately following *sahai*. A *lo pahis* prestation was given by the dead person's children and siblings to all of his or her kindred, in order to commemorate their participation in the mourning. Like all of the mortuary prestations, *lo pahis* had no return prestation. It was, in a sense, a final prestation from the dead person to his or her family.

---

[2] Simple forgetfulness also was endemic, especially for the more distant kin relations that bound people to each other. This too was apparent in the arrangement of displays.

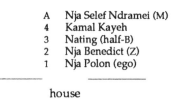

A   Nja Selef Ndramei (M)
4   Kamal Kayeh
3   Nating (half-B)
2   Nja Benedict (Z)
1   Nja Polon (ego)

house

Figure 40   Lo pahis *for Nja Polon*

The first of these is portrayed in figure 40, which shows the arrangement used for the distribution of *lo pahis* for Nja Polon, an old widow. This display is simple and straightforward, for the death and attendant prestations were unclouded by conflict or dissent. The distribution was divided among only five groups: her child, two siblings, *kamal*-mates and maternal kin. These gifts were arranged in a strictly genealogical sequence. At the base came the gift for Nja Polon herself, which was distributed to her child and affines. Following this, the gifts for others were arranged in terms of genealogical distance, concluding with a gift for her maternal kin.

The effect of disputes on gift displays is brought out very clearly by comparing this display with another, this one made for an elderly widower, Pe-nja Kapen. Like Nja Polon's, his *lo pahis* contained only five shares, for himself and his children, for his siblings, for his *kamal*-mates and for his maternal kin. The genealogy illustrating these relationships appears in figure 41. If the shares for these groups had been arranged in a purely genealogical manner, it would have appeared almost identical to the one arranged for Nja Polon. However, this display was not arranged in this neutral genealogical manner, but was arranged instead in a way that illustrated the controversy surrounding Pe-nja Kapen's death. Figure 42 shows a hypothetical, purely genealogical display, and the display that was actually made.

In chapter 5 we described the *sahai* given for Pe-nja Kapen and some of the troubles that beset his funeral. We noted that the more societal orientation of the funeral *sahai*, presented to Ponam as a whole, did not really allow the expression of personal conflicts (though it did allow commentary on the state of Ponam's *kamals*). However, the *lo pahis* display does allow such conflicts to be portrayed. Recall that Pe-nja Kapen's funeral celebrations were led by his sister, Augusta Pinambong, who attributed his death to a recent dispute between Pe-nja Kapen and some of his *kamal*-mates over his wish to give his mother's

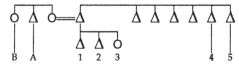

B   A   1   2   3   4   5

Figure 41   *Pe-nja Kapen's genealogy*

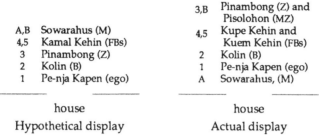

A,B	Sowarahus (M)	3,B	Pinambong (Z) and Pisolohon (MZ)
4,5	Kamal Kehin (FBs)	4,5	Kupe Kehin and Kuem Kehin (FBs)
3	Pinambong (Z)	2	Kolin (B)
2	Kolin (B)	1	Pe-nja Kapen (ego)
1	Pe-nja Kapen (ego)	A	Sowarahus, (M)

house   house

Hypothetical display   Actual display

Figure 42   *Hypothetical and actual* lo pahis *for Pe-nja Kapen*

kamal-mates some land on which to build a new men's house. The entire arrangement of the display, and in fact the entire funeral, was shaped by Augusta Pinambong's desire to portray the way that her relations with her kin had been reshaped by this dispute.

The gift at the base of the display, the first to be announced, went to Pe-nja Kapen's maternal kin (line A in figure 41). This was a most unusual move, for this position in the display normally belonged to the *ke-gwok*, the person on whose behalf the prestation was being made. By placing her mother's gift here, Augusta Pinambong made an unequivocal statement of her allegiance to her maternal kin and her opposition to her paternal kin. They were, after all, those very *kamal* members who, she said, were responsible for Pe-nja Kapen's death. She placed Pe-nja Kapen's own gift (1 in figure 41) second in the line. Pe-nja Kapen's brother's gift (2 in figure 41) followed his own. Normally Augusta Pinambong's own gift (3 in figure 41) would have followed her brother's, but she had another point to make, and she put her share elsewhere, so the fourth place in the line went instead to Pe-nja Kapen's *kamal*-mates (4, 5 in figure 41).

However, it went to only some of them. As the hypothetical display in the left of figure 42 shows, after the gift for Pe-nja Kapen's siblings one would expect to find gifts for his father's siblings, with each of his six brothers getting an equal share or, as in Nja Polon's display, all being asked to share a single portion (these are "Kamal Kayeh" in Nja Polon's display, figure 40). However, because Pinambong was in dispute with some of her agnates, she gave to only two of the brothers (4, 5 in figure 41). The others received nothing at all. The single gift at the crown of the line went jointly to Augusta Pinambong and her mother's sister (3, B in figure 41), whose only descendant, Chris Pelekai, was her speaker (*sohou*). In placing her own gift jointly with Chris Pelekai's, instead of next to her brother's as one would have expected, Augusta Pinambong illustrated that she and Chris Pelekai had worked together closely. Just as her mother's agnates were given the place of her own agnates, so her mother's sister's descendants were given the place of her maternal agnates.

The same kind of revealing social commentary exists in the arrangement of the contributions to the return prestation for Sowahanu Tapo's engagement gift (figure 32, page 169). Under more normal circumstances this prestation would have been led by Sowahanu's elder married brother, and his gift would have been placed at the base. Equally, under more normal circumstances Sowahanu's father, Michael Tapo, would have had no name in the display (just as, for example, Tony Kakaw's father had no name in his brideprice prestation: see figures 36–39). Sowahanu's mother's contribution would have been placed separately, probably in the far-right line next to Sowahanu's father's mother's contribution, in a manner analogous to the separate placement that Tony Kakaw gave his mother's gift in figure 39 (page 177).

However, as we have described, the circumstances of the return prestation for Sowahanu Tapo's engagement gift were not normal: her father, Michael Tapo, was in dispute with his son. Because of this, he refused to allow his son to participate in the exchange and he arranged the display in such a way as to make this very clear. His arrangement of the display suggested that he, Tapo, was Sowahanu's brother. Michael Tapo placed his own contribution at the base of the line, and Sowahanu's mother's contribution was included with this rather than being placed separately. Michael Tapo and his wife could have chosen to place his gift at the base and her gift in the line with his mother's, an arrangement that would have implied some sort of openness to compromise.[3] But instead they laid out an arrangement that completely eliminated Michael Tapo's son from his sister's kindred, by contracting the genealogy and placing her father in her brother's place.

We could repeat such examples *ad nauseum*. The reality of Ponam life was that circumstances were seldom "normal", and the beauty of the Ponam system of display was that its complexity (admittedly within a fairly simple basic formula) allowed, and in a sense required, the expression and public declaration of the state of these complex and frequently tense social relations.

Although these two displays deviated from the genealogical rules we have described, although they did not accurately portray the two kindreds according to convention, they were not in any sense wrong. No one made an error or a social *faux pas*. In fact, given the circumstances of these two prestations, the arrangers would have been wrong to arrange the displays in a conventional manner. This was so because gift displays were a form of communication as much as anything else.

Possibly Ponams could have simply heaped their gifts into a big pile as they were accumulated and then taken the pile apart again gift by gift for

---

[3] Placing his own contribution at the base would have shown his exclusion of his son. Placing his wife's in the line with his mother's, which is where it would go were there no dispute and were his son leading the prestation, would have shown that a more normal state of relations within his family was not ruled out.

distribution.[4] But such a simple procedure would be tediously uninformative when compared with the wealth of information and insinuation that gift displays actually provided. As the examples in this chapter show, the arrangement of displays provided considerable information about the structure and composition of individuals' kindreds, about who was related to whom and how. However, they also provided a great deal of more subtle information about the actual state of play of social relations among kin. This kind of social commentary was possible because islanders were familiar with both the conventional structure of display and the genealogical composition of most people's kindreds. As a result they had fairly clear expectations of what any given gift display would look like.

In other words, these displays had to be couched in a set of structured principles if they were to be used and understood as statements about the nature of people's relationships with their kin. It was these principles that allowed islanders to arrange displays in a meaningful way, as it was these that allowed islanders to read the meaning in the displays they saw. Consequently, it would be wrong to approach these displays in purely processual terms. In fact, it would be impossible to interpret them solely in light of the contingencies of the relationships between the person making the display and his or her kin. Certainly Ponams did not approach them in this way. Equally, however, these displays were not simply the formulaic representation of kin relations, comprehensible in purely structural terms. While a few, relatively insignificant displays could be interpreted in this way, most displays could not. Instead, they had to be approached with a knowledge of the contingencies of the relationships they represented; they had to be approached with process in mind.

Structure and process, then, interacted in these displays. The structure of kin relations and the principles of display created a framework of expectations, a framework that gave meaning to the deviations from those expectations that were so common in actual displays. Equally, however, the fact that these deviations were meaningful to people knowledgeable about contingent circumstance reaffirmed the significance of the very expectations from which they deviated. Thus, for example, it was because people expected to see Augusta Pinambong put the gift for her mother's kin at the crown of the line of gifts, that they could see the significance of her decision to put it at the base of the

---

[4] They did not think that they could. They said that the process of arranging displays is, in addition to being expressive, an essential step in figuring out how distributions should be made — figuring out to whom and how much to give. In view of the complexity of these distributions, some sort of procedure such as this does seem necessary. Pre-planning with pen, paper and calculator had become more important, but working out distributions on the ground in the way that they did would probably always be easier than planning them on paper.

line instead. If there were no expectations about what she would do, then there could be no grounds for evaluating the significance of what she did do; if the deviations were not meaningful, there would be no valid structure against which to identify deviation, only randomness.

CONCLUSION

The abstract model of genealogical relations that Ponams presented to themselves in ceremonial exchange was real and significant to them, as were the abstract models that they saw underlying other aspects of island life and social relations. However, they were also clearly aware that this structural model was partial, that it did not always encompass the way people actually behaved.[5] Thus, Augusta Pinambong was fully aware of the differences between the abstract model of ideal social order that she held and the behaviour of her own kin, and she used display to illustrate this; to illustrate, for example, that in her family her agnates were not behaving as proper agnates, and that her maternal kin had taken this supportive role instead. Further, though we have not discussed this point, she and others did have articulate ideas about the kinds of more processual factors that influenced behaviour and made the ideal, structural model a partial one.[6]

Islanders were also aware of ways that their abstract model of social relations disadvantaged certain groups in favour of others in ways that possibly no one had intended. In other words, they saw their system as external to them and as having logical consequences that could, at times, constrain action (J. Carrier 1987a: 128). This is the significance of the point made earlier in this chapter about Michael Tapo and Julie Pipohok's division of the engagement tobacco they received. Women, in their roles as wives and mothers, were disadvantaged in exchange, and this was made abundantly clear in every prestation display. Happily-married couples, which is to say most couples, commonly found this disadvantage uncomfortable, and therefore discovered for themselves a loophole by which they could transform the wife's public disadvantage into a private advantage. The share of a distribution that a wife could not receive publicly was transformed into a gift that she gave her husband privately. This private transaction did not, of course, eliminate the disadvantage, but it does illustrate that people identified it and felt constrained

---

5 For these reasons we do not think that this model of social order can really be described as mystifying, though this is implied in our earlier description of it as fitting Bourdieu's notion of "official kinship", in chapter 5.

6 We comment upon Ponams' articulate notions of both the structural and processual aspects of their lives in *WT&E*: 48–52.

by it, but not overwhelmed by it. They could attempt to deal with it by contrivances of their own.

Ponams, then, were sophisticated about the operation of their system of kinship and exchange, just as they were aware of the ways that actual behaviour often deviated from it. We expect, however, that the depth of their sophistication about these structures and processes of social life was largely a function of the scale and complexity of their society. Ponam was a small society in which people were related in many ways, and it was one in which people exchanged frequently in terms of their various kin links to each other. As a result, people were likely to stand in many different relations to each other as they participated in different exchanges, just as they were able to see the operation of their system in terms of these different relations and their different actions in different exchanges.

Their consciousness of themselves and their society was not, in other words, framed by their occupation of but a single, relatively unambiguous position in relation to a single and relatively unambiguously-defined set of others. Consequently, they could not help but know their system intimately and perceive it from many sides. This may help account for the difference between Ponams, with their clearly structural conceptions of the nature and operation of their social order, and the societies, especially in the New Guinea Highlands, of the sort described by Marilyn Strathern (1988). She argues that in these societies there is little conception of social structure of the kind we have described for Ponams. This may be because of the relative importance of a single set of social groups, clans, in many of these societies, groups that provided people with something like a single, relatively unambiguous position (the importance of clans in the region is summarised in Whitehead 1986: 89–95). This situation is in contrast to the multi-faceted nature of Ponam society, especially since the decline in this century in the significance of the resources that Ponam *kamal*s controlled. Prior to that decline, Ponams may have been as a-sociological as Strathern's Highlanders.

However, Ponams' awareness of larger structures was by no means as adequate as what they knew of the structures of their island society. Their participation in the structures that had come to impinge upon and even encompass them in marked ways by the middle of the twentieth century was much more limited. Islanders were not so able to see these structures from a range of different perspectives, they were not so able to see the consequences of their different actions in different circumstances. Instead, they were likely to be the victim of ideological misrepresentations of, for example, the state and the national economy, which were defined for them largely by school and the news media and whose processes they experienced only partially and from a single position, processes that they were, thus, less able to comprehend fully.

CHAPTER SEVEN

The process of exchange

Chapters 5 and 6 described the way that Ponams displayed the gifts they gave in their major prestations and return prestations. These displays are important, we showed, because they embody islanders' conception of the key categories of kin that make up their social universe, as well as the more processual factors that affected the status and state of relations among and between these kin categories. The present chapter continues the task of describing the practices that were part of Ponam exchange. It does so by describing the ways that Ponams carried out the major prestations in which displays were so important, and then by looking at the ways that gifts were accumulated and distributed before and after the main event. Our purpose is partly ethnographic, to complete the picture of exchange by describing some of the steps and activities that preceded and followed major prestations. But our purpose is also to look at exchange from the perspective of the individuals who planned and conducted them, and so qualify and complement our previous focus on structural relationships among groups. As might be expected, given the highly structured system of exchange that we have already described, this chapter will show that even at the individual level, structural considerations were very important. We will get at these processes and transactions by describing some of what went on as part of two large, but by no means extraordinary, prestations. One was a funeral prestation in May 1979, the other was a brideprice prestation in January 1981.

FINAL FUNERAL PRESTATION FOR CAMILIUS PARI

Camilius Pari died just after the New Year in 1979. He was only in his mid-fifties, his children were still young, his death was sudden and a great shock to everyone.[1] Like most men, he was in the midst of disputes with a

---

[1] We got information on contributions to Camilius Pari's funeral prestation by interviewing at least one active adult member of 50 of the households that had at least one member on the island during the prestation. Because exchange activity was almost always a joint household decision, we judged that interviewing one member was adequate. We have no interviews for the 19 remaining households which had resident members. Of these, four were only nominally independent (containing one senile old person and no one else), five were headed by single women (including the widow herself, who was not available to be interviewed),

number of his *kamal*-mates, and people quickly seized on these disputes as the cause of his death. As we have described, funerals were often the occasions of controversy, as the dead person's kin quarrelled about who was to blame, and funeral exchanges were often disrupted as one party or another refused to participate or refused to allow others to do so. The intensity of feeling surrounding Camilius Pari's death might easily have led to open controversy of this kind, but it did not.[2] This was because his brother, Self Njohang, who led the funeral celebrations, was a most skilful manager. The same skill that enabled him to manage the funeral had enabled him to be an effective *lapan* of his *kamal*, Nilo, and had enabled him to remain village councillor for fifteen years.

Immediately after Camilius Pari's death, the councillor arranged his burial and the burial prestation (*lutung*) to his *tamatu*. But he did not follow convention and conclude the mourning period immediately after this. Instead, he extended it over a number of months and held the final prestations in early May. This long mourning period was said to be typical of the past, when the body was kept in the men's house for months before finally being buried under the deceased's house. This practice was forbidden during German times, and mourning periods became progressively shorter. By the 1980s they normally lasted a few days for a long-predicted or unimportant death and up to several weeks for an important one. The long period of mourning for Camilius Pari's death was concluded in May with a day of major prestations.

PREPARING FOR THE *KAAPET MAHAN*

Public preparations for the final funeral prestations, the *kaapet mahan*, began in late April, when the councillor inaugurated a series of collective

---

and ten were of ordinary married couples. Although we gained information about contributions given by all but three of these households from others who had received them, their contributions may well be under-represented. For another reason, however, the data may over-represent contributions more generally: the data are derived from interviews, not observations, and we have included all contributions that people claimed to have made. Despite their shortcomings, the data are adequate to our purpose, which is indicative rather than rigourously quantitative.

[2] The fact that this prestation was a success made it possible to investigate it with extensive interviews with participants about their contributions. Although we attempted these kinds of interviews many times, we only managed to complete them on four exchange occasions: the two engagements reported in appendix 3, the funeral reported here, and another funeral *lutung* in 1986. Other attempts had to be given up when disputes broke out that made it impossibly rude to interview people about the gifts they had given and received. However, in its general outlines this prestation was like others; its contributions were accumulated and later distributed according to the same principles used in all other prestations.

expeditions to provide fish to be included in the final food distributions. Men fished almost every day for a week, using the two fishing techniques in which Pari and the councillor had hereditary rights (see *WT&E*: 111–118), while women smoked and stored the fish (this was the only important intra-island prestation during our period of fieldwork that relied on smoked fish rather than tinned fish). When they were not catching or preparing fish, Camilius Pari's kin were busy trying to accumulate sago and coconuts from the mainland, for cooked sago dressed with coconut oil was the main item to be given on this occasion. The councillor and his wife had already accumulated the bulk of what they would give, 100 bundles of sago and 1000 coconuts for oil, before they announced the date for the prestation. But others who were more distantly related and did not have such great obligations usually waited until the last minute to find what they would give.

The final prestation was held on the second of May. There was no public activity that morning. Instead, most of the men stayed in bed, still exhausted from their sleepless nights of fishing, and most of the women stayed home to cook the enormous quantity of food that was later to be given away. More than 1200 kg of sago and 120 kg of rice were cooked that morning, enough to feed the island's three hundred residents for about a week. At about noon, women slowly began moving around the island, carrying their dishes of sago and baskets of fish to the houses of the senior members of the cognatic stocks that would participate in the funeral prestations, so that gradually each stock accumulated its entire contribution in one spot. Some people displayed the contributions to a stock on the ground in the manner described in the preceding chapter. Others did not bother with this, but simply pushed all their gifts into a heap. The major contributors to a stock tended to stay at the house of their senior member after they had brought their contribution, chewing betel nut, smoking, chatting and waiting for something else to happen. But minor contributors usually rushed off again to bring another gift elsewhere, or perhaps to go hang about where they were a major contributor. Generally women arrived earlier and were more active in these preparations than men.

At 2.30 one of the Nilo men beat out the Kamal Nilo rhythm on the slit gong at the Nilo men's house, the signal for all the participating *ken sis* to bring their contributions. Women frantically fried their last dishes of sago and ran to wash up. Men who did not have any important part to play in the proceedings woke up from their naps and went off for a wash as well. The leaders of the various stocks began to check up on who had brought their contributions and who had not. And within an hour the leaders of all stocks had marshalled their followers and brought them and their stocks' contributions to the clearing in front of the Nilo men's house. (We discuss this process in detail later in this chapter, after describing the overall sequence of events in the exchange.) These contributions were laid out at the men's house door, but not in any very orderly form. Contributions included a number of very large dishes of cooked sago, about a metre in diameter, and baskets of smoked fish for the major prestations, as well as many smaller dishes of fried sago, sago pancakes, cooked taro and sweet potato, and small amounts of money and second-hand clothes for the smaller prestations. Shortly after these contributions arrived, the afternoon's work began, with two distributions called *songa* and *toweni heping*.

THE PRESTATION OF *SONGA* AND *TOWENI HEPING*

Prestations called *songa* were usually the opening stage of major prestations, such as those for marriages, brideprice payments and funerals. During the days leading up to a prestation, anyone who chose to could bring small gifts, called *njafang*,[3] to people working to prepare for the prestation. Conventionally people brought things like hot tea, cooked food, cigarettes and tobacco to the workers. In this case people brought, among other things, gifts of tobacco for Camilius Pari's agnates as they set off fishing, tea to the councillor's wife and her sisters as they smoked fish, and food for the widow and her family as they sang mourning songs. In the *songa* prestation the recipients repaid each of these gifts with small amounts of money and second-hand clothes before the major prestations took place.

Songa did not involve displays of the kind described in the preceding chapter. Instead, individual men who were members of the main *ken si*s that had received *njafang* gifts stood in front of the Nilo men's house, each with a collection of small gifts. They took turns calling out the names of particular individuals to whom they wished to give, and identifying the reason for the

---

3 Broadly speaking, *njafang* meant any kind of informal gift, such as those given between friends, spouses and parents and children, as well as those given on this kind of occasion. A popular metaphor for *njafang* was *kusun*, the stem end of a fruit, the implication being that this gift was the small end of something, with a larger return gift to follow. Another image (of our own) may help show the relationship between *njafang* and the exchanges around which it took place. That image is the game of Lucky (a variant of three-card brag), routinely played on Saturday and Sunday afternoons in Ponam men's houses. While Lucky involves a central pool in which all players put their bets, this was complemented by a flurry of side-bets between individual players in every hand, side-bets that attracted more interest and were often of greater value than the central pool. It appeared to us that *njafang* was of growing importance as a complement to ceremonial exchange on Ponam. If so, it suggests that the formal, central structure of these exchanges was increasingly being complemented by, and perhaps even displaced by, more individual, peripheral transactions, though unlike the game of Lucky, the total value of goods passing through *njafang* was still much smaller than the value of goods passing through the central ceremonial exchanges.

gift. The Ponam word for "call out", *songa*, gave this prestation its name. The giving proceeded fairly seriously at first, then became quicker and less serious as members of the audience warmed up and began to remember *njafang* gifts that they wanted to reciprocate. As this happened, members of the audience began to come forward to one or another of the men acting as a speaker and hand over a small gift with a request for an announcement. Often those who received something quickly passed it on to someone else.

Before these gifts of *songa* were completely finished, some of the speakers began to announce the gifts called *toweni heping*. Here the speakers gave small dishes of cooked sago or small sago pancakes to the men and women who had come to sleep with and care for the bereaved during the mourning period. The name *toweni heping*, which means "waiting for morning", referred to the fact that mourners came to sleep each night with the dead person's close kin, waiting for morning to go back to their own houses and chores. While the series of *songa* gifts began soberly, this one began with hilarity and continued until people had laughed themselves silly and the sago had run out. *Toweni heping* was funny because the person whose name was announced as the recipient of a gift was not actually allowed to collect it. Instead, it had to be collected by one of the recipient's *tamatus*. But since every Ponam had a number of *tamatus*, they were expected to race for the gift, a competition that was purposefully funny. Everyone laughed to see doddery old ladies hurl themselves into the race against fit young men and waddling pregnant matrons, all of the competitors making a joke of themselves and of each other. And people laughed to see which *tamatu* actually entered the race and who won, full of speculation that there was some special relationship between the recipient and the victorious *tamatu*. It was all part of the persistent theme of cross-cousin joking, used here to lighten the mood of the mortuary ceremonies.

THE PRESTATION OF *SAHAI* AND *LO PAHIS*

As the prestation of *toweni heping* gifts began to peter out, the councillor and a few of his close kin, particularly one old *asi*, started to work. In front of the door of the Nilo men's house, they began arranging the large dishes of sago and baskets of fish for the first of the day's two major prestations, the *sahai*, the gift to all Ponams that was distributed by *kamal*s. We described the display of this prestation in chapter 5 and it is shown in figure 27 (p. 153), so there is no need to describe it again here. Arranging this took over an hour. When the arrangement was complete, the councillor announced the shares and people quickly took them away. In most cases, however, they were not redistributed until later that evening or even the next day. Within an hour everyone was back again, to watch the councillor as he worked to prepare the last and most difficult distribution, the *lo pahis*. This time he worked outside his own house,

		C	So'on (FFM)		
			anthropologists		
		B	Asaf Ndrakalahan (FM)		
		6	Drapuon (FBDS)	14	Kosohi
		5	Hirong (FBSD)	13	Toloso'on
		3	Pakou (FBS)	12	Buhai
A	Fuluvii (MMZS)	4	Maie (FBSS)	11	Molou ("FFFB")
2	Councillor (B)	8	Sangul II (FFB)	10	So'onlao (FFFB)
1	Nja Pari	7	Aluf Sangul (FFZ)	9	Ndrahol (FFFB)

men's house

Figure 43   *Distribution to Camilius Pari's kindred*

not outside the Nilo men's house. This took even longer to arrange, and the audience sat in silence while he did it. The *lo pahis* was distributed to all of the *ken si*s of Camilius Pari's kindred. That is, it was redistributed to exactly those same stocks that had contributed to it. Thus, it was not an exchange. It was a redistribution, a final prestation from and to all those stocks that had ever contributed to Camilius Pari during his lifetime.

When the councillor announced this distribution, people from each stock came quickly to grab their shares and run back to the house of the receiving stock's senior member, for by this time it was late, dark, and everyone wanted to go home. Some stocks set straight to work distributing their share that evening, others put the whole thing off until the next day.

Figure 43 shows this *lo pahis*. At the base of the left line was the share (1 in figure 43) for Pari's widow and children, representing Pari himself. Next was a share (2) for the councillor, last was a share (A) for Camilius Pari's MMZS. Pari and his brother were in dispute with their mother's agnates and gave nothing to them, so this MMZS, their mother's maternal kin, took their place.

In the central line were shares for various groups within the two Nilo companies, Sangul I and Sangul II, both descended from Nilo's eldest son, Sangul. Sangul II, the stock descended from Sangul's second son, received a single share (8), as did the descendants of his daughter, Aluf Sangul (7). Camilius Pari was in Sangul I, and the members of that company got individual shares. We have already mentioned the shares for two members of that company, Pari's widow and the councillor, which were in the left line. The remaining members of this company were descendants of Camilius Pari's father's brother, Kapita (see figure 44), and their shares are numbered 3–6 in the figure.

In the right line were shares for the three other Nilo companies (9, 10, 11); for Kamal Buhai (12), which, as we described in chapter 5, had been a dependent of Kamal Nilo in the last generation and still felt close ties to Nilo; and for the descendants of Nilo's brothers Toloso'on (13) and Kosohi (14), from whom Nilo had broken away in order to found his own *kamal*. Relations among these groups are shown in figure 44.

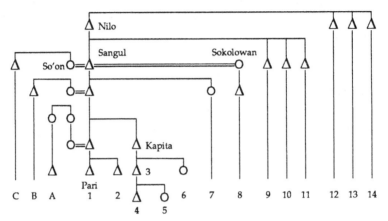

Figure 44   *Camilius Pari's genealogy*

Note: So'on was Sangul's first wife, Sokolowan was his second.

ACCUMULATING THE CONTRIBUTION FOR THE *KEN SI* NDRAHOL

The contributions to Camilius Pari's funeral prestations made by these stocks had been accumulated during the morning before the prestations, described in the previous section. The members of each stock had gradually come together at the house of their senior member, each person bringing his or her own contribution, a contribution that was often accumulated with help from other kin or affines who were not members of that stock. These small personal contributions were all joined together to make a single contribution which the members of the stock carried to Camilius Pari's men's house as a group.

The accumulation of these contributions followed the same genealogical principles that were used when any individual accumulated contributions for a major prestation, the principles described in chapter 6. In order to show this process, we describe in detail the contributions to Ndrahol, one of the stocks that participated in the final prestations for Camilius Pari. Ndrahol was both large enough to be interesting and small enough to be described fairly simply, but all of the stocks that were related to Camilius Pari through males accumulated their contributions in exactly the same way that the Ndrahol stock did. Ndrahol himself, the stock's focal ancestor, was Camilius Pari's FFFB. He was the second son of the *kamal*'s founder, Nilo, and was the focal ancestor of one of Kamal Nilo's five constituent agnatic companies.

CONTRIBUTIONS TO NDRAHOL FROM HIS AGNATIC DESCENDANTS

The core of the *ken si* descended from Ndrahol consisted of Ndrahol's male and unmarried female patrilineal descendants, as shown in figure 45. All

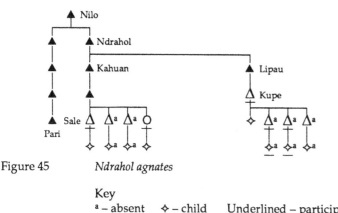

Figure 45   *Ndrahol agnates*

Key
ᵃ – absent   ✦ – child   <u>Underlined</u> – participant

of these people were members of Kamal Nilo, were *kamal si* to each other and to
Camilius Pari, as the figure shows. They were all expected to contribute to
Ndrahol whenever a prestation was made for someone to whom they were
related through Ndrahol.

Although all Ndrahol agnates were expected to contribute to the Ndrahol gift, they did not contribute simply as independent individuals. Instead,
they were organised into smaller stocks and contributed on the road of each
stock's senior member. Thus, Ndrahol included two distinct smaller stocks,
descended from Ndrahol's two sons, Kahuan and Lipau, as the figure shows.
Kahuan's descendants met at the house of Gerrard Sale, his senior descendant,
to assemble their contributions. Lipau's descendants met the house of Mark
Kupe, his only son, to assemble their contributions there. Later in the morning
the descendants of the junior brother, Lipau, brought their contribution to the
house of the descendant of the senior brother, Kahuan, to wait until it was time
to carry them all to Camilius Pari's men's house as a single contribution under
the name of Ndrahol.

Each contributor to these stocks gave to Ndrahol on the road of his or her
father — that is, on the road of his or her nearest male link.[4] Kahuan's grandchildren (Gerrard Sale and his sister) and Lipau's son (Mark Kupe) all gave
directly to Ndrahol on the road of their deceased fathers. Because there was no
living ascendent between them and Ndrahol, they had the absolute right to
give directly to Ndrahol as they chose.

---

[4] This is not the form of contribution we described in chapter 3, from parent to
child to parent to sibling etc. That form was the way that contributions moved
laterally, and its purpose was to get a contribution to someone, like Mark Kupe
or Gerrard Sale, who could contribute vertically to an ancestor who was related
appropriately to the focal party of the prestation. As we will describe, those
people who were not descendants of Ndrahol gave contributions in the lateral
way to those who were.

Their children, however, did not have this right. Thus, Mark Kupe's mature sons contributed to Ndrahol through their father. However, if for some reason Mark Kupe had refused to participate in the Ndrahol contribution, he could have blocked his sons' road to Ndrahol by refusing to accept and pass on their contributions. If those sons wished to defy their father and participate anyhow, they would have had to find some other road by which to send their contributions. (This issue did not arise in the case of Gerrard Sale, Ndrahol's other direct agnatic descendant. This was because his children were minors and did not participate at all, while his unmarried sister's only child, a son, was himself unmarried and did not participate.)

Although all those shown in figure 45 could have contributed to Camilius Pari's funeral exchanges as Ndrahols, only the people whose diagram symbols are underlined actually did so. Those who did not participate fall into two categories: unmarried minors and absentees. As we have said, Ponams generally did not participate in exchange on their own behalf until they were married or, if single, until they were mature, usually at around thirty years of age. (However, as we also said, unmarried minors of any age could be passive participants in exchange if their parents chose to use them as a road for exchanges between each other.)

Those who were absent from Ponam at the time of an exchange, on the other hand, still could participate actively by sending a gift of money or goods with specific instructions regarding its use and with specific instructions that the sender's name be proclaimed with the contribution. However, they did not often do this unless they were close relatives of the person on whose behalf the exchange was being held. More commonly they did not bother to send such detailed instructions, but simply sent money home for their kin to use as they saw fit, in which case their names were not usually proclaimed in the accumulations and distributions. However, migrants who had Ponam spouses had an important role to play in exchange, regardless of whether or not they sent any money, for they were used by others as roads between their own and their spouse's kin. In this accumulation for Ndrahol, none of the absentees who were single or who were married to foreigners were used as passive roads in this way, while all of the absentees with Ponam spouses were used as roads between sets of affines.

It was perfectly conceivable to Ponams that some might decline to contribute to a prestation; that some who were Ndrahol agnates might decline to contribute to Ndrahol out of anger, indifference or poverty. All other things being equal, people were expected to contribute to the stocks of which they were a member, but this did not always happen, as the discussion of Michael Tapo's treatment of his son in the preceding chapter showed. In this case, however, all resident Ndrahols did participate.

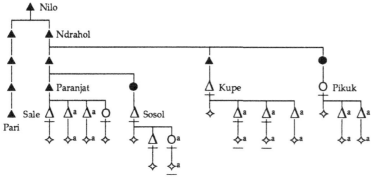

Figure 46   *Ndrahol agnates and line-of-the-woman*

Key
ᵃ – absent   ◇ – child   <u>Underlined</u> – participant

CONTRIBUTIONS TO NDRAHOL FROM LINE-OF-THE-WOMAN

Although Ndrahol's agnatic descendants formed the core of his stock, they were not the only active contributors to it: Ndrahol's descendants through women contributed as well. These descendants through women were line-of-the-woman to Ndrahol's descendants through men. Figure 46 shows both the agnatic members of Ndrahol and their associated line-of-the-woman.

Under normal circumstances there were no apparent differences in the behaviour of line-of-the-woman and Ndrahol agnates. All acted together on terms that were apparently equal and line-of-the-woman appeared to give directly to Ndrahol as the senior generation of agnates did. However, line-of-the-woman did not have the same right to contribute to Ndrahol that agnates did. As we said, contributions had to be sent through male roads. Thus, the children of male agnates gave on the road of their fathers, while the children of female agnates gave on the road of their nearest male Ndrahol agnate: a mother's brother, father's mother's brother, and so forth.

The case of Herman Sosol illustrates this. He participated in Ndrahol on the road of his mother's brother, Paranjat (shown in figure 46). Because Herman Sosol's mother and her brother both were long dead, his contribution was accepted in Paranjat's name by his son, Gerrard Sale. Gerrard Sale could refuse this if he chose and thus prevent Herman Sosol from participating in Ndrahol on the road of his mother's brother. If this happened, Herman Sosol could try to contribute to Ndrahol by giving to one of Ndrahol's other descendants, Mark Kupe or Cecelia Pikuk, and only if all of the Ndrahol descendants refused to accept a contribution would he be totally prevented from giving via Ndrahol. None of these people were obliged to accept his contribution, however.

Although it was unlikely that Herman Sosol would ever find all of his roads to Ndrahol cut off, it was certain that he would find himself prevented

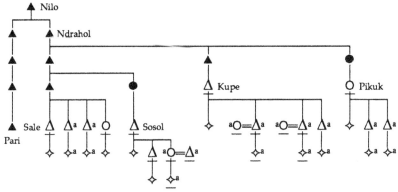

Figure 47   *Ndrahol agnates, line-of-the-woman and spouses*

Key
ª – absent   ✧ – child   <u>Underlined</u> – participant

Note: Non-participating spouses are excluded from this figure.

from giving via his mother's brother at least from time to time. This could happen for two reasons: because of a dispute between Herman Sosol and Gerrard Sale or because of a dispute between Gerrard Sale and someone else. Gerrard Sale might refuse to accept Herman Sosol's contribution because of a dispute between them, though this was relatively unlikely, for were there such a dispute, Herman Sosol would be unlikely to try to give and risk a refusal. Gerrard Sale was more likely to refuse to accept Herman Sosol's gift because he did not want to contribute to Ndrahol at all. Thus, for example, if Gerrard Sale were involved in a serious dispute with Camilius Pari's brother, the councillor, he might refuse to make any contribution to the funeral. Having decided this, he might then refuse to allow Herman Sosol's contribution to pass along his road.

All who should have contributed to Ndrahol on this occasion did so, and no contributions were refused. But several other people did not participate on some of the expected roads. The most prominent of these involved Pari's FBSS (number 4 in figure 44). This young man was recently engaged, and should have received a substantial contribution to his *ken si*'s prestation from his future wife and her family. Unfortunately, the young man's father and the young woman's father were at loggerheads over the wedding arrangements and her father refused to allow her to give anything to her betrothed. Consequently she sat at home most of the morning miserably turning away contributors. Those who were sympathetic to her case, however, managed to find some other road on which to give to her betrothed, as indeed she did herself.

CONTRIBUTIONS TO NDRAHOL FROM OTHERS

The contributors described thus far were direct descendants of Ndrahol, *ken si*, one origin, *lowa-* to one another. They were the prime contributors, the

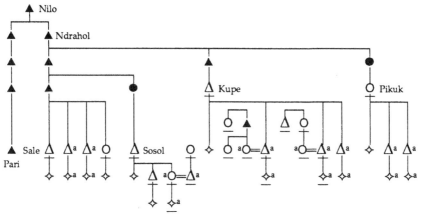

Figure 48   *Ndrahol agnates, line-of-the-woman and all contributors*

Key
ᵃ – absent   ✧ – child   <u>Underlined</u> – participant

Note: Non-participating spouses are excluded from this figure.

only ones who said they were contributing directly to Ndrahol. However, the range of Ndrahol contributors was much broader, for each of these members of the Ndrahol *ken si* could also receive contributions from other people. Figure 47 shows one aspect of this, contributions from their spouses.

While the descendants of Ndrahol thought of themselves as contributing directly to Ndrahol *ken si*, rather than to particular individuals, these secondary contributors thought of themselves as giving to individuals rather than to Ndrahol. Thus, when asked to whom they were giving, members of the Ndrahol *ken si* answered, 'to Ndrahol', to the stock. But others answered with the names of individual members of Ndrahol, not with the name of the *ken si* itself.

The contributions from those not descended from Ndrahol were all given to a Ndrahol from a spouse on the road of their unmarried child. As described in chapter 3, as a couple's children began to marry, that couple was used less and less often as a road for contributions between others. The fading of the use of husband and wife as a road for the exchange of gifts between inter-marrying families is clear in this case. None of the four senior married couples were used in this way. The children of Kupe, Pikuk and Sosol were all adult, and only one or two of the children of each remained unmarried. While Sale's children were all unmarried, both his wife and her only sibling were away, so he received nothing from them, as he might have in other circumstances. Only those whose children were still young continued to serve as roads for other people.

The spouses who contributed to Ndrahols could themselves receive assistance from any of their own kin. Figure 48 shows the extent of the contributions from these more distant relatives to Ndrahol.

This example of the accumulation of contributions for the *ken si* Ndrahol illustrates clearly the point made in chapter 3 about the asymmetrical relations between line-of-the-woman and line-of-the-man. The contributors to Ndrahol were agnatic members and those who were the descendants of sisters, line-of-the-woman. Those related to Ndrahols as line-of-the-man, as the descendants of the brothers of women who had married Ndrahol men, did not contribute. Following this logic, when those who were line-of-the-woman to Ndrahol contributed to the stocks of their fathers, they would receive nothing from Ndrahols. Cecelia Pikuk, for example, would contribute to Ndrahol whenever that stock made a contribution to someone else, but would almost never receive a contribution from Ndrahol when she contributed to her own father's company. Should Pikuk herself make a major prestation, however, she would receive from her mother's brother's descendants in the name of her mother.

Herman Sosol, though standing as line-of-the-woman to Ndrahol, was in a slightly different position. His father was from Ahus Island, and Sosol had been born and brought up there but had come to live on Ponam after his marriage to a Ponam woman. Sosol thus had no Ponam *kamal*-mates. He made up for this by his whole-hearted participation in Ndrahol *ken si*, and Ndrahols in turn contributed to him in exchange as they did to other agnates. Even so, his whole-hearted participation in Ndrahol *ken si* did not give him rights in the property-owning *kamal* of which Ndrahol was also a part, and Sosol and his sons were very much aware of their status as line-of-the-woman, of the fact that they had no property rights.

ORGANISING AN INDIVIDUAL'S CONTRIBUTIONS

Twenty-one people gave to the contribution that was eventually presented to the councillor by the *ken si* Ndrahol. Of these, three were minors who played no role other than that of providing a road for the transfer of contributions between their parents. Of the remaining 18 adults, 12 were resident on the island. The remaining six were migrants, and their role, like that of the children, was largely the passive one of providing a road for the movement of contributions between affines. Thirteen other stocks also contributed to Camilius Pari's prestations and received shares of the *lo pahis* when it was distributed. The number of contributors to these stocks varied considerably, from the 81 people who contributed to Camilius Pari's widow, to the single person who contributed in the name of Pari's FFM.

Table 1 shows the contributors to each of the participating stocks. For each, it lists the total number of participants: adults and children, residents and absentees. It shows that resident adults made a total of 266 contributions to Camilius Pari's funeral prestation, even though the resident population at the

Ken si[1]	Resident Ponam child	adult	Absent Ponam child	adult	Non-Ponam adult	Total
Nja Pari (1)	10	62	2	7	0	81
Councillor (2)	7	43	2	8	4	64
Kapita[2] (3,4,5,6)	5	24	0	0	0	29
Aluf Sangul (7)	2	9	0	0	0	11
Sangul II[2] (8)	4	29	1	6	0	40
Ndrahol[2] (9)	0	12	3	6	0	21
So'onlao (10)	1	12	1	2	0	16
Molou (11)	2	7	0	2	0	11
Buhai (12)	4	16	1	2	0	23
Toloso'on (13)	1	6	1	2	1	6
Kosohi[2] (14)	2	7	0	1	0	10
Fuluvii (A)	1	18	1	2	0	22
Asaf Ndra-kalahan (B)	3	20	1	3	4	31
So'on (C)	0	1	0	0	0	1
Total	42	266	13	41	9	366

Table 1   *Age and residence of contributors to Camilius Pari's funeral prestations, by ken si*

1 The figure in parentheses beside each *ken si* refers to its position in figures 43 and 44 (pages 191 and 192).

2 Some individuals made more than one contribution to this *ken si* by different roads.

time of the prestation included only about 125 mature adults,[5] or less than half the number of contributions. Thus it is apparent that many people contributed to more then one stock (and a few contributed more than once to the same stock). An example of the contributions given and received by one Ndrahol agnate illustrates this.

ONE INDIVIDUAL CONTRIBUTES TO MANY STOCKS

Mark Kupe received contributions on two different roads and, using these two roads and three others, he made contributions to five different stocks. He passed on the contributions that he had received to the stocks that the givers requested, adding a small contribution of his own to them. In addition, he also made contributions of his own to three other stocks. The evening of the prestation and the next day he received portions of the food redistributed

---

5 As we have said, there were substantially fewer socially mature adults on Ponam than physically mature ones. Young people on the island became important roads for exchange, and appear as adults in our data, from the moment their engagements were announced, regardless of their age. However, as we have described, unmarried men and women rarely played any independent role in exchange until they were middle–aged.

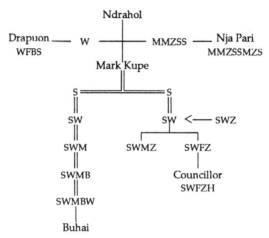

Figure 49   *Contributions to and from Mark Kupe*

Note: Except where otherwise indicated, parallel lines show contributions
flowing in both directions; a single line shows a contribution flowing away
from Mark Kupe.

to each of these stocks, as well as a portion of the *sahai* given to Kamal Nilo.
He returned the appropriate portions to his contributors and kept the rest for
himself and his family.

Figure 49 shows this. Mark Kupe received contributions from both of his
endogamously-married absent sons, on the roads of their wives. Of course,
neither these sons nor their wives actually gave to Mark Kupe themselves.
Instead the wives' kin gave on the road of these couples. They brought their
contributions directly to Mark Kupe at his house, along with their instructions
about the roads on which they wanted Mark Kupe to forward their contributions. Both chose to give to Ndrahol because that was the stock to which Mark
Kupe's sons had their greatest obligation. Mark Kupe himself also made contributions of his own to each of his sons, which went on the roads of their wives
and were passed along by their kin to the stocks to which the wives had their
greatest obligations. These two sets of contributions to and from Mark Kupe
were independent: his contributions were not return payments for the contributions from the sons' affines. Instead, each contribution would receive its own
separate share of the redistributed *lo pahis*. Mark Kupe also gave, together with
his wife, to her FBS, Drapuon, and to his MMZSS, who was a major contributor to
Camilius Pari's widow.

Thus, like many other participants in the prestation, Mark Kupe served
as a kind of interchange, an intersection of a number of roads along which
contributions were sent, all destined for one or another of the stocks contributing to Camilius Pari's funeral. The image of an interchange is an appropriate
one, not only because it reflects the Ponam metaphor of roads, but also because

	— *Number of roads used by contributors* —										
	1	*2*	*3*	*4*	*5*	*6*	*7*	*8*	*9*	*10*	*Total*
All contributors											
%	43	26	13	9	5	3	1	0	1	0	101
(n)	(64)	(38)	(19)	(14)	(7)	(4)	(1)	(0)	(1)	(0)	(148)
Resident contributing women											
%	40	17	19	15	5	1	1	0	1	0	99
(n)	(30)	(13)	(14)	(11)	(4)	(1)	(1)	(0)	(1)	(0)	(75)
Resident contributing men											
%	36	36	11	7	7	4	0	0	0	0	101
(n)	(16)	(16)	(5)	(3)	(3)	(2)	(0)	(0)	(0)	(0)	(45)
All contributing residents											
%	38	24	16	12	6	3	1	0	1	0	101
(n)	(46)	(29)	(19)	(14)	(7)	(3)	(1)	(0)	(1)	(0)	(120)
Resident contributing households											
%	11	9	18	20	11	8	9	6	6	2	100
(n)	(7)	(6)	(12)	(13)	(7)	(5)	(6)	(4)	(4)	(1)	(65)

Table 2   *Number of roads used by contributors to Camilius Pari's funeral*

Note: We have no record of any contribution made by 6 residents, 3 men and 3 women, and by any member of 4 resident households. These are excluded from the totals.

it reflects Mark Kupe's largely passive role in the transmission of contributions. Those who contributed to him did not really give to him as a person, expecting him to decide for himself where to send their contribution. Rather, they gave to him as a road, with very explicit expectations about where he would send what they gave. And if there was any doubt about what he should do, they gave explicit instructions about where their contribution was to go.

Although Mark Kupe contributed on more roads than most people, his performance was not particularly remarkable. Table 2 shows the number of roads used by the contributors to Camilius Pari's funeral prestations. More than half of the resident participating individuals gave on two or more roads. Further, almost two-thirds of the households that participated gave on four or more roads.[6]

When reduced to the simple diagram shown in figure 49, the organisation of Mark Kupe's contributions appears simple and unproblematic, but this was never so. The contributions that people made were always the result of

---

[6] Information on participation in two engagement distributions is given in appendix 3. The figures for multiple participation there are somewhat lower. However, in part this reflects the fact that these were initial distributions of gifts marking an engagement, and hence reflected the ability of distributors to remember all the stocks of their kindreds, rather than the willingness of individuals to activate roads by contributing. We discussed this difference in chapter 6.

conscious decisions, for no matter how avidly other expected contributions, it was always possible to withhold them.

DECIDING HOW MUCH TO GIVE TO WHOM

Like Mark Kupe, most people could have participated in Camilius Pari's funeral prestations by contributing on a variety of different roads. Everyone was a member of, or related by marriage to, many different contributing stocks. Thus, when the call for contributions came, each adult had to decide to which of his or her many relatives to give. Because the number of possible roads almost always exceeded the giver's resources, people devoted a great deal of thought to working out to whom they would give. Our first understanding of the process by which people made decisions about how much to give to whom came during the days of preparation leading up to Camilius Pari's funeral prestations, when we interviewed the major participants about the nature of the planned exchange and their part in it. People were very willing to talk about the general principles of the prestations but all insisted that they had no idea what they would eventually give or to whom. They would make that decision, they said, on the day of the exchange itself. We assumed at first that they were merely being secretive, but it gradually became clear that people really did not know what they would give, and could not know until the last minute. They could not know because each individual's contributions were contingent in complex ways on the contributions given by others.

Although most people refused even to speculate about what they would do, one couple was willing to do so. But they were prepared to speculate only in a most hypothetical way about what they might do if they had only a very limited amount to give. Charles Polangau and Augusta Pinambong explained things this way. On the morning on which it was announced that all participants should bring contributions, they would sit down together and plan what to give. They would plan jointly, they said, because a married couple was like one person, and if one made an error the other would share the blame. The first step in planning to whom they should give was to take stock of what they had to give. Therefore we asked them to explain to whom they would give if they had only a single 1-kg bag of rice (effectively an indivisible unit), to whom they would give if they had only two 1-kg bags, if they had only three, and so on. Figure 50 shows their choices.

Unlike Mark Kupe, Charles Polangau and Augusta Pinambong were not directly descended from the founders of any of the contributing stocks, therefore all of their contributions went to individuals, rather than directly to a stock. If they had between them just one 1-kg bag of rice, they said, it would go to his brother (see gift 1 in figure 50), for two reasons: the relationship between brothers was a close one, and this brother was very close to the centre of the

1. One kilogram of rice to C. Polangau's brother, for the *ken si* Nja Pari.

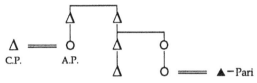

2. One kilogram of rice to A. Pinambong's FBSS for the *ken si* Nja Pari.

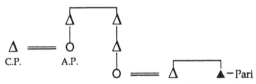

3. One kilogram of rice to A. Pinambong's FBSD for the *ken si* Councillor.

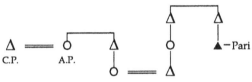

4. One stick of tobacco to A. Pinambong's BD for the *ken si* Kapita (Drapuon).

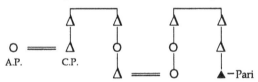

5. One stick of tobacco to C. Polangau's FBDS for the *ken si* Sangul II.

Figure 50   *A married couple's prospective contributions to Camilius Pari's funeral prestations, in rank order*

exchange, being married to Camilius Pari's wife's only sister. If the couple had two 1-kg bags of rice, they would give the first to his brother and the second to the relative who formed the next closest link to Camilius Pari. This was Augusta Pinambong's FBSS (see gift 2 in figure 50), another of Camilius Pari's wife's relatives. A third 1-kg bag of rice would go to her FBSD (see gift 3 in figure 50), who was married to Camilius Pari's brother, the councillor.

When we asked to whom they would give a hypothetical fourth such bag of rice, they were silent for a considerable time. Then they answered: they could not give it to anyone. Their first three roads were approximately equal in importance, and could reasonably be given identical contributions, but their other roads (see gifts 4 and 5 in figure 50) were clearly less important, and they would have to recognise this by giving smaller contributions. These were less important because they went through people who were less closely related to

H

1. To C. Polangau's brother, for the *ken si* Nja Pari.
    As gift 1 in figure 50.
2. To A. Pinambong's FBSS for the *ken si* Nja Pari.
    As gift 2 in figure 50.
3. To A. Pinambong's FBSD for the *ken si* Councillor.
    As gift 3 in figure 50.
4. To A. Pinambong's BD for the *ken si* Kapita (Drapuon).
    As gift 4 in figure 50.
5. To C. Polangau's FMBSD for the *ken si* Sangul II.

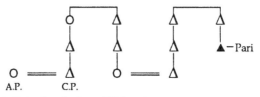

6. To A. Pinambong's FMBSD for the *ken si* Toloso'on.

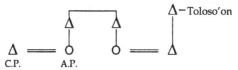

Figure 51   *A married couple's actual contributions to Camilius Pari's funeral prestations, in rank order*

Augusta Pinambong and Charles Polangau, less closely related to Camilius Pari, or both.

Thus, like others, Augusta Pinambong and Charles Polangau ranked their obligations by two genealogical criteria: the genealogical distance between giver and recipient, and the genealogical distance between the recipient and the leaders of the prestation. Contributions of the first rank were important because they went to closely-related recipients who were important members of major stocks, contributions of the second rank went to more distantly-related kin or those who were less-central members of less-significant stocks.

This, at least, was the arrangement that Augusta Pinambong and Charles Polangau hypothesised on the day before the prestation. What they actually gave was somewhat different, and these differences are shown in figure 51. They gave to their three most important roads and one of their lesser ones, though obviously not in the very small amounts of our hypothetical discussion before the event. In addition, they left out one of the lesser roads and added two extras. According to their explanation, the two they added had simply been forgotten in their original hypothetical discussion, but should have been there. The one they left out, however, was left out for a reason.

Charles Polangau gave nothing to his FBD (contribution 5 in figure 50) because on the morning of the prestation she came round to see him to say that she was sorry that she was going to have to leave him off her list this time, and she hoped he would not take offence. This tactic of sending talk instead of a contribution was an established and formally-legitimate one. In fact, people said that, in principle, sending talk should be considered equivalent to sending a contribution, and those who sent talk should receive a portion of the return gift equivalent to that of other contributors. In practice it did not always work out like this, of course. No one could get away with it all of the time, and some families had a reputation for trying this on far too often. Charles Polangau was perfectly willing to accept his FBD's talk without prejudice, and in fact he used it as an excuse to economise on his own contributions, sending nothing to her, and giving her none of his share of the redistribution. He was able to do this conveniently because no one else had attempted to use him as a road to contribute to his FBD. Had someone else done so, however, he might very well have been more critical of her talk, feeling that he was being manoeuvred into giving something for nothing.

Deciding to whom to give was much simpler than deciding how much to give. This was complicated because the answer was definitely not 'as much as possible'. As Augusta Pinambong and Charles Polangau explained, it was necessary to give larger contributions to more important roads and smaller contributions to lesser roads, so that the recipients on the more important roads would not feel slighted. However, while the size of a contribution was judged in relation to the size of all of the giver's other contributions, it was judged also in relation to the size of the contributions that the recipient got from others. It was important to try to give a relative more than he or she received from kin who were related less closely, and it was only slightly less important to try to give a relative less than what he or she received from contributors who were related more closely. That is, a recipient expected to get the largest contribution from siblings, somewhat smaller ones from FBC, somewhat smaller yet from MBC, and so on, and contributors had to bear this in mind.

People judged the size of A's contribution to B in relation to the size of A's other contributions to W and X, and also in relation to B's other contributions from Y and Z. Thus it was easy for A to be faced with the dilemma of offending B by giving too little or offending W and X by giving too much. And it was not possible to wriggle out of this dilemma simply by giving more and more to everyone, for the more a person gave, the more closely others scrutinised his or her performance, and the more they hoped to receive. This gave Ponam exchange a tragic dimension, for people often gave offence where no offence was intended, started off a day of exchange with pleasure and excitement at the prospect of giving to and sharing with their kin, only to end it in bitterness and disillusionment, with the discovery that their efforts were misread by others, that they could not do well without also doing ill.

This indeterminacy was an important feature of Ponam exchange, particularly apparent in the anxiety, frustration and anger that were so marked on these occasions. High levels of tension probably arc inevitable in this classic double-bind situation, in which the rules rigidly circumscribe action, limiting innovation and imagination, but do not provide any right answers; and *cannot*, because it is only by knowing the future that one can judge how the rules ought to be applied in the present. This tension also helps to explain the curious stop-and-go rhythm of Ponam exchanges. The day, often even the hour, for some events was marked well in advance, yet people seemed to wait and wait, doing nothing for a very long time. Then suddenly someone would break, and the event would lurch forward very quickly as everyone fell into line, following positions defined by that initial actor. And then there would be another long period of inaction, as people waited and watched for the next step.

Thus far we have described the problem of deciding how much to give to whom in purely genealogical terms, as a matter of a complex, but purely logical, kinship algebra. Such considerations were of great significance, but they were not the only considerations. The contingencies of personal relationships between the giver and recipient were just as important — not in any illegitimate way, but openly. One person's contribution to another was not a unique event, something to be understood solely in terms of the prestation of which it was a part. Instead, it was almost certainly one of a long chain of contributions, stretching back years, or even generations, and a giver's contribution reflected and had to be understood in terms of his or her evaluation of the history of that relationship.

Generally, Ponam exchange had an inflationary tendency, for if the relationship was a positive one, a person tried to give a recipient slightly more than that recipient had given to him or her in the last similar exchange, at least in so far as possible without offending someone else. But all of the things that had happened since the last exchange were also taken into account. Particularly, everyone thought that it was reasonable, or even a good thing, to refuse to give to someone who had refused to give to them the last time they had a similar obligation. No one, however, ever suggested to us that one might give an exceptionally large gift in these circumstances in order to shame the recipient. On the contrary, when we put this suggestion forward people saw it as slightly ridiculous, since the transactions were private and the recipient could claim the credit for passing on a large contribution without ever having to reveal its embarrassing origins.

All of these problems of individual decision-making were magnified as contributions moved toward the stocks that would ultimately present them to the leaders of the prestation. This was because all of the members of those stocks would have to agree about what was the appropriate size and content of the gift, manner and timing of its presentation, and a number of other factors. Given all of the complications we have described, this agreement was by no means simple to achieve.

On one occasion, for example, we saw an argument break out among members of a stock about the size of a contribution they proposed to give. All the members had brought their prospective contributions to the house of the stock's senior member. After having looked at the amount that everyone had brought, one man who was line-of-the-woman announced that there was too much, and therefore he would withdraw one of his bales of sugar. The senior member of the stock disagreed and insisted that the sugar should be included. After some argument, the senior member declared that if the man who was line-of-the-woman withdrew his bale of sugar, then he would withdraw one of his own bags of rice, and said that if other members insisted on taking his rice while leaving the sugar, he would break the rice bag open and spill it on the ground. With that, he took his axe out of his tool case, laid it down on top of the rice and stalked away. Without further discussion the others picked up their contributions and carried them off, leaving both the rice and the sugar behind. As one might expect, this dispute was provoked by a number of considerations in addition to the immediate one about the appropriate amount to give, but this concern was still significant. And it is significant that most members of the stock agreed to a smaller contribution, agreed that it would be better to leave the rice and the sugar than to include them.

THE SIZES OF CONTRIBUTIONS
TO A BRIDEPRICE PRESTATION

Having described some of the issues involved when people made decisions about how much to contribute toward a prestation, we now want to describe a single case in some detail, want to describe how much was accumulated, distributed and returned as *kahu* in a single exchange.[7] That case is the

---

7 We do not have the kind of complete data on this topic that we would like. It was difficult to investigate the quantities given in major prestations in any systematic way. The two major prestations in which we were able to trace out the contributions thoroughly were a funeral *kaapet* in which people gave cooked sago, and a funeral *lutung* in which they gave baskets of minor valuables. In neither of these cases was it possible to investigate the quantity or value of what was given with any rigour. People's reported gifts of 'large', 'very large', or 'not so very large' dishes of cooked sago were impossible to quantify. Woven baskets filled with small change, second-hand clothes and second-hand household goods, the major gifts given in the *lutung,* were similarly unquantifiable. The types of prestations that would be logical to look at in order to study the quantity or value of people's

transactions of one of the *ken si*s involved in the brideprice prestation by Tony Kakaw described in chapter 6, and we will look in particular at one of the important stocks involved. We describe the fate of the gift accumulated by that stock — how it was accumulated, presented, distributed, and how the return prestation came back again.

The prestation of Tony Kakaw's brideprice was led by his sister and brother, Teresia Pisile and Otto Kakaw. On the day set for the accumulation of contributions to the brideprice, Teresia Pisile and her husband, Francis Navii, stayed at home waiting for his kin to bring their contributions. Teresia Pisile relied entirely on her husband's kin for help with her contribution to her brother, because all of her own kin could give to her brother Tony Kakaw more directly on their own roads, and so would not give through her. Thus, an investigation of the activity of her stock in this brideprice means, in effect, an investigation of the activity of her husband's kin.

Those kin came in two groups: Francis Navii's paternal kin met and arranged their contribution in one room of his house, and his maternal kin (whom we investigate most closely in this description) met and arranged their contribution in another room. Eighteen of his paternal kin came, contributing a total of K96, in gifts ranging in size from K1 to K10. Seventeen of his maternal kin came, including his mother, who was still living, and his mature but un-married sister who came with her. They brought K137 in contributions that ranged in size from K1 to K52.

Figure 52 shows the genealogical relations among Francis Navii's maternal kin, the amounts they contributed, and the percentage each gift was of the total gift from all his maternal kin. On average, Francis Navii's mother's siblings (Salimet Palu and Sowa Palu in figure 52) and their children gave more than his mother's father's sibling's (Kela's) descendants, who gave more than his mother's father's father's (Tapo's) sibling's descendants. However, large contributions came from a *ken si*, Drakolok, that had only a most distant genealogical connection. This group was small and isolated genealogically, and its members maintained an old tie of patronage to Francis Navii's maternal kin with great determination. Francis Navii received nothing from his mother's mother's kin, who were from the nearby island of Sori.

Once the contributions from Francis Navii's paternal and maternal kin had been formally presented to him, he brought out his own contribution, and gave them all to his wife. She then brought out her own contribution, which included K40 and a belt of dog's teeth. Francis Navii then took all the cash that

---

contributions are those in which the major gift was cash, but predictably these generated a great number of disputes and so were difficult to investigate thoroughly.

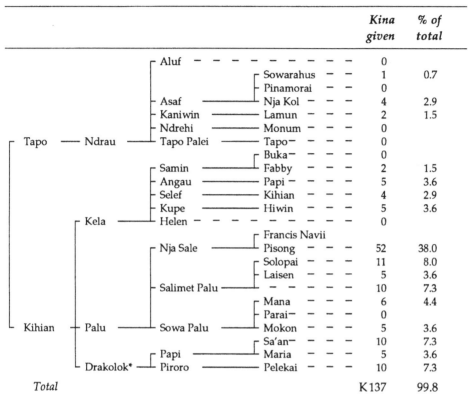

	Kina given	% of total
Aluf	0	
Sowarahus	1	0.7
Pinamorai	0	
Nja Kol	4	2.9
Lamun	2	1.5
Monum	0	
Tapo	0	
Buka	0	
Fabby	2	1.5
Papi	5	3.6
Kihian	4	2.9
Hiwin	5	3.6
Helen	0	
Francis Navii		
Pisong	52	38.0
Solopai	11	8.0
Laisen	5	3.6
—	10	7.3
Mana	6	4.4
Parai	0	
Mokon	5	3.6
Sa'an	10	7.3
Maria	5	3.6
Pelekai	10	7.3
Total	K 137	99.8

Figure 52   *Contributions to Teresia Pisile from the maternal kin of her husband, Francis Navii, for Tony Kakaw's brideprice*

* The connection between Palu and Drakolok was one of patronage.

had been collected, K334, and divided it into four piles. He put three lots of K100 each into envelopes, labelled each with Teresia Pisile's name and the amount, and kept the remaining cash loose.

After this was done the entire group went together to the groom's men's house, where a long rope (*haliki*) had been hung up stretching from the doorpost of the men's house to a tree some distance away. The contributions already brought by other stocks had been pegged onto the rope for all to see. Teresia Pisile handed the envelopes containing her contribution to one of the men supervising the display, to be hung on the line. The remaining loose cash was handed over to help with incidental expenses such as food. She then spoke briefly, saying that not everyone in her line had contributed as she expected, so that her contribution was not as large as it should have been, and she was angry about it. The groom's father's brother made a brief speech thanking her for the money. Then he put her three envelopes together into an empty plastic rice bag and pegged them in their place on the rope.

Relation	Name	Portion of Total	Contributions	
			Money	Additional Items
M	Kiki	18.2%	K 793	
FB	Kupe Lul and	9.2	70	1 pig (K 330)
FM	Nja Sanuen	4.6	200	
	Lahai	0.2	8	
	Sowawura	0.3	12	
	Nilo	0.7	30	
	Toloso'on	3.0	130	
FFFBD	Pisile Warai	1.0	45	
FFFBS	Kailawin	1.9	84	
	Fofou	6.3	277	
	NjaHaluai NjaMaloh Aluf Musim Pe'af	0.2	10	
	Sowarahus	1.0	45	
	Soguop	0.6	25	
FFZ	Pingomet	0.5	24	
FFB	Mbrum	2.7	120	
FB	Sepat Kaso	1.0	42	
FZ	Himasau	1.0	43	1 belt shell money
FZ	Pimeses	1.4	60	
FB	Nakaw	3.4	150	
Z	Pisile	6.9	300	1 belt dog's teeth
B	Otto	22.9	270	1 outboard motor (K 730)
ego	Tony	13.7	600	1 belt dog's teeth
Total		100.7%	K 4398	

Table 3   *Amounts of contributions to Tony Kakaw's brideprice*

Later in the afternoon, when all the contributors seemed to have arrived, the groom and some of his kin took the money down from the line, counted it, hung it up again, and then announced how much had been collected. Table 3 shows the contributions in the order in which the envelopes were displayed on the rope. This should be compared with the other information on Tony Kakaw and his brideprice that is given in figures 35 and 38 (pages 174 and 177).

The total value of the contributions displayed was K 4398, which included K 3338 in cash, an outboard motor with an announced value of K 730 and a pig announced at K 330. There were also two belts of dog's teeth and one of shell money. These were much prized and desired and were important contributions. However, we do not include them in the value of the contributions because we cannot calculate their cash value.

The largest contribution came from the groom's brother, an employed professional in the national capitol. The groom's own contribution of K 600 was next in size (this was only a small fraction of the money he really spent; far greater sums went on air fares, canoe charters, food, drink, clothes and similar presents, and so on). Teresia Pisile gave K 300 on the rope, and would have liked to give more, but she, her husband and her young children were all island residents without incomes to bolster the contributions received from others.

Following Pisile's gift came those from the groom's father's siblings, with one exception all smaller that Pisile's. The eldest brother, Nakaw, with several successfully-employed children, gave K150. The others, without such children, gave much less. The last-born brother, Kupe Lul, was a single man in his fifties employed as a carpenter. Because he was unmarried his contribution was displayed at the end with his mother's. We have valued his contribution at K400, which includes the announced price of the pig that he contributed. It may well be, however, that the pig did not actually cost him this much money.

Most of the contributions from beyond the range of the groom's father's siblings were very small, less that one per cent of the total brideprice, but there are several pertinent exceptions. The contribution from Kailawin, the groom's FFFBS's descendants, was irregularly large, but was predictably so. This stock included a wealthy widow who was the island's most compulsive exchange player, consistently giving more on more roads than almost anyone else on the island. Also, two substantial contributions were made by two distantly-related stocks, Fofou and Toloso'on, that included the groom's two closest personal friends, men who were, like him, wealthy and successful civil servants.

Although we have argued that exchange relations were predominantly organised on the basis of genealogy rather than more personal relations, these contributions to the brideprice payment show that this is not entirely true. Personality and personal relationships did affect what people contributed in exchange. However, the general genealogical pattern is clear enough to establish the point that these personal relations serve to modify a pattern that is shaped predominantly by genealogical structure. The reverse is not the case.

By the time the groom's kin had announced all of the contributions displayed on the rope, it was late in the afternoon, so they took all the money down off the rope and stowed it away ready to make the prestation itself the following day.

People spent the morning of the next day preparing for the prestation, making decorations for dancing, cooking food and so on. The formal prestation finally began at about one o'clock in the afternoon, as the groom's kin set off from his men's house, dancing to the music of slit gongs and carrying the money, a pig and the groom's children. The total amount of cash announced when the prestation to the bride's family was made the next day was K3275, somewhat less than had been announced the night before. The total amount announced when the prestation was distributed the following day was K3290.[8]

---

[8] This figure in turn was different from the actual amount of money distributed subsequently among the bride's kin. From what we have observed, Ponams are

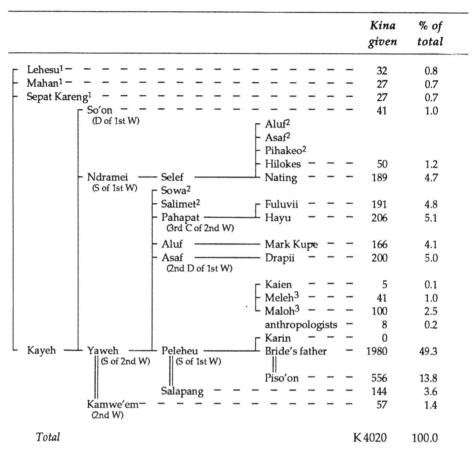

Figure 53   *Distribution of brideprice by bride's father and brother*

1 These *ken sis* were all affiliated to Kayeh in the distant past.

2 The descendants of these sisters did not participate.

3 Peleheu joined these brothers when he ran away from his father. Kaien was related to them.

The celebrations, speeches and dancing went on until about four o'clock, and then the bride's father began to think about distributing the money.

He, his wife and his young sons contemplated the money for a long time, but by dusk he announced that he could make no final decisions, and everyone should go home and come back again the next day. One thing that made his decision difficult, as it made the distribution of all brideprice payments

careful to calculate and re-calculate the size of such gifts for so long as was necessary to reach agreement on the amount. Therefore, we conclude, albeit only tentatively, that people were changing the amounts of money in the various envelopes, including late contributions or bringing the size of a gift up or down to what they thought was more appropriate.

Recipient	Brideprice received		Kahu returned			
	Kina amount	Percent of total brideprice	Kina value	As percent of brideprice received	total kahu	Items
Bride's F	1980	49.3[1]	586	30	44.2	(a)
Meleh	41	1.0	delayed			
Maloh	100	2.5	33	33	2.5	(b)
Drapii	200	5.0	28	14	2.1	(c)
Mark Kupe	6	4.1	90	54	6.8	(d)
Hayu	206	5.1	47	23	3.5	(e)
Fuluvii	191	4.8[1]	83	43	6.3	(f)
Nating	189	4.7	32	17	2.4	(g)
Hilokes	50	1.2	12	24	0.9	(h)
So'on	41	1.0	delayed			
Sepat Kareng	27	0.7	18	67	1.4	(i)
Mahan	27	0.7	delayed			
Lehesu	32	0.8	delayed			
Kaien	5	0.1	4	80	0.3	(j)
Kamwe'em	57	1.4	delayed			
Piso'on	556	13.8[2]	342	62	25.8	(k)
Salapang	144	3.6	43	30	3.2	(l)
Achsah	8	0.2	7	88	0.5	(m)
Total	K 4020	100.0%	K 1325		99.9%	

Table 4   *The return prestation for Tony Kakaw's brideprice*

1 Plus one belt of dog's teeth.

2 Plus one belt of shell money.

Items given, in kilograms, except tobacco, in sticks, and sago, in bundles:
(a) 360 rice, 30 flour, 60 sugar, 40 sago, 105 tobacco, 1 pig (= K 400); (b) 25 rice, 15 sugar, 15 tobacco; (c) 35 rice, 10 flour, 16 sugar, .25 tea, 20 tobacco; (d) 130 rice, 10 flour, 16 sugar, 20 sago, 30 tobacco; (e) 65 rice, 20 flour, 1 case biscuits, 45 tobacco; (f) 188 rice, 30 sugar, 25 sago, 1 case betel nut, 1 rope bananas; (g) 60 rice, 30 sugar, 5 tobacco; (h) 20 rice, 5 sugar, 5 tobacco; (i) 27 rice, 15 sugar, 1 tobacco; (j) 3 rice, 1 sugar, .5 tin fish, 3 tobacco; (k) 235 rice, 100 flour, 52 sugar, 10 sago, 5 bottles oil, 1 pig (= K 200); (l) 75 rice, 17 sugar, 15 tobacco; (m) 10 rice, 10 flour, 3 tobacco.

difficult, was that the distributor was not allowed to break open the envelopes of money that he received, but had to make the distribution in the units he was given. This made it possible for the recipient stocks to know whose contribution they had received, and hence to whom their return prestation should go, but made it difficult to distribute exactly the amounts one wanted to.

People began to return to the bride's father's men's house the next morning at around nine o'clock, but it was not until about eleven that her father announced how he had decided to distribute the money. Figure 53 shows the genealogical pattern of this distribution. The bride's father gave nothing to his true brother, with whom he was in dispute. The very large portion reserved to his sons (who were the nominal leaders of this work, though precluded by their youth from taking a very active role), he later redistributed among the stocks of his kindred, but this distribution was made separately later, and was not part of the formal distribution described here.

After the bride's father had finished his distribution, he announced that he would bring his return prestation, *kahu*, that afternoon. The members of four of the recipient stocks announced that they were unable to bring *kahu* until later (in the event, a fifth stock delayed its *kahu* as well). This was a common occurrence. These four stocks were relatively insignificant and their members all had more important commitments to other stocks. Furthermore, their members all had the expectation of receiving a share of the return prestation as members of one or more of the stocks on the groom's side. They hoped to use the *kahu* they received as a member of the groom's family to pay off their debts as a member of the bride's family, and thus avoid having to spend any more money.

Table 4 shows the value of the return prestations (*kahu*) given by each of the recipient stocks. As *kahu* was primarily raw food, with only a small amount of money, we have used the prevailing price for foodstuffs to compute the value of these return prestations. This table relates the size of each return gift to the value of the portion of the brideprice that each stock received, and it also relates the size of each return gift to the value of the total return gift accumulated. There was a wide range in the value of return prestations: the smallest was equal to 14 per cent of the share of the brideprice the stock received, the largest was equal to 80 per cent. Overall, however, the size of return prestations clustered between about 25 and 45 per cent.

Figure 54 shows the way that the return prestation given to Teresia Pisile was divided among her contributors. One important point about this is that Teresia Pisile and Francis Navii kept nothing for themselves, but redistributed it all to their contributors. Another is that, for the most part, the return prestation was redistributed roughly equally, rather than in proportion to the contributions made. Thus, Francis Navii's maternal kin received only marginally more than his paternal kin, despite their larger contribution. His maternal contribution was divided into two parts, one for his mother and sister, who had given a very large contribution, and the remainder for all the others. This last was divided by the technique called *huruhut*. All the contributors came back to Francis Navii's house with dishes, and the rice, sugar and flour were dealt out into them equally by cupfuls. This method of redistributing *kahu*, which was commonly used, had an equalising effect. Those who made the smallest contributions, normally the poorest contributors, received *kahu* that was equal to, or perhaps greater in value than, the contribution they had given; those who made the largest contributions, normally those who were better off, received *kahu* that was much less valuable than their contributions. (Some of the implications of this are discussed in *WT&E*: 217–220).

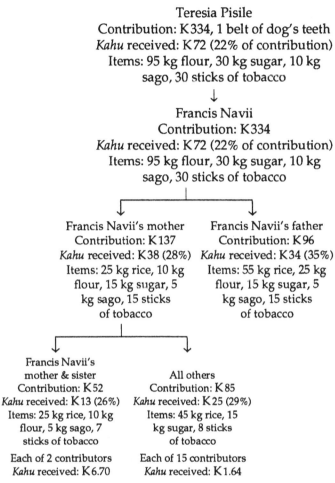

Teresia Pisile
Contribution: K334, 1 belt of dog's teeth
Kahu received: K72 (22% of contribution)
Items: 95 kg flour, 30 kg sugar, 10 kg
sago, 30 sticks of tobacco

↓

Francis Navii
Contribution: K334
Kahu received: K72 (22% of contribution)
Items: 95 kg flour, 30 kg sugar, 10 kg
sago, 30 sticks of tobacco

Francis Navii's mother
Contribution: K137
Kahu received: K38 (28%)
Items: 25 kg rice, 10 kg
flour, 15 kg sugar, 5
kg sago, 15 sticks
of tobacco

Francis Navii's father
Contribution: K96
Kahu received: K34 (35%)
Items: 55 kg rice, 25 kg
flour, 15 kg sugar, 5
kg sago, 15 sticks
of tobacco

Francis Navii's
mother & sister
Contribution: K52
Kahu received: K13 (26%)
Items: 25 kg rice, 10 kg
flour, 5 kg sago, 7
sticks of tobacco

Each of 2 contributors
Kahu received: K6.70

All others
Contribution: K85
Kahu received: K25 (29%)
Items: 45 kg rice, 15
kg sugar, 8 sticks
of tobacco

Each of 15 contributors
Kahu received: K1.64

Figure 54   *Distribution of* kahu *by Teresia Pisile*

COMPETITION AND HIERARCHY:
THE IMPLICATIONS OF THE SYSTEM

We mentioned previously that the Ponam system of exchange did not produce the sort of competition between the partners to an exchange that is common in some other parts of Papua New Guinea, and thus did not have the same potential for producing competitive hierarchies of big men. Ponam exchange did lead, however, to intense competition among kin, which served to give exchange the air of urgency and importance that it had.

In a sense, the leaders of a major prestation saw themselves as being in competition with all of those who had previously made a similar prestation, especially their own kin, and the ambitious strove to give a larger gift than had ever been given before on a similar occasion (though not necessarily a larger gift than they had ever given to the same person before). By doing this they hoped to demonstrate their wealth, the earning power of their migrant kin and their ability to attract contributions from others, a proof of their generosity in the past (see, e.g., *WT&E*: 129–133). By this they gained a reputation, or as Ponams described it, a "big name", *langan mahan*. This striving for reputation fuelled a steady inflation in the size of prestations, particularly of brideprice prestations. Thus, at least among migrants, each brideprice paid between 1978 and 1986 was larger than the one that preceded it.

This competition over the size of prestations meant that it was roughly possible to hierarchise individuals or sibling sets according to the size of the different sorts of prestations they made. But this was not the only aspect of competition among kin in exchange, and it was not the most important one, for Ponams competed not only over the amounts they gave, but also over the amounts they received.

Descriptions of ceremonial exchange in Melanesia tend to focus on major prestations and the striving for prestige and power that are central to them, and they tend to ignore the subsequent distributions and redistributions of what has been presented. For Ponams, the issues of prestation and prestige were interesting and important, but in some sense the icing on the cake. For example, even though people gossiped about the size of major prestations, we never saw or heard a dispute over this issue. The real issues were accumulation and distribution, which were the subject of endless and often vehement controversy. It was here, and particularly in distribution, that the real competition in Ponam exchange lay. Erik Schwimmer (1973: 49) summed up what may be the nub of the matter in his book on Orokaiva exchange:

> Westerners often criticise Melanesians for being too grasping and mean in gift exchange. Absurd though this criticism may seem, it arises from a real cultural difference: Westerners depend on institutions other than gift exchange for the acquisition of desired scarce resources. Hence the institution of exchanging Christmas presents need serve no other end but the fostering of social exchange relations. For the Melanesians ... gift exchange must serve economic as well as social ends.

Thus, while the leaders of a major prestation, particularly migrant leaders, may have seen themselves as engaged in a kind of abstract competition for prestige with the leaders of all previous similar prestations, the more peripheral participants felt themselves to be competitors with the prestation leaders and all other participants in a mad scramble for the food and money that they needed for survival. The larger and more important the prestation, the madder and more competitive the scramble became. Thus, Tony Kakaw's brideprice included about K3338 in cash, of which about K2000 was imported to the island from outside. At this time Ponams (who, remember, had no gardens) were spending on average K1.20 per person per week at trade stores and the local market to purchase their essential staple starch, as well as other minor necessities like tea and soap (*WT&E*: tables 8, 11). So, this K2000 would meet islanders' basic cash survival needs for more than five weeks. The food given in the *kahu* was enough to feed them for more than one week exclusively on luxury foods: rice, flour, sugar, biscuits. For people who depended for their survival largely on what they could induce others to give them, six weeks' food supply was a lot to fight about. Compared to this, the relatively abstract issue of the prestige of major (and usually migrant) leaders paled into insignificance. Instead, each leader's kin were set into competition with him or her over the eventual distribution of the goods and cash that had been presented.

CONCLUSION

In chapters 1 to 4 we described the importance of economic and political processes for understanding Ponam kinship and exchange. We argued that the organisation and significance of kinship and exchange were constantly altered as people attempted to deal with and take advantage of their changing circumstances. The logic and structure of exchange were important in determining the direction of these changes, but did not in and of themselves determine them. The changes cannot be understood by an analysis that focuses on the internal logic of kinship and exchange alone. Instead they can only be understood within the broader context that shaped individual actions and decisions.

In the last three chapters, however, we have taken quite a different perspective and showed how the particular exchanges that we witnessed, exchanges that took place within a relatively short span of time, were tightly structured within a strongly genealogical framework. They cannot be understood adequately in terms of individual and idiosyncratic relations or in terms of individuals' positions in the larger political and economic system. In other words, they cannot be understood adequately in terms of the historical and economic factors that concerned us in chapters 2 and 4. This is because individuals' decisions and actions were tightly bound by the genealogical, structural rules of exchange. Chapters 5 and 6 described ways that these rules were manifest in the overall process of exchange, while this last chapter has described the way that these rules shaped the actions of individual participants. Taken together they show that Ponam exchange can by no means be reduced to or explained in terms of idiosyncratic or individual transactions and contingencies.

This was true in Ponams' conceptions of exchange as well as our own. A person might refuse to give to another for purely personal reasons, but when he or she did give, structural considerations were of great importance. People did not give simply to individuals, but gave instead to status holders, to "roads", as they described it. The discussion of the various transactions involving Mark Kupe during Camilius Pari's funeral illustrates this. People did not contribute to him simply as a person, as an individual who might use what he received for his own best advantage as he understood it. Instead, they gave to him as a road by which they could reach a desired destination. If there had been any suspicion that he might divert their gifts to some other end, people would have avoided him and found some other road. And people understood the various roads on which they might give as being in structured relationships to one another, as Charles Polangau and Augusta Pinambong's discussion of their planning for the funeral indicated. Even at the level of process, structural relations were foremost in people's minds.

The web of genealogically-structured statuses was a dense and complicated one. In Tony Kakaw's brideprice, for example, 21 different *ken si*s were involved as kin of the groom, and 17 as kin of the bride, a total of 38. Although we do not have complete records on this, it is certain that most roads had at least ten contributors; Teresia Pisile's had 35. Thus, a very large number of genealogical statuses was invoked in this exchange, though the actual number of individual participants could not have been more than about 150.

The apparently discrete and identifiable *ken si*s that appeared in gift displays were, thus, not at all discrete, but overlapped in numerous ways, with many individuals having obligations in a number of them. People were, of course, well aware of this, and were somewhat ambivalent about it. They used a nice metaphor to describe a person who participated on both sides of an exchange and who egged the givers on to give more and more, only to pop up on the other side to receive what was given. They called this *katihing*, after a small creature that lived in the sandy bottom of the lagoon in a burrow with two entrances. It would bite your foot if you trod on one entrance, but when you reached down in anger to grab it, you would see it peeping up from the other entrance some distance away, laughing at you.

In this they, and we, can see the tension between structure and process that arose as individuals filled a number of possibly conflicting statuses and attempted to play them off one against the other. Ponams' acute awareness and persistent involvement with this tension partially explains, we think, their highly sociological, objectivist, structural view of their own society. People were forced to occupy so many different, contradictory statuses that they came to see their society from many points of view, in a way characteristic of the sociological viewpoint.

We also suspect that this multiplicity of overlapping statuses helps to explain why the system appears so neat and orderly, so rule-bound. Each person was a member by right of many *ken si*s and no one's fate was totally tied to any one of them. If a person occupying one position found that his or her interests were threatened, it was not necessary to fight hard to defend them: it was always possible to find some other road, some other way to circumvent the threat. Thus, for example, when the young woman described earlier was forbidden to contribute to her fiancée as she expected to do, she got around this by contributing to him on another circuitous, but legitimate, route, and she urged others who wished to help her to contribute on this road as well. She did not have to violate the structural rules in order to do as she wished. Similarly, we expect that this logic will explain the rigidly agnatic composition of modern *kamal*s. As they became less significant economically, so there was less pressure to manipulate them to achieve individual ends.

In conclusion, then, Ponams saw their structured system as important, and as a system it was important, but for each individual any given unit was relatively insignificant. The system as a whole was more important than any of its parts. Individuals' interest in the system as a whole allowed this elaborately-structured system to flourish. Structure depended on process, just as process depended on structure.

The tension of
structure and process

We have organised our description of Ponam kinship and exchange in this book to illuminate the distinction between structural and processual approaches to social organisation and practice. Our concern with these two approaches springs in part from two sources. It comes first from our dissatisfaction with the repeated failure of Melanesian ethnographers to move beyond a fairly simple, synchronic, structural approach to kinship and exchange. As well, it comes from the way that Ponams themselves appeared to approach their own lives and practices.

Ponams regularly objectified and represented the structural units that they saw as making up their society when they displayed gifts in ceremonial exchange, and they regularly organised themselves and acted in terms of the groups portrayed in these displays. Perhaps for these reasons, islanders had a strikingly structural view of their society. That is, they were comfortable predicting and interpreting social behaviour in light of what one might call the consequences of the logical properties of their social arrangements. Ponams, then, took a Fortesian view of their world, seeing it as being very much like 'a unity made of parts and processes that are linked to one another by a limited number of principles of wide validity' (Fortes 1953: 39). They did not see their society in processual terms as the epiphenomenal consequence of 'concrete social activity [and of] the process of [the] ordering of action and of relations in reference to given social ends' (Firth 1964 [1954]: 45).

But even though Ponams took a structural view of themselves, they did not do so naively. To begin with, they did not accord any special ontic status to their social arrangements. Instead, they saw them as reflecting in important ways the volition of islanders. Their social arrangements had not been ordained by gods or spirits. Instead, they had been created by ancestors who were as human as modern Ponams, and who had adopted social institutions that best fit their needs.[1] Further, they were aware of the fact that people do not always

---

[1] To complicate matters, their explanations of these origins often had a sociological air. Thus, we have described the popular hypothesis that the institution of *kamal* began when ancestors decided to exclude women from the inheritance of real property in order to reduce what they saw as an undesirable pressure toward the

behave in the way that the model dictates. In some circumstances they explained this nonconformity in terms of a structural conflict: the conflict between allegiances to affines and to agnates was a recurring theme. But they did not articulate a set of coherent and independent motives that conflicted with their structural view. Some people were thought to be lazy or selfish, ignorant or indifferent. None, however, were thought to be responding to an alternative structure or scheme of motivation. Ponams did perceive that some villagers did not play the game properly; they did not perceive that anyone was playing a different game.

The complexities of islanders' structural approach were especially apparent in Ponam gift display, because in those displays they represented social order to themselves. But while islanders used these displays to represent their social structure to themselves, at the same time they used gift display to make political statements, to express their contingent circumstances in terms of their representation of the relations between the groups contained in their displays. However, in their own minds this political dimension of display appears to have been but a useful by-product of a more mundane and immediately functional purpose. That is, while they used the complex procedure of arranging displays to reveal their thoughts, they saw these displays primarily as a way to help arrange those thoughts in the first place, to help themselves to remember how all the many different participants were related to one another, and thus who should give or receive how much.

As our descriptions of Ponam exchange showed, the tension between structure and process in Ponam kinship and exchange was not something that became apparent only as a result of diligent fieldwork and careful analysis by a pair of trained anthropologists. Rather, it was a tension that, without too much distortion, could be said to have existed for Ponams themselves, a tension that they expressed regularly to themselves and to us. All that was really required of us was to pay attention to what they were doing and saying.[2]

---

fragmentation of holdings. In other words, Ponams explained this institution in terms of the concomitants of the principles of their social arrangements, and in many ways they appeared to see their society as one made up of people who manipulated their social arrangements in light of their understanding of these principles and concomitants (this point is pursued in J. Carrier 1987a).

[2] In her description of the Mendi, in the New Guinea Highlands, Rena Lederman (1986) indicates that they are aware of another tension within anthropological analysis, that between individual and group orientations. Her work and ours, like that of others (e.g. the description of aroe and bope as images of structure and process among the Bororo of Brazil, in Crocker 1985) indicates that these tensions are something more than just artifacts of scholarly analysis or even Western thought, and that resolving or transcending them may entail more than scholarly advance or freeing ourselves from our cultural presuppositions.

The tension between structure and process that Ponams wrestled with in exchange was particularly intriguing to us as ethnographers because it so clearly recalled the tension between structural and processual approaches to social organisation that dominated Melanesian ethnography in the 1960s, the 1970s and the 1980s. Structure was seen to subsume process; structure was taken to be an epiphenomenon of process; structure and process were deemed to be radically different from each other. In the 1980s, however, a different anthropological approach to this tension began to emerge, and though this emergence occurred outside of Melanesian studies, it was influential in the ethnography of the region. This approach sought to transcend the tension between these two orientations by developing a more inclusive model that would encompass both structure and process. The leading candidate for this higher frame was the notion of practice ("praxis" in an older terminology). Indeed, in her review, 'Theory in anthropology since the sixties', Sherry Ortner predicted that "practice" would be the most important theoretical orientation of the 1980s. The notion of practice was seen to bring together the processualist concern with human action and interaction and the structuralist interest in system. Writers concerned with practice contended that people's activities are not simply a reflection of their interests, a view often assumed by early processualists, but are guided by their structured, cultural understanding of their situation, an understanding that springs from and feeds back on the practical situations in which people find themselves.

Ortner picked out two writers, Marshall Sahlins and Pierre Bourdieu, as being of special interest. The work of these two men is particularly appropriate for the themes of this book. Sahlins was concerned especially with the relationships between structure and historical process, the subject of our first four chapters on Ponam kinship and exchange; Bourdieu was concerned especially with the relationship between structure and immediate contingency, the subject of our last three chapters.[3] We will deal with these writers partly because their

---

[3] The other obvious candidate for inclusion in the ranks of practice theorists is Anthony Giddens, mentioned in the introduction. While his theory of structuration attempts to transcend the distinction between structure and process, at least one critic has argued that, 'Far from transcending the dichotomy, Giddens's approach presupposes it' (Hekman 1990: 158). In any event, we will not consider Giddens here, for structuration has had little impact on Melanesian anthropology. This may reflect the fact that Giddens is too sociological for the extremely cultural orientation of much recent, influential work in Melanesia. In addition, his writing is so abstract that it is difficult, at least for us and some others (e.g. Stinchcombe 1990), to decide the actual content and implications of his arguments, though it seems unlikely that he makes a significant advance over Sahlins and Bourdieu. Telling criticisms of Giddens's work appear in Clark, Modgil and Modgil (1990).

work is important in its own right, and partly because we can express our own views through a discussion of theirs.

Sahlins argued that, seen from the perspective of history, the distinction between structure and "event" (which corresponds to process) is false because people's actions are culturally-informed praxis, so that 'all events are culturally systematic.... [That is,] an event is indeed a happening of significance, and *as significance* it is dependent on the structure for its existence' (1985: 153). By exemplifying cultural categories, events act to reproduce culture. Thus, in his discussion of how the Hawaiian cultural understanding of the events of Western colonisation affected Hawaiian society, he said: 'Encompassing the extraordinary event in traditional cultural forms they would thus recreate the received distinctions of Hawaiian status' (1985: 138). However, event is not simply shaped by culture: it acts back upon culture as well. This is because 'the world is under no obligation to conform to the logic by which some people conceive it.' When people act, their 'cultural categories acquire new functional values.... [T]he cultural meanings are thus altered. It follows that the relationships between categories change: the structure is transformed' (1985: 138).

Sahlins thus wanted to dissolve the contradiction between structural and processual approaches by defining cultural structures and circumstantial actions as dialectically related: a structured ideology produces action in an environment which reproduces (but slightly modifies) the ideology, and so on. However, in setting up this dialectic Sahlins eliminated from consideration the form of structure that had most concerned the early writers, *social* structure. Like many of the later anthropologists discussed in the introduction, he was concerned with the structure of symbols, meanings and understandings rather than the structure of society. Sahlins did not attempt to analyse structures, patterns and regularities of behaviour that are not part of people's cultural stock.

Thus, his approach leaves no room for an old question from the 1960s, how well does people's interpretation of their social order match that order itself? After all, there is no *a priori* reason to assume that people see their social arrangements accurately and adequately. Sahlins says that reality need not accord with people's structured culture, but he does not pursue the point and address the questions of how this mismatch might come about (other than as a result of external accidents like Cook's arrival in Hawaii), how it is or is not maintained, and what the social consequences of its maintenance might be. As a result, questions of ideology and false-consciousness are difficult to frame using his approach. Thus, Sahlins cannot easily see if or how people are systematically misled by their structured culture.

This point is illustrated by Raymond Kelly in his discussion of the social organisation of the Etoro, a New Guinea Highlands society. The Etoro were organised into a number of small patrilineal lineages. They used classificatory sibling terminology extensively, prohibited marriage with sisters, preferred sister exchange and agnatic parallel marriage, and insisted on reciprocity in gifts of women. These marriage practices caused the lineages to be aligned into two identifiable marriage-class moieties, which were the predominant structural feature of Etoro society. Strikingly, however, these moieties were not recognised by Etoro people (Kelly 1974: 118–119). Thus, the logical properties of Etoro marriage rules generated a particular identifiable social structure that could be analysed independently of the cultural principles of the Etoro themselves.[4]

The point that social structures may not march with cultural perceptions emerged with particular force in the later 1980s, in a debate about gender relations. In her study of the Kewa, of the New Guinea Highlands, Lisette Josephides (1985) argued that there was an objective gender inequality, a structure of gender relations, springing from the way that men appropriated women's products in the process of exchange and used them to their own benefit. Those who dissented from Josephides's analysis (e.g. Errington & Gewertz 1987a; M. Strathern 1987, 1988) generally argued that it was necessary to consider the cultural interpretation of these events, and they asserted that things would look different from an indigenous perspective. These dissents raise an important issue: To what degree are the analytical categories of anthropologists adequate to describe and explain life in Melanesian societies? In raising that issue the dissenters appear to claim, at least tacitly, that indigenous cultural constructions define and delimit the questions that an anthropologist should ask. However, we think that the fact of material gender inequality, of the sort that Josephides identified, is important. It merits anthropological attention regardless of whether or not it may be visible from the cultural perspective of the Kewa themselves.

Kelly's work on the Etoro and the debate about gender inequality point to an important flaw in Sahlins's approach. If there are structural regularities that are either invisible to or un-noticed by members of society, and if these regularities have practical consequences, then a focus on cultural structures will be inadequate to explain social life. Indeed, this criticism can be lodged against the general turn away from social anthropology and toward cultural anthropology in Melanesia (and elsewhere) over the past twenty years.[5]

---

[4] As Knauft (1985) describes it, the Gebusi, of lowland Papua, present an analogous case. They were unaware of the objective connection between certain sorts of marriage that they considered desirable, and recurrent sorcery and violence between affines.

[5] Another shortcoming in Sahlins's model deserves mention. His writing on Hawaii presents an image of people who are totally absorbed by their cultural structures. These structures are so pervasive and determinant that people are

This shortcoming is not really apparent because of the momentous and unique nature of the historical event that Sahlins has chosen to analyse and explain, the Hawaiian encounter with Captain Cook and the cultural changes that ensued. The inadequacy of this approach *would* be apparent if Sahlins had chosen, for example, to study not the encounter with Captain Cook, but the encounter with the Dole Pineapple Company. In order to understand this long-term encounter with an agent of capitalist colonisation one has to understand the structures of nineteenth-century capitalism, structures that were significant in ways that the actors involved neither knew nor understood, and thus could not be analysed within Sahlins's framework. Similarly, such a topic would probably have required a broader consideration of the ways that people reflected on their own society and practices, and the ways that they used these in political debate and in response to growing colonial presence.[6] In other words, while Sahlins's historical orientation is important, his work fails to consider social facts and structures that are not apparent in people's own cultural frameworks.

The second of the writers Ortner identified who used practice as a key concept to incorporate structure and process was Pierre Bourdieu. In *Outline of a theory of practice*, published in the 1970s, Bourdieu, like Sahlins, argued that analyses based on either structure or process alone are inadequate and even deceptive. Bourdieu sought to transcend the distinction between the two through the study of practice, action that shapes and is shaped by culture, as well as shaping and being shaped by objective social conditions. Also like Sahlins, Bourdieu gave a central place to structured understanding, his concept of habitus, by which he meant the set of structured beliefs and values that predispose members of society to act in certain ways.

Bourdieu differs from Sahlins, however, in that he united habitus (structured culture) and practice (action in the world) without discarding either social structure or strategic uses of culture as Sahlins seems to have done. Thus, he did not adopt Sahlins's mentalistic tendency to locate structure only in culture. Instead, his model includes a dimension that Sahlins's lacks, one that links him

---

unable to (or at least fail to) distance themselves from them. Hence, his model makes it difficult to pursue another question of the 1960s. That is, how are people's models of social order consciously used as instruments of rhetoric and tools in political struggles? This use of people's models of social order is important for understanding the way that Ponams used gift display to make political comments, as well as for understanding the political use of *kastom* in Melanesia (Keesing & Tonkinson 1982). It is also, of course, an important part of Scheffler's argument in *Choiseul Island social structure*.

[6] These points echo Thomas's earlier (1982) criticism of Sahlins. They are pursued in Linnekin (1983) and Thomas (n.d.), and in a related form in Kaplan (1990).

with those old-fashioned structuralists (such as Marx) who believed there is a structured reality apart from that of ideology.

This is expressed in Bourdieu's criticism of phenomenologists (who denied the existence, and hence the power, of social structure), a criticism that applies equally well to those, like Sahlins, who locate structure exclusively in ideology and the interpretations it makes of the world. Bourdieu argues that the concern with representation and understanding (or "accounts") is misleading to the degree that analysts assume that these representations are coterminus with the social world. He says:

> One is entitled to undertake to give an "account of accounts", so long as one does not put forward one's contribution to the science of pre-scientific representation of the social world as if it were a science of the social world.... Only by constructing the objective structures (price curves, chances of access to higher education, laws of the matrimonial market, etc.) is one able to pose the question of the mechanisms through which the relationship is established between the structures and the practices or the representations which accompany them, instead of treating these "thought objects" as "reasons" or "motives" and making them the determining cause of the practices (Bourdieu 1977: 21).

Although Bourdieu does avoid an important shortcoming in Sahlins's attempt to transcend the distinction between structure and process, his work has an important shortcoming of its own. That is, a failure to move beyond a relatively synchronic framework, a failure to deal with historical time, the problem that Sahlins addresses, however inadequately he may do so. In his criticism of Lévi-Strauss's reformulation of Mauss's model of gift exchange, Bourdieu (1977: 4–8) distances himself from the totallising synchronic approach of what he calls objectivist social science. Instead, he argues, it is necessary to incorporate 'time into the theoretical representations of a practice [i.e., gift exchange] which, being temporally structured, is intrinsically defined by its *tempo*' (1977: 8). But as Bourdieu uses it in his illustrative arguments, this time is a time of individual strategies and calculations, it is not a time of historical change. It is a micro-social time defined and given meaning by the interaction, not one that easily incorporates events taking place outside of it. Because of this, it is difficult to use his model to analyse the consequences of systematic changes in people's circumstance, just the sort of changes that were so important in shaping Ponam kinship and exchange in the twentieth century.

Thus there appear to be important flaws and limitations in both Bourdieu's and Sahlins's attempt to transcend the tension between structure and process. One attempt lacks social structure (as the complement to ideological structure), the other lacks history (the complement to synchronic process). Yet, we argue, even by introducing all four analytical component — cultural structure, social structure, historical process, synchronic process — we cannot make a picture that resolves the conflict between structure and process. While Bourdieu's and Sahlins's attempts do contain important insights, it seems most appropriate to consider them as ways to address the tension between structural and processual approaches, rather than satisfactory ways of subsuming that tension under some higher-order set of terms. In a sense, then, we are not much farther along than we were when Marx observed, in the beginning of *The eighteenth Brumaire*, that people make their own history, but not in circumstances of their own making. This should not come as a surprise. This tension has dogged social analysis for a long time, and we see no reason to assume that scholars of the present generation are really able to solve the problem that worried so many of their predecessors. It is for this reason that we approached structure and process in the way that we have in this book — an approach that echoes that of Ponam Islanders themselves. Like them, we see structure and process as alternative, complementary approaches to the ways that islanders lived and ordered their lives; both valid within their own limits, but both limited. The two approaches together modify each other, and help us, at least, to understand what Ponam society was, how it operated, and how it came to be that way.

We want to illustrate this complementarity more concretely in terms of Ponam society.

STRUCTURE AND PROCESS ON PONAM

In accord with both Bourdieu's and Sahlins's point that the structures contained in culture are real and motivating and cannot be discounted, we showed the importance of kinship structures as Ponams conceived them. Ponam kinship was not what Scheffler suggested in *Choiseul Island social structure*, a system of rhetoric that offers post-hoc justifications for self-interested actions. It constrained and defined people's behaviour far more than that. The power of Ponam kinship structures is most evident in our discussion of the exchanges and gift displays that served to create and externalise kinship structures which then shaped action.

Bourdieu used the phrase 'the dialectic of objectification and embodiment' (1977: 87–95) to describe the way that structured ideologies acquire an external reality that makes them determining and motivating in a way that a purely internal ideology, however structured, can never be. His argument rests on the premise that the external world is shaped by human beings, and human beings are not mindless. Thus, when they shape that world they do so in terms of their cultures, which thereby achieve concrete manifestation. In this way, says Bourdieu, structured ideologies become objectified. The world is stamped with human culture and contains in an objective and constraining form the culture of members of society. Actors in this world then embody, or take back into themselves as empirical and real, the same structures that they have put into it; or, 'the mental structures which construct the world of objects are constructed in the practice of a world of objects constructed according to the same structures' (1977: 91). In other words, structures such as those of Ponam *kamals* and *ken si*s are perceived as real, objective, and constraining because for the people involved in the system they are indeed so.

In the acting out of ceremonial exchange Ponams continuously object-ified and re-embodied the structures of kin relations in a process that was no less powerful for being at least in part a conscious intellectual endeavour. This objectification and re-embodiment took place in two ways. First, contributions to prestations were not simply lumped together at their final destination, but all were carried carefully from house to house through a whole series of stages as they moved gradually nearer the leaders of the exchange. Contributors too walked through this series of relationships, following out the "roads" by which they were connected to their kin, re-embodying them as they did so. Second, at each stage in the proceeding contributions were displayed in diagrams that made explicit the relationships that were being acted out. Thus, Ponam eti-quette made it mandatory that participants should declare at each stage exactly what roads they were following, and that they should build upon the ground with their gifts a map of their relationships to one another. The external world of *ken si*s and their structure was there to be embodied. And of course all of this was played out once more in reverse as the prestation was distributed and redistributed. These constant re-enactments and objectifications of those kin relationships in ceremonial exchange gave them a power and reality that was quite external to the mind of any individual.

In exchange and gift display we can see the reality and power of culture, the way that it structured action. However, exchange and gift display also illustrate the essential link between cultural structures and practical action. Cultural ideologies are not created just by thought, but are themselves created by action in the world and so must be analysed in the context of the actions and environment that produce them. This means that we cannot understand human action through the study of ideology alone. Studies of kinship and exchange often seem to take this view, but we believe they are misdirected when they do so. The structured ideology of Ponam kinship served to structure action in the world *because* the world itself was, in many ways, structured in terms of that ideology. However, because ideology itself is created and re-created through action in the world, through social process, to understand ideology it is there-fore necessary to look at the action that produces it. That is, it is necessary to look at both sides of the dialectic between cultural structures and social processes. Looking at both, however, brings out a third essential subject, social structure. To re-phrase a point we made earlier in this chapter, attention to the processes of action in the world brings out the power and importance of structures that are not necessarily part of the cultural ideology of the people being studied.

Attention to concrete practices encourages observers not only to see how the structures they study are made real in daily life, but also to see how the structures they study are situated in a world of practical human concern and activity, a world that may itself be structured in ways and by forces that actors do not understand. However self-evident this point may appear, it needs re-petition. Practical human activity is, after all, shaped by factors beyond the immediate scope of our concerns, whether we are people acting or anthropo-logists studying people acting. Thus, we need to be aware of the situation of the society and its structures, to see those structures as themselves situated in a larger world.

In chapters 2 and 4 we investigated the larger world in which Ponam was situated in the twentieth century.[7] We showed that Ponams' relationship to this larger world had a profound effect on the structure of their kinship and exchange, an effect that occurred because colonial change affected the practical situations in which they had to live their lives. These effects were so far-reaching that by the time we went there Ponam was in many ways a colonial creation. This is not to say that Ponam was in any sense a simple reproduction of the Australian society that colonised it. On the contrary, the interaction of Ponam and Australian societies had produced a course of change that was unique to Ponam. (And, of course, by virtue of their prominence in the new national elite, Manus people, Ponams included, contributed to the national social structures that will shape Ponam's future.)

Though we have criticised Sahlins for some things, what we have said about Ponam echoes what he said about the way that Hawaiians respond to external events. They responded to colonial contact as Hawaiians, so that the impact of colonisation there, like the impact of colonisation on Ponam, led to a new indigenous order, an order that was no longer traditional, but was not that of the coloniser either.

---

[7] Here we emphasise the effect of colonisation on Ponam. In the study of a society like Ponam in the twentieth century, it is reasonable to point the causal arrow in that direction. It is important to remember, however, C.A. Gregory's point in *Gifts and commodities*: over the region as a whole, the structure of Melanesian societies had an effect on the structure of the intruding capitalist system. And also, even at the level of individual villages like Ponam, the ability of the en-croaching capitalist system to penetrate is affected by village cultural structure and social organisation (see, e.g., Epstein 1968; Finney 1973). Some of the ways that Ponam kinship and exchange structures restricted the imposition of capital-ist social relations and enterprises are described in part in *WT&E*.

We have argued here that attention to the detail of social process is important in two distinct ways. First, it is important because it is in social processes that people act out their cultural structures, and so make them real and constraining — what Bourdieu calls objectification and embodiment. Consequently, a study of cultural structures that is not tied to the processes by which they are enacted will be highly artificial. In saying this we are only echoing Bourdieu's warnings (1977: 1–2) about the danger of studying these structures without also studying process: ideology studied in the abstract this way is particularly likely to reflect the abstracting requirements of anthropology and the techniques of fieldwork as much as it reflects the understanding that actually motivates the people being studied.[8] We have tried to heed this by deriving Ponam kinship structures from the representations that they made to and for one another in exchange, representations in which ideology and process were clearly and inextricably linked together.

The second reason for paying close attention to the detail of social process is that it is there that one observes the impact of structures that are not part of local culture, or that are not closely linked to the aspect of culture under study. We have described, for example, the way that the colonial demand for young male labour and the colonial need to sell imported commodities altered both the practice and the ideology of marriage negotiations and brideprice payments. While it certainly is *possible* to appreciate these larger contextual factors in the absence of close attention to process, such attention clearly facilitates an awareness of how context shapes the enactment of cultural structures and thereby affects those structures themselves.

Taken together, these points indicate that the study of social process is essential for the understanding of culture and ideology because it is by the study of process that we locate ideas in the context in which people use them, in the context in which they mean something to people. We stress this here because we believe that a methodical attention to process could help to draw the study of kinship and exchange in Papua New Guinea out of the self-contained world of ideology in which it is now enclosed and into the main stream of activities in Papua New Guinea, where it belongs.

CONCLUSION: PROCESS AND HISTORICAL CONTEXT

We have argued that both structural and processual approaches are important to the study of kinship and exchange, and indeed social life more generally. Yet here we want to stress the importance of the study of process and

---

[8] LiPuma (1983) demonstrates the force of this point in the context of Melanesian ethnography.

what we see as its corollary, the location of one's subject in a realistic historical context. While we are mindful of Radcliffe-Brown's point (1935: 400–401) that structural and historical analyses each can be valid in terms of the different questions they address, we think an historical awareness is helpful both in showing the transience of these structures (especially in areas like Melanesia in the twentieth century) and in restraining the sort of extrapolations based on the structural logic of systems that we criticised in chapter 4. Thus, we conclude this work with a discussion of process not because we think that it is inherently more important than the study of ideological or social structures, but because process and history, rather than structure, are missing from so much contemporary research. We believe that this absence has led to an incomplete portrait of the realities of kinship and exchange in Papua New Guinea, one that often seems to take little or no account of the changes that have taken place there in the last hundred years and their effect on peoples' structured understanding or behaviour. (These points are pursued in J. Carrier n.d.).

This failure is apparent in many of the influential works on kinship and exchange in the New Guinea Highlands. Here we discuss two that are interesting especially because they review large bodies of ethnographic literature, but the tendency that concerns us is there in ethnographic monographs as well. The first of these works is Paula Rubel and Abraham Rosman's *Your own pigs you may not eat*. They analysed thirteen societies, ranging from the Banaro, for whom they use data published in 1916, to the Melpa, using data from the 1960s and 1970s. They compared societies using a number of different variables, including: 'rules regarding the nature of descent and descent-group formation, rules regarding post-marital residence, rules regarding exchange of women and goods with affines, rules regarding ceremonial exchange, rules regarding exchange of goods with spirits, the structure of the spirit world, the organization of leadership, and kinship terminology' (Rubel & Rosman 1978: 7). And, as we reported in the introduction, they concluded: 'The structure that underlies ceremonial exchange is the same structure underlying other cultural domains.... The structure of ceremonial exchange also organizes behavior in other cultural domains, which is why it can be singled out as the dominant structure' (1978: 319–320).

The key to any study like this is the selection of variables for analysis, for of course that selection limits the conclusions one can draw. Here, all the variables were institutions and relations that anthropologists have associated with pre-colonial Papua New Guinea. Rubel and Rosman failed to include in their analysis variables that appear to be consequences of colonisation, such as wage labour, migration, cash cropping, education, church affiliation, national and local politics and so on. Of course these factors were probably not of the same significance for the Banaro in the 1910s as they were for the Melpa in the 1970s, but we think it is likely that in almost all the places that the colonial admin-istration allowed anthropologists to work, these kinds of factors were too significant to be ignored.

We expect that Rubel and Rosman ignored these variables in the belief that outside, Western influences would be at least superfluous, and probably confusing, given their plan to analyse the possible evolution of pre-colonial Highlands forms of social organisation. Unfortunately, when they selected only apparently-traditional variables they compromised their ability to accomplish their purpose. This is because accomplishing it requires that the traditional variables they studied were truly in a traditional state, an assumption that we find untenable. One cannot wash out the effects of colonisation on a society simply by ignoring features that are obviously products of colonisation, because even apparently-traditional aspects of life will necessarily bear the marks of colonisation, as we showed in the discussions of Ponam history and as we argue at length in *WT&E*. Consequently, by ruling out of consideration those variables likely to reflect Western influence, Rubel and Rosman made it most difficult to determine whether the variables that did concern them remained in a relatively traditional state or had been modified in significant ways by colonisation. Their study illustrates the problems of dealing with kinship and exchange in an artificially-traditional context. Had Rubel and Rosman paid greater attention to the practical processes of kinship and exchange they would have been better able to see what was influenced by Western impact and how it was influenced, and so would have been better able to avoid their sterile traditionalism.

The difficulties of this kind of de-historicised analysis, the difficulties that follow when anthropologists ignore contemporary circumstances in favour of traditional-seeming ideology, are also apparent in Marilyn Strathern's review essay, 'Marriage exchanges: A Melanesian comment'.[9] Like the writers she reviewed, Strathern ignored the processes of modern exchange and their contemporary economic, political and symbolic context. She focused instead on a complex cultural problem, 'understanding the role of exchanges in items other than persons when these items are part of or move in conjunction with transactions (such as marriage) conceptualised as exchanges of persons' (1984b: 42), and she located the problem entirely within a traditional context. Reflecting the interests of the writers whose work she reviewed, none of the issues she discussed concern the changes that have taken place in Melanesian marriage in the last hundred years, or attempt to relate any aspects of marriage to non-

---

[9] Similar points could be made using Strathern's *The gender of the gift*. We restrict ourselves to her review essay here, both because it is more accessible than the book and because it more clearly addresses the topics of kinship and exchange.

traditional spheres of life. It is indicative of this traditionalism that in this review Strathern did not address the question of money, one of the key 'items other than persons ... [that] move in ... exchanges of persons.'

Strathern did deal with the use of money among the people of Mt Hagen, in the New Guinea Highlands, in another paper, 'Subject or object'. She argued that Hagen people's use of money and property, in marriage exchange and elsewhere, cannot be understood in terms of Western models, particularly models of the relationship of persons and objects. This is because money must be interpreted in terms of indigenous values. This point is not contentious. Our concern, however, is that she did not undertake the inverse analysis, analysis of the ways that the importation of money into ceremonial exchange is accompanied by the importation and creation of novel values and associations. These come from the activities and places and social relations where money is mostly made and spent. For the Hagen villagers that concerned Strathern these include cash crops, trade stores, markets, local government councils and rural wage labour, and probably Hagen town itself. For almost all Papua New Guineans, money carries associations springing from its use in the urban world, the social realm most closely associated with money, both in fact and in common cultural conception.

Colin Filer's analysis (1985) of a series of letters to the editor in the main Papua New Guinea newspaper, the *Post-Courier*, illustrates some of the cultural values that have become associated with money in the urban world. In the letters he studied, the use of money in brideprice is tied up with issues of prostitution, domestic violence, ethnic identity, family solidarity, divorce, wage labour, remittances and much more. Urban life is the scene of the creation of new meanings for money, exchange, gender and so on, meanings that un-doubtedly have significance for all but the most remote villages. Neither Filer's article nor the letters reviewed in it provide symbolic detail or completeness of the sort given in the conventional anthropological analyses that Strathern reviewed. But they illustrate that those more conventional analyses are likely to be incomplete if they write about marriage exchange in Papua New Guinea without considering any of these issues.

In the preceding pages have we have illustrated what we see as a continuing, misleading timelessness in studies of kinship and exchange in Papua New Guinea. We stress it here because we think that it is facilitated by what we identified in the introduction as the dominant concern in studies of kinship and exchange in Papua New Guinea in the 1980s, the structure of cultural beliefs. Both the concern with structure and the concern with culture discourage attention to practical processes, the sort of attention that was instrumental in bringing down the old Fortesian structuralism in the 1960s and the sort of attention that helps make visible the broader social, political and economic contexts in which villagers like Ponam Islanders lead their lives. For us, this attention to practical processes has meant, among other things, looking at what valuables are used in marriage exchange and through whose hands they move as they are transacted: what they are, where they come from and where they go, and thus how exchange is linked to the valuable-producing world outside of Ponam. Once this connection is made, it is no longer possible to think of exchange solely in terms of its own internal structures or in terms of the structures of kinship.

As our discussion of Filer's work indicates, we do not think that the whole of anthropological work on Melanesian kinship and exchange is coloured by the same inattention to process and the effects of history. For example, in 'The division of labor and processes of social change in Mount Hagen', Andrew Strathern discusses changes in the ways that money moved through male and female hands and the way that these changes have affected conceptions of exchange, conceptions of gender and relations to the world outside. Daryl Feil (1982) also looked at this kind of connectedness between systems of exchange and the wider world in his paper on the transformations brought to Highlands exchange systems by colonisation. Of course there is other work that avoids the problems that we have described here, some of which we mentioned in the introduction to this book.

However, most of the writing on kinship and exchange has failed to attend to the modern context. This is unfortunate because it is not at all clear that we can make sense of kinship and exchange as ideologies, structures or processes, unless we recognise the context in which they now necessarily exist, the context provided by the modern, capitalist economy and state. This context and its consequences are, of course, not everything, not all that should be studied. But they are everywhere and influence everything, even the heart of traditional village life, kinship and ceremonial exchange.

Social indicators from the 1980 census

| Indicator | Census Districts | | | National | |
	Manus	Kavieng	Rabaul	Max.	Min.
Population density per sq km	11.3	9.0	21.9	80.7	0.3
Sex ratio (males/100 females)	103.2	132.7	124.7	148.6	85.5
Youth dependency ratio[a]	893	712	810	1038	561
Aged dependency ratio[b]	59	75	49	189	13
Child–woman ratio[c]	738	810	810	981	499
Average distance of district population to nearest town,[d] in km.	114.3	63.4	17.5	457	8.9
% of pop. in rural non-village sector	3.6	17.9	1.5	54.9	0.0
% of pop. in urban area	20.8	16.6	20.5	55.0	0.0
Inter-provincial in-migration[e]	83.3	163.6	184.1	388	4.2
% 10 years+ in wage employment	12.0	20.2	19.8	34.2	1.2
% 10 years+ in big or small business	0.7	1.9	2.0	12.8	0.1
% 5–25 years at school	34.4	32.6	32.0	34.4	4.8
% not at school who completed grade 6	29.2	23.3	31.3	31.3	1.0
Males 7–12 years, % in school	61.1	60.0	66.3	69.9	10.8
Females 7–12 years, % in school	59.2	59.2	65.1	65.1	3.8
% more than 1 hour from school	91	91	86	100	13
% more than:					
1 hour from health centre or aid post	95	91	78	100	32
15 min. from primary drinking water source	64	35	48	100	2

a (pop. 0–15 yrs x 1000) / (pop. 15–59 yrs)

b (pop. 59+ yrs x 1000) / (pop. 15–59 yrs)

c (pop. 0–4 yrs x 1000) / (fem. pop. 15–44 yrs)

d 500+ population, density of 250/km^2, urban characteristics. The figure for Manus is distorted by the fact that a small fraction of the population lives on distant atolls. The bulk of the population lives within 50 km of town.

e (born outside province x 1000) / (enumerated in district)

Source: de Albuquerque 1986: 59–70

Definitions of kinship terms

Term/ reciprocal		Genealogical meaning	Example
Abu/ abu		tama-tama	FF
		tama-tine	MF
		asi-tama	FFZ
		asi-tine	MFZ
	(m-s)*	naro-naro-	CC
	(m-s)	naro-naro-nato-	//-sib's CC
	(w-s)	tama-woro- (informally)	HF

Note: When used formally, for distant kin or for affines the appropriate term was tombru- .

* m-s = term used by a man speaking; w-s = term used by a woman speaking.

Anifo-/ anifo-		naropiso-tine	MB
	(m-s)	naro-naropiso-	ZC

Note: The term of address is kali.

Asi/ natue- (f) narohamero-(m)		naropiso-tama	FZ
		tine-tama	FM
		naro-parif asi	FZD

Lasepo-/ lasepo-	(w-s)	woro-naro-parif	DH
	(m-s)	tine-woro-	WM

Note: This term was apparently used only for close daughter's husbands and wives' close mothers. Distant affines of this class were called njana-.

Lowa-		cognate other than descendant, not term of address.	

Malesowa-/ malesowa-	(m-s)	naropiso-woro-	WB
	(w-s)	woro-naropiso-	ZH

Marike-/ marike-		(a) any relative by marriage	
		(b) traditionally, especially spouse's //-sex affines, e.g. WBW, HZH	

Mbrutile-/ mbrutile-		naro-asi	FZC
		naro-anifo-mahan	MBC

Note: Cross-cousins in a joking relationship.

Narohamero-/ asi	(w-s)	naro-kamal naro-kamal	SS
	(w-s)	naro-kamal naro-piso-	BS
	(w-s)	naro-kamal naropiso-tine	MBS

Term/ reciprocal		Genealogical meaning	Example
Naro-/		own child	
tama (m)		naro-nato-	//-sib's C
tine (f)		naro-woro-	H/W's C
	(m-s)	naro-anifo-	MBC/ZCC
		nato-marin-woro-	WyZ/HyB
Naropiso-/		opposite sex sibling	
naropiso-	(w-s)	naro-kamal tama	FS
	(w-s)	naro-kamal tine	MS
	(m-s)	naro-parif tama	FD
	(m-s)	naro-parif tine	MD
Nato-/		same-sex sibling	
nato-	(w-s)	naro-parif tama	FD
	(w-s)	naro-parif tine	MD
	(m-s)	naro-kamal tama	FS
	(m-s)	naro-kamal tine	MS
Natue-/	(w-s)	naro-naropiso-	BD
asi	(w-s)	naro-naro-kamal	SD
	(w-s)	naro-parif anifo-	MBD
Nja-kali/		woro-anifo-kamal	MBW
nja-kali	(m-s)	woro-anifo-marin kamal	MBSW
Njalepa-/	(w-s)	naropiso-woro-	HZ
njalepa-	(w-s)	woro-naropiso-	ZH
Njana-/		tine-woro-	H/WM
njana-		tama-woro	H/WF
		woro-naro-	DH/SW
		asi-woro-	H/WFZ
		woro-asi-woro-	H/WFZH
		anifo-woro-	H/WMB
		woro-anifo-woro-	H/WMBW
	(w-s)	woro-natue-	BDH
	(w-s)	woro-narohamero-	BSW
	(m-s)	woro-anifo-marin parif	ZDH
Pahamwelie-/		woro-nato-	//-sib H/W
pahamwelie-		nato-woro-	H/W //-sib
		woro-naropiso-woro-	H/W //-sib H/W
Palue- (pelu)/		woro-asi	FZH
palue-		woro-nato-tine	MZH
	(m-s)	natue-woro-	WMBS
	(m-s)	narohamero-woro-	WMBD
Pito- (to-)/		tine tine	MM
pito-	(w-s)	naro-naro-parif	DC
	(w-s)	naro-natue-	MBDC

Term/ reciprocal		Genealogical meaning	Example
Poro-/ poro-		marike-marike-	
	Note:	Affine of one's affine.	
Tama/ naro-		father	F
		nato-tama	FB
		naro-kamal asi	FZS
	(w-s)	woro-naro-parif	DH
	(w-s)	woro-nato-mahan	oZH
Tine/ naro-		mother	M
		tine-nato-	//-sib's M
		woro-tama	FW
		nato-tine	MZ
	(m-s)	woro-nato-mahan	oBW

Source: A. Carrier 1987: appendix 5.

Recipients of
two engagement distributions

Most prestations were not as involved or as important as that for Camilius Pari, but all had a similar number of participants and a similar pattern of participation. The table shows participation in two distributions of engagement tobacco in which we interviewed all recipients. More than 85 percent of resident mature adults participated in each distribution, and in each nearly 30 percent received more than one share of the tobacco distributed.

	—— Number of roads on which recipients received ——							
	1	2	3	4	5	6	7	Total
Engagement: July 1979[1]								
All adult participants:								
%	62	21	10	4	1	1	1	100
(n)	(83)	(28)	(14)	(5)	(1)	(1)	(2)	(134)
Resident female adult participants:								
%	54	22	14	6	2	2	2	102
(n)	(35)	(14)	(9)	(4)	(1)	(1)	(1)	(65)
Resident male adult participants:								
%	56	29	10	2	0	0	2	99
(n)	(27)	(14)	(5)	(1)	(0)	(0)	(1)	(48)
All resident adult participants:								
%	55	25	12	4	1	1	2	100
(n)	(62)	(28)	(14)	(5)	(1)	(1)	(2)	(113)
Engagement: January 1980[2]								
All adult participants:								
%	71	15	11	1	1	0	0	99
(n)	(95)	(20)	(15)	(2)	(2)	(0)	(0)	(134)
Resident female adult participants:								
%	67	14	13	3	3	0	0	100
(n)	(48)	(10)	(9)	(2)	(2)	(0)	(0)	(71)
Resident male adult participants:								
%	69	20	12	0	0	0	0	101
(n)	(35)	(10)	(6)	(0)	(0)	(0)	(0)	(51)
All resident adult participants:								
%	68	16	12	2	2	0	0	100
(n)	(83)	(20)	(15)	(2)	(2)	(0)	(0)	(122)

1 Of adult residents, 12 women and 7 men did not participate.

2 Of adult residents, 11 women and 6 men did not participate.

Glossary

ANOF.[1] Gift of valuables or property made in order to compensate another person or group for injury or loss. Property given this way is alienated and, unlike other gifts of property, cannot be reclaimed.

ARIBIHI SAL, "open the road". An engagement, and sometimes the prestation made for it. This prestation is also called simply "tabac", for its main element, twist tobacco.

BROLOFAU. Prestation made by a person's maternal kin to paternal *tamatus*, on the occasion of his or her return to the island from a new and distant place.

BRONA-PARIF, "woman price". The money and valuables paid by a husband and his kin to his wife's kin to confirm her transfer to her husband and his kin. This is usually paid in a ceremony called *njakenjak*. By itself, *brona* can refer to the price in cash or kind of any object, such as rice in a store, fish or sago in a market.

FILI'I. To avoid a person or thing because of some special relationship. People avoid their cross-sex affines, and they often avoid particular people, places or things that remind them of a dead relative for whom they mourn greatly. This latter kind of avoidance can be terminated by an exchange.

HURUHUT. A method of distributing goods by dealing them out equally in hands- or cups-full to all recipients.

JOSO. A customary marriage ceremony, also marriage and marriage ceremonies of all kinds.

KAAPET. The period of mourning and the ceremony involved in it.

KAHU. The return prestation of raw food made by the recipient of a major prestation.

KAHUWE TABAC, "return prestation for the tobacco". The return prestation for an engagement prestation.

KAMAL, "male". Male gender and sex, also men's house and the group belonging to it.

---

[1] For ease of presentation, we define and illustrate terms using the present tense, except to refer to usages that had ceased by the 1980s. The reader should recognise, however, that the meanings Ponams gave to these terms, like the practices to which they refer, were not immutable.

240

KANA. All kinds of food. *Kana mahan* is a big gift of cooked food, such as was given at funerals, after *polot* seclusion and at other times.

KANA PE-HAU, "food for the door". The pig feast once held to celebrate the raising of a new men's house.

KAWAS. A kinsman or kinswoman from outside Ponam, particularly one with whom a person has an established trading and exchange relationship.

KE-GWOK, "origin of the work". The person or people who are the leaders or main sponsors of a prestation or return prestation. The imported word *gwok* is used much more often than the indigenous term *marai*.

KEN. This term is virtually identical to the Pidgin term "as". It means: base, bottom, behind, origin, starting point and a range of similar concepts. We translate it different ways in different circumstances.

KEN SI, "one origin". Two or more people who share a common ancestor.

KENDI'I. Literally, to count the number of something. In the contexts described here, to distribute, to count out to people.

LANGOU. Traditional valuables normally given in ceremonial exchange, primarily belts of shell money and dog's teeth, woven baskets filled with clothes, dishes, and small amounts of money, and traditional decorations, such as skirts and beadwork.

LAPAN. A leader, important person, rich person. The senior member of a *kamal* is *lapa-kamal*. The Manus Provincial Government Assembly is called the Lapan Assembly.

LAU ARA KAMAL, "line of the man". The descendants of a brother, when spoken of in relation to the descendants of a sister. In the context of affinal relations this term also means husband's kin.

LAU ARA PARIF, "line of the woman". The descendants of a sister, when spoken of in relation to the descendants of a brother. In the context of affinal relations this term also means wife's kin.

LO PAHIS, "on the coconut mat". A funeral prestation made to the deceased's kindred.

LOWA-. Cognates or kindred. All of those people with whom one shares a common ancestor, other than one's own children and descendants.

LULUAI (Pidgin). The village leader appointed by German and Australian colonial governments. The *lapans* of Kamal Kehin were luluais of Ponam from German times until the 1970s.

LUTUNG. The prestation of woven baskets and lesser valuables made by a person's children, affines and maternal kin to his or her *tamatus* in order to compensate them for carrying out the work of his or her burial.

MARA MAK AHIN / MAK MALANGAN, "lower bed / upper bed". These terms distinguish between true members of a *kamal* (*mak malangan*) and those who are there through patronage (*mara mak ahin*).

MARASUS, "nipples". The prestation sometimes made by husband's kin to wife's kin on the occasion of her first pregnancy.

MASAF. Major prestation of valuables made by husband's kin to wife's kin after many years of marriage, abandoned some time in the 1930s.

MARIKE-. Affines. People to whom one is related through one's spouse, the spouse of any cognate or the spouse of any descendant.

NJAFANG. A gift, particularly a gift of help and care, such as parents give their children or husbands and wives give to each other. In exchange, *njafang* gifts are given to those doing the preparatory work for the prestation. These are repaid in *songa* when the major prestation began.

NJAHARUN, "accumulate, bring together". The process of bringing together all the various contributions that will be used to make a major prestation.

NJAKENJAK, "crawl". The ceremony in which a husband's kin bring brideprice to his wife's kin.

NJOMIS. A gift of cooked food prepared by the recipients of a major prestation or return prestation for those who bring it.

NONOU, "decoration". Any form of decoration, such as traditional dress to decorate dancers, flowers to decorate a table, pictures to decorate a house and so on. Also, the ceremony in which a bride is decorated in traditional finery and carried to her husband's house with a major prestation of baskets and lesser valuables.

PARAKAU. In earlier affinal exchanges the contributors and recipients of gifts on the bride's and groom's sides were matched in partnerships. Those of the bride's kin who contributed to the *nonou* would expect to get something from the member of the groom's kin who had received their contribution in the *masaf* made years later. The people paired in such a partnership were called *parakau*. This kind of relationship was relatively insignificant in the 1980s.

PARUHU. The prestation sometimes made by husband's kin to wife's kin on the occasion of her first pregnancy. Another name for *marasus*.

POHO-KOL, "voice of the place". Another name for *kamal*.

POLANGAI, "to name, to call". To name something, such as a person or a pet. To announce or reveal something, particularly, in this case, to announce the names of contributors or recipients of shares of prestations. To give something over to the use of someone else, particularly to give valuable property, such as land or fishing rights, to someone else.

POLOT. The period of ritual seclusion of a mother and her first-born child in which they are cared for by members of her *kowun* and by her child's *tamatu*s.

RIF. To arrive, and thus to be descended from.

ROVWEL. The final prestation of cash and valuables from a husband's kin to his wife's kin, made after the funeral of the first of the couple to die.

SAHAI. A form of prestation in which shares are given to each of the island's *kamal*s. This is most important on the occasion of the building a new men's house, but is also done on other occasions, especially funerals.

SAL, "road, way". Any road, path, door, gate. Also any characteristic way of acting or thinking. Most important in the context of this book is the meaning of a genealogical (or other kind of) link between two people.

SOHOU. A public speaker, particularly one who speaks at prestations.

SONGA "to call out". The prestation of individual gifts to those who have given *njafang* made before most major prestations.

SOR. A contribution made toward a prestation or return prestation.

TAMATU. People whom a person addresses as *asi* (FZ, FZD, FMZD etc) and *tama* (F, FB, FZS, FMZS etc).

TOWENI HEPING, "waiting for morning". A prestation of cooked food to individuals who slept with the deceased's family during the mourning period.

TULTUL (Pidgin). Assistant to the village leader appointed by German and Australian colonial governments.

Bibliography

Barnes, John A.

    1962   African models in the New Guinea Highlands. *Man* (o.s.) **62**: 5–9.

    1980   Kinship studies: some impressions on the current state of play. *Man* **15**: 293–303.

Barnes, R.H.

    1976   Dispersed alliance and the prohibition of marriage: reconsideration of McKinley's explanation of Crow-Omaha terminologies. *Man* **11**: 384–98.

Battaglia, Deborah

    1985   'We feed our father': paternal nurture among the Sabarl of Papua New Guinea. *American Ethnologist* **12**: 427–41.

Béteille, André

    1990   Race, caste and gender. *Man* **25**: 489–504.

Bourdieu, Pierre

    1973   The Kabyle household. In Mary Douglas (ed.) *Rules and meanings*: 98–110. Harmondsworth: Penguin.

    1977   *Outline of a theory of practice*. Cambridge: Cambridge University Press.

Brown, Paula, and Georgeda Buchbinder (eds)

    1976   *Man and woman in the New Guinea Highlands*. (American Anthropological Association Special Publication 8.) Washington: American Anthropological Association.

Carrier, Achsah

    1984   Structural and processual models in Oceanic kinship theory. *Research in Melanesia* **8**: 57–87.

    1987   The structure and processes of kinship: a study of kinship and exchange on Ponam Island, Manus Province, Papua New Guinea, 1920–1980. Doctoral thesis, University of London.

    1989   The place of Western medicine in Ponam theories of health and illness. In Stephen Frankel and Gilbert Lewis (eds) *A continuing trial of treatment: medical pluralism in Papua New Guinea*: 155–80. Dordrecht: Kluwer Academic Publishers.

Carrier, James

    1987*a* History and self-conception in Ponam society. *Man* **22**: 111–31.

    1987*b* Marine tenure and conservation in Papua New Guinea: problems in interpretation. In Bonnie McCay and James Acheson (eds) *The question of the* *commons: the culture and ecology of communal resources*: 142–67. Tucson: University of Arizona Press.

1988   *The Ponam fish freezer.* (Occasional Paper No. 4.) Port Moresby: Department of Anthropology and Sociology, University of Papua New Guinea.

n.d.   Introduction. In J. Carrier (ed.) *History and tradition in Melanesian anthropology.* Berkeley: University of California Press. Forthcoming.

Carrier, James, and Achsah Carrier

1989   *Wage, trade, and exchange in Melanesia: a Manus society in the modern state.* Berkeley: University of California Press.

1990   Every picture tells a story: visual alternatives to oral tradition in Ponam society. *Oral Tradition* 5 (special issue): 354–75.

Clark, Jon, Celia Modgil and Sohan Modgil (eds)

1990   *Anthony Giddens: consensus and controversy.* London: Falmer Press.

Comaroff, John

1980   Introduction. In J. Comaroff (ed.) *The meaning of marriage payments*: 1–47. London: Academic Press.

Crocker, Jon Christopher

1985   *Vital souls: Bororo cosmology, natural symbolism, and shamanism.* Tucson: University of Arizona Press.

Damon, Frederick

1980   The kula and generalised exchange: considering some unconsidered aspects of *The elementary structures of kinship. Man* 15: 267–92.

1983   Muyuw kinship and the metamorphosis of gender labour. *Man* 18: 305–26.

Damon, Frederick, and Roy Wagner (eds)

1989   *Death rituals and life in the societies of the kula ring.* Dekalb: Northern Illinois University Press.

Davenport, William

1959   Nonunilinear descent and descent groups. *American Anthropologist* 61: 557–69.

de Albuquerque, Klaus

1986   *Spatial inequalities in Papua New Guinea: a district-level analysis.* (IASER Discussion Paper 49). Boroko: Institute for Applied Social and Economic Research.

de Lepervanche, Marie

1967–68   Descent, residence and leadership in the New Guinea Highlands. *Oceania* 38: 134–58, 163–89.

Department of External Territories

1946   Australian Archives: Department of External Territories (1): CRS A518, Correspondence files, Y840/1/1; New Guinea Natives: Re Deputation of natives (Manus) requesting Americans to take over island.

Epstein, T.S.

　1968　*Capitalism, primitive and modern: some aspects of Tolai economic growth*. Canberra: The Australian National University Press.

Errington, Frederick

　1974　*Karavar*. Ithaca, NY: Cornell University Press.

Errington, Frederick, and Deborah Gewertz

　1987*a*　*Cultural alternatives and feminist anthropology*. Cambridge: Cambridge University Press.

　1987*b*　Of unfinished dialogues and paper pigs. *American Ethnologist* **14**: 367–76.

Feil, Daryl

　1980　When a group of women takes a wife: generalized exchange and restricted marriage in the New Guinea Highlands. *Mankind* **12**: 286–99.

　1982　From pigs to pearlshells: the transformation of a New Guinea Highlands exchange economy. *American Ethnologist* **9**: 291–306.

　1987　*The evolution of Highland Papua New Guinea societies*. Cambridge: Cambridge University Press.

Filer, Colin

　1985　What is this thing called brideprice? *Mankind* **15** (special issue): 163–83.

Finney, Ben

　1973　*Big-men and business*. Canberra: The Australian National University Press.

Firth, Raymond

　1964 (1954)　Social organisation and social change. In R. Firth, *Essays on social organisation and values*: 30–58. London: Athlone Press.

　1968 (1957)　A note on descent groups in Polynesia. In Paul Bohannan and John Middleton (eds) *Kinship and social organisation*: 213–23. Garden City, NY: Natural History Press.

Forge, Anthony

　1972　The golden fleece. *Man* **7**: 527–40.

Fortes, Meyer

　1953　The structure of unilineal descent groups. *American Anthropologist* **55**: 17–41.

　1959　Descent, filiation and affinity: a rejoinder to Dr Leach. *Man* (o.s.) **59**: 193–97, 206–12.

　1962　Introduction. In M. Fortes (ed.) *Marriage in tribal societies*: 1–13. (Cambridge Papers in Social Anthropology No. 3.) Cambridge: Department of Anthropology and Archaeology, University of Cambridge.

　1969　*Kinship and the social order*. Chicago: Aldine.

Fortune, Reo

　1935　*Manus religion*. Philadelphia: American Philosophical Society.

Foster, Robert

　1985　Production and value in the Enga *tee*. *Oceania* **55**: 182–96.

Fox, Robin

1989   *The search for society: quest for a biosocial science and morality.* New Brunswick: Rutgers University Press.

Freeman, J. Derek

1961   On the concept of the kindred. *Journal of the Royal Anthropological Institute* **91**: 192–220.

Gammage, Bill

1975   The Rabaul strike, 1929. *Journal of Pacific History* **10** (3 & 4): 3–29.

Gell, Alfred

1982   The market wheel: symbolic aspects of an Indian tribal market. *Man* **17**: 470–91.

Gewertz, Deborah

1983   *Sepik River societies.* New Haven: Yale University Press.

Giddens, Anthony

1977   *Studies in social and political theory.* London: Hutchinson.

Godelier, Maurice

1986   *The making of great men: male domination and power among the New Guinea Baruya.* Cambridge: Cambridge University Press.

Goodenough, Ward H.

1955   A problem in Malayo-Polynesian social organization. *American Anthropologist* **57**: 71–83.

1962   Kindred and hamlet in Lakalai, New Britain. *Ethnology* **1**: 5–12.

Gregory, C.A.

1982   *Gifts and commodities.* London: Academic Press.

Harding, Thomas

1967   *Voyagers of the Vitiaz Straits.* (American Ethnological Society Monograph 44). Seattle: University of Washington.

Harrison, Simon

1989   Magical and material polities in Melanesia. *Man* **24**: 1–20.

Hekman, Susan

1990   Hermeneutics and the crisis of social theory: a critique of Giddens's epistemology. In Jon Clark, Celia Modgil and Sohan Modgil (eds) *Anthony Giddens: consensus and controversy*: 155–65. London: Falmer Press.

Hempenstall, Peter

1975   The reception of European missions in the German Pacific empire: the New Guinea experience. *Journal of Pacific History* **10** (1 & 2): 46–64.

Howell, Signe

1989   Of persons and things: exchange and valuables among the Lio of eastern Indonesia. *Man* **24**: 419–38.

Hughes, Ian
1977   *New Guinea stone age trade*. (Terra Australis 3). Canberra: The Australian National University Press.

Jolly, Margaret
n.d.   Banana leaf bundles and skirts: a Pacific Penelope's web? In James Carrier (ed.) *History and tradition in Melanesian anthropology*. Berkeley: University of California Press. Forthcoming.

Josephides, Lisette
1985   *The production of inequality: gender and exchange among the Kewa*. London: Tavistock.

Kaplan, Martha
1990   Meaning, agency and colonial history: Navosavakadua and the *Tuka* movement in Fiji. *American Ethnologist* 17: 3–22.

Keesing, Roger
1966   Kwaio kindreds. *Southwestern Journal of Anthropology* 22: 346–53.
1985   Kwaio women speak. *American Anthropologist* 87: 27–39.
1987a   African models in the Malaita highlands. *Man* 22: 431–52.
1987b   Ta'a Geni: women's perspectives on Kwaio society. In Marilyn Strathern (ed.) *Dealing with inequality: analysing gender relations in Melanesia and beyond*: 33–62. Cambridge: Cambridge University Press.

Keesing, Roger, and Robert Tonkinson (eds)
1982   Reinventing traditional culture: the politics of kastom in island Melanesia. *Mankind* 13: special issue.

Kelly, Fr Peter
n.d.   Brief history of the diocese of Kavieng. MS. (New Guinea Collection, University of Papua New Guinea Library.)

Kelly, Raymond
1974   *Etoro social structure*. Ann Arbor: University of Michigan Press.

King, V.E.
1978   The end of an era: aspects of the history of the Admiralty Islands, 1898–1908. BA (Hons) thesis, Macquarie University.

Knauft, Bruce
1985   *Good company and violence: sorcery and social action in a lowland New Guinea society*. Berkeley: University of California Press.
1990   Melanesian warfare: a theoretical history. *Oceania* 60: 250–311.

Kuluah, Albert
1977   The ethnographic history of the Kurti people on Manus Island, Papua New Guinea, to 1919. MA thesis, University of Victoria.

Langness, L.L.

1967 (1964)   Some problems in the conceptualisation of Highlands social structures. In
Ian Hogbin and L.R. Hiatt (eds) *Readings in Australian and Pacific anthropology*:
130–58. London: Melbourne University Press.

Lansdell, Keith

1981   Summary of commerce and industry: discussion and tentative plan. Lorengau:
Manus Province. Mimeo.

Leach, Jerry, and Edmund Leach (eds)

1983   *The kula: new perspectives on Massim exchange*. Cambridge: Cambridge
University Press.

Lederman, Rena

1986   *What gifts engender: social relations and politics in Mendi, Highland Papua New
Guinea*. New York: Cambridge University Press.

1989   Contested order: gender and society in the southern New Guinea Highlands.
American Ethnologist 16: 230–47.

Lévi-Strauss, Claude

1968   Do dual organizations exist? In C. Lévi-Strauss, *Structural anthropology*: 132–63.
Harmondsworth: Penguin.

Linnekin, Jocelyn

1983   Defining tradition: variations on the Hawaiian identity. *American Ethnologist* 10:
241–52.

LiPuma, Edward

1983   On the preference for marriage rules: a Melanesian example. *Man* 18: 766–85.

1988   *The gift of kinship: structure and practice in Maring social organization*. Cambridge:
Cambridge University Press.

Mcdowell, Nancy

1980   It's not who you are but how you give that counts: the role of exchange in a
Melanesian society. *American Ethnologist* 7: 58–70.

Malinowski, Bronislaw

1922   *Argonauts of the western Pacific*. London: Routledge and Kegan Paul.

Marshall, Mac

1981   Introduction. In M. Marshall (ea., siblingship in Oceania: 1–15. Ann Arbor:
University of Michigan Press.

1984   Structural patterns of sibling classification in island Oceania: implications for
culture history. *Current Anthropology* 25: 597–637.

Mead, Margaret

1930   Melanesian middlemen. *Natural History* 30: 115–30.

1934   Kinship in the Admiralty Islands. *American Museum of Natural History
Anthropological Papers* 34: 189–358.

1963 (1930)   *Growing up in New Guinea*. Harmondsworth: Penguin.

1968 (1956)   *New lives for old*. New York: Dell.

Mitchell, William
  1963   Theoretical problems in the concept of kindred. *American Anthropologist* **65**:
          343–54.

Modjeska, Nicholas
  1982   Production and inequality: perspectives from central New Guinea. In Andrew
          Strathern (ed.) *Inequality in New Guinea Highlands societies*: 50–108. Cambridge:
          Cambridge University Press.

Moore, Sally Falk
  1987   Explaining the present: theoretical dilemmas in processual ethnography.
          American Ethnologist **14**: 727–36.

Mosko, Mark S.
  1989   The developmental cycle among public groups. *Man* **24**: 470–84.

Murdock, George
  1968 (1960)   Cognatic forms of social organisation. In Paul Bohannan and John
          Middleton (eds) *Kinship and social organization*: 235–53. Garden City, NY:
          Natural History Press.

O'Hanlon, Michael
  1983   Handsome is as handsome does: display and betrayal in the Wahgi. *Oceania* **53**:
          317–33.
  1989   *Reading the skin: adornment, display and society among the Wahgi*. London: British
          Museum Publications.

Ortner, Sherry
  1984   Theory in anthropology since the sixties. *Comparative Studies in Society and
          History* **26**: 126–66.

Otto, Ton
  1989   A sociological study of the baitfish areas in New Ireland and Manus Province.
          Report prepared for the Papua New Guinea Department of Fisheries and
          Marine Resources. Canberra: Department of Anthropology, Research School of
          Pacific Studies, The Australian National University.
  1990   The politics of tradition in Baluan: social change and the appropriation of the
          past in a Manus society. Doctoral thesis submission, Department of
          Anthropology, Research School of Pacific Studies, The Australian National
          University.

Papua New Guinea
  1980   *National census: Manus Province*. Port Moresby: Bureau of Statistics.

Pehrson, Robert
  1971 (1954)   Bilateral kin groupings as a structural type: a preliminary assessment. In
          Norman Graburn (ed.) *Readings in kinship and social structure*: 192–95. New
          York: Harper and Row.

Petersen, Glenn
  1982   Ponapean matriliny: production, exchange and the ties that bind. *American Ethnologist* **9**: 129–44.

Pokawin, Polonhou
  1983   Community government in Manus: people's participation in government. *Yagl-Ambu* **10**: 8–16.

PR = Patrol reports, various, held in Lorengau and Port Moresby.

Radcliffe-Brown, A.R.
  1935   On the concept of function in social science. *American Anthropologist* **37**: 394–402.

Rubel, Paula and Abraham Rosman
  1978   *Your own pigs you may not eat*. Canberra: The Australian National University Press.

Sahlins, Marshall
  1981   *Historical metaphors and mythical realities: structure and the early history of the Sandwich Islands kingdom*. (Association for Social Anthropology in Oceania Special Publication No. 1). Ann Arbor: University of Michigan Press.
  1985   *Islands of history*. Chicago: University of Chicago Press.

Sankoff, Gillian
  1985   Touching pen, marking paper: Queensland labour contracts in the 1880s. In Deborah Gewertz and Edward Schieffelin (eds) *History and ethnohistory in Papua New Guinea* (Oceania Monograph 28): 100–26. Sydney: University of Sydney.

Scheffler, Harold
  1965   *Choiseul Island social structure*. Berkeley: University of California Press.
  1986   The descent of rights and the descent of persons. *American Anthropologist* **88**: 339–50.

Schneider, David M.
  1965   Some muddles in the models: or, how the system really works. In Michael Banton (ed.) *The relevance of models for social anthropology*: 25–85. London: Tavistock.
  1981 a   Conclusions. In Mac Marshall (ed.) *Siblingship in Oceania*: 389–404. Ann Arbor: University of Michigan Press.
  1981 b   *A critique of the study of kinship*. Ann Arbor: University of Michigan Press.

Schwartz, Theodore
  1962   The Paliau Movement in the Admiralty Islands, 1946–1954. *Anthropological Papers of the American Museum of Natural History* **49**: 211–421.
  1963   Systems of areal integration: some considerations based on the Admiralty Islands of northern Melanesia. *Anthropological Forum* **1**: 56–97.

Schwimmer, Erik
  1973   *Exchange in the social structure of the Orokaiva*. London: C. Hurst and Company.

Seligmann, C.G.

1910   *The Melanesians of British New Guinea*. Cambridge: Cambridge University Press.

Stinchcombe, Arthur

1990   Milieu and structure updated: a critique of the theory of structuration. In Jon Clark, Celia Modgil and Sohan Modgil (eds) *Anthony Giddens: consensus and controversy*: 47–56. London: Falmer Press.

Strathern, Andrew

1973   Kinship, descent and locality: some New Guinea examples. In Jack Goody (ed.) *The character of kinship*: 21–33. London: Cambridge University Press.

1979*a*   Gender, ideology and money in Mount Hagen. *Man* **14**: 530–48.

1979*b*   'We are all of one father here': models of descent in New Guinea Highlands societies. In Ladislaw Holy (ed.) *Segmentary lineage systems reconsidered* (Queen's University Papers in Social Anthropology 4): 145–55. Belfast: Department of Social Anthropology, Queen's University.

1980   The central and the contingent: bridewealth among the Melpa and the Wiru. In John Comaroff (ed.) *The meaning of marriage payments*: 49–66. London: Academic Press.

1982   The division of labor and processes of social change in Mount Hagen. *American Ethnologist* **9**: 307–19.

Strathern, Marilyn

1972   *Women in between: female roles in a male world, Mount Hagen, New Guinea*. London: Academic Press.

1984*a*   Domesticity and the denigration of women. In Denise O'Brian and Sharon Tiffany (eds) *Rethinking women's roles: perspectives from the Pacific*: 13–31. Berkeley: University of California Press.

1984*b*   Marriage exchanges: a Melanesian comment. *Annual Review of Anthropology* **13**: 41–73.

1984*c*   Subject or object: women and the circulation of valuables in Highlands New Guinea. In Renée Hirschon (ed.) *Women and property — women as property*: 158–75. London: Croom Helm.

1988   *The gender of the gift: problems with women and problems with society in Melanesia*. Berkeley: University of California Press.

Strathern, Marilyn (ed.)

1987   *Dealing with inequality: analysing gender relations in Melanesia and beyond*. Cambridge: Cambridge University Press.

Thomas, Nicholas

1982   A cultural appropriation of history: Sahlins among the Hawaiians. *Canberra Anthropology* **5** (1): 60–65.

1989   *Out of time: history and evolution in anthropological discourse*. Cambridge: Cambridge University Press.

n.d.   Substantivization and anthropological discourse: the transformation of practices into institutions in neotraditional Pacific societies. In James Carrier (ed.) *History and tradition in Melanesian anthropology*. Berkeley: University of California Press. Forthcoming.

Thompson, E.P.

1968   *The making of the English working class*. Harmondsworth: Penguin.

Thornton, Robert

1982   Modelling of spatial relations in a boundary-marking ritual of the Iraqw of Tanzania. *Man* **17**: 528–45.

Titus, Elijah

1980   *Manus handbook*. Lorengau: Manus Province.

Trompf, Garry

1983   Independent churches in Melanesia. *Oceania* **54**: 51–72.

Wagner, Roy

1967   *The curse of Souw*. Chicago: University of Chicago Press.

1986   *Symbols that stand for themselves*. Chicago: University of Chicago Press.

Walsh, A. Crosbie

1983   The volume and direction of interprovincial migration. *Yagl-Ambu* **10**: 77–89.

Weiner, Annette

1980   Reproduction: a replacement for reciprocity. *American Ethnologist* **7**: 71–85.

Weiner, James

1979   Substance, siblingship and exchange: aspects of social structure in New Guinea. *Social Analysis* **11**: 3–34.

1982   Restricted exchange in the New Guinea Highlands. *Canberra Anthropology* **2**: 75–93.

Whitehead, Harriet

1986   The varieties of fertility cultism in New Guinea: part I. *American Ethnologist* **13**: 80–99.

Young, Michael

1971   *Fighting with food*. Cambridge: Cambridge University Press.

1983   'Our name is women: we are bought with limesticks and limepots': an analysis of the autobiographical narrative of a Kalauna woman. *Man* **18**: 478–501.

Author index[*]

Barnes, John 16, 22–23
Barnes, R.H. 31
Battaglia, Deborah 97
Béteille, André 10n
Bourdieu, Pierre 23n, 111n, 140, 142–43, 184n, 222, 225–28, 230
Brown, Paula xvii
Buchbinder, Georgeda xvii

Carrier, Achsah xv, xvi, 1–7, 10, 30–33, 42–43, 52, 55n, 58, 70n, 75–77, 79, 93, 98, 139, 143, 156n, 159, 184n, 188, 214, 216–17, 229n, 232, 238
Carrier, James xv, xvi, 1–7, 24, 30, 40, 42–43, 52, 55n, 58, 67, 70n, 75–77, 93, 98, 126, 139, 143, 156n, 184n, 188, 214, 216–17, 220n, 229n, 231–32
Clark, Jon 222n
Comaroff, John 87, 124
Crocker, J. Christopher 221n

Damon, Frederick 20, 98, 107–08, 110
Davenport, William 12
de Albuquerque, Klaus 235
de Lepervanche, Marie 16–17
Department of External Territories 74

Epstein, T.S. 229n
Errington, Frederick 53, 115n, 161, 163n, 224

Feil, Daryl 19, 24n, 234
Filer, Colin 233–34
Finney, Ben 229n
Firth, Raymond 9, 13, 220

---

[*] In this index the dash marks a run of numbers, not necessarily an extended discussion of an author.

Forge, Anthony 19, 89n, 98
Fortes, Meyer 9, 11–15, 87–88, 220
Fortune, Reo 66
Foster, Robert 141–42
Fox, Robin 31
Freeman, J. Derek 14

Gammage, Bill 129n
Gell, Alfred 140
Gewertz, Deborah 23n, 24, 53, 115n, 163n, 224
Giddens, Anthony 24, 222n
Godelier, Maurice 20, 53, 89
Goodenough, Ward 12–14
Gregory, C.A. 20, 110n, 229n

Harding, Thomas 57
Harrison, Simon 155
Hekman, Susan 222n
Hempenstall, Peter 68
Howell, Signe 111
Hughes, Ian 57

Jolly, Margaret 112
Josephides, Lisette xvii, 20, 52–53, 224

Kaplan, Martha 225n
Keesing, Roger xiv, 11n, 14, 163n, 224n
Kelly, Peter 69
Kelly, Raymond 19, 223–24
King, V.E. xxii, 67
Knauft, Bruce 23n, 224n
Kuluah, Albert 58

Langness, L.L. 16
Lansdell, Keith 1, 7
Leach, Edmund 57
Leach, Jerry 57
Lederman, Rena 48n, 53n, 98, 172, 221n
Lévi-Strauss, Claude 18, 140

Subject index

256

For Product Safety Concerns and Information please contact our EU
representative GPSR@taylorandfrancis.com Taylor & Francis Verlag GmbH,
Kaufingerstraße 24, 80331 München, Germany

Batch number: 08158921

Printed by Printforce, the Netherlands